Rethinking Gender, Ethnicity, and Religion in Iran

Sex, Family and Culture in the Middle East Series

This innovative series explores the connections and influences impacting ideas about marriage, sexuality, and the family throughout history in the MENA region, and until the present day. Individual volumes consider the ancient, early Islamic, medieval, early modern, and contemporary periods to investigate how traditions and practices have evolved and interacted across time and countries.

Series Editors:
Janet Afary, Professor and Mellichamp Chair in Global Religion and Modernity, UC Santa Barbara
Claudia Yaghoobi, Roshan Institute Assistant Professor in Persian Studies, The University of North Carolina at Chapel Hill

Rethinking Gender, Ethnicity, and Religion in Iran

An Intersectional Approach to National Identity

Azadeh Kian

I.B.TAURIS
LONDON • NEW YORK • OXFORD • NEW DELHI • SYDNEY

I.B. TAURIS
Bloomsbury Publishing Plc
50 Bedford Square, London, WC1B 3DP, UK
1385 Broadway, New York, NY 10018, USA
29 Earlsfort Terrace, Dublin 2, Ireland

BLOOMSBURY, I.B. TAURIS and the I.B. Tauris logo are
trademarks of Bloomsbury Publishing Plc

First published in Great Britain 2023
This paperback edition published 2025

Series design by Adriana Brioso
Cover image: SARA, in the Golestan Province, Iran, 2016, by Sohrab SARDASHTI

A catalogue record for this book is available from the British Library.

A catalog record for this book is available from the Library of Congress.

ISBN: HB: 978-0-7556-5025-5
          PB: 978-0-7556-5029-3
          ePDF: 978-0-7556-5026-2
          eBook: 978-0-7556-5027-9

Series: Sex, Family and Culture in the Middle East

Typeset by Integra Software Services Pvt. Ltd.

To find out more about our authors and books visit www.bloomsbury.com
and sign up for our newsletters.

To subaltern women of Iran who struggle subtly for their rights
To my mother and to the memory of my uncle Mehdi

Contents

Figures

Tables

Maps

Acknowledgments

This research would not have been possible without the help of several people and institutions. I am deeply indebted to my interviewees, mostly ordinary women from lower- or middle-class ethnic and religious minorities, and lower-class Persian/Shi'ites who accepted to share with me their personal lives, experiences, thoughts, sufferings, and hopes. In order to respect the anonymity of the respondents, the names have been changed.

I would like to thank Iran Center for Statistics for their precious contribution to the quantitative national survey we conducted in Iran in 2002 and my qualitative survey in 2004. I'm also grateful to the French Center for Scientific Research (CNRS) and the French Research Institute in Tehran (IFRI) for their invaluable support.

I am grateful to Sadigheh Sheikhzadeh, then a PhD student and my assistant in 2007–8, who kindly conducted open-ended interviews with a sample of educated and active Baluch women in Iranshâhr, Châhbahâr, and Khâsh on my behalf. She also accompanied me to Golestân province in 2008.

My special thanks to my family and friends for their support.

I would like to thank the Faculty of Societies and Humanities of université Paris Cité for granting me an exceptional full-year sabbatical which allowed me to write this book, a project that I had been forced to postpone due to my administrative and teaching responsibilities.

I also would like to thank the anonymous readers of earlier versions of the manuscript for their precious comments.

Introduction

I returned to Iran in 1994, fourteen years having passed in the United States and France. Once in Iran, I realized that everything had changed, starting from the spoken Persian. New words had been invented; in public spaces, people no longer greeted one another. Parts of Tehran were no longer recognizable to me. Some new skyscrapers were built, entire neighborhoods were divided by freeways, the images of the martyrs of the revolution or the Iraq-Iran war lined the walls. Streets and roads were full of people, often young, many of whom were rural migrants unacquainted with urban culture. For example, crossing highways by foot had become common.

In the early 1990s, many women still wore the black compulsory headscarfs and long coats, which, along with the polluted blackened buildings, gave an extremely sad view of the capital. Shortly after my arrival in Tehran, a group of ten female relatives came to visit me at the home of my parents. As I watched them cross the garden, all dressed in black from head to toe, I began to cry and asked my mother why she had not told me that a family member had passed away. In my mind it was the only explanation as to why these women wore black! This image changed when their veils and coats were removed to show their fashionable clothes worn underneath. This simple incident illustrated the extent to which under the Islamic regime private and public spaces are considered different and separated, each with its own rules, life, and culture. Later, upon traveling to Isfahan (called half the world for its splendor), where parts of my extended family live, I realized the scope of cultural change just by counting the number of women driving on major streets. I remembered how back in the 1970s the few women I witnessed driving their cars in Isfahan were verbally harassed by traditionalist men who did not appreciate "westernized Isfahani women."

It occurred to me that a society which has become modern in its socio-demographic, political, and cultural behaviors threatens the state's cultural and ideological hegemony.

Observations of different neighborhoods in Tehran and later other parts of Iran also showed that despite the Islamic state's claim, social inequalities were paramount, and that the discourse of unity uttered by the leaders at the beginning of the revolution could no longer stand in an increasingly fragmented society. In order to sustain the social and political order, the state has pursued a repressive policy against active social groups.

My research therefore particularly focused on societal transformations, including gender relations, the emergence of new social movements with youth, women, and intellectuals as their main vectors, and their interactions with political and religious institutions.

Following Erving Goffman's teachings, my research also led me to embrace sociological studies that reject a distinction between micro- and macro-levels of analysis, combining qualitative and quantitative methods. This combined method aided in the ability to grasp the articulations between social determinants and women's individual subjectivities. In Iran, gender inequality is the paradigmatic form on which the Islamic regime is based. Given the main stake that women and their statuses represent for political Islam, my research and interrogations have focused on the new strategies of women, mothers, wives, citizens, workers, and their constitution as social actors and political subjects.[1]

My research on post-revolutionary Iran, largely based on fieldwork, emphasizes the reciprocal influences of society and political institutions. In contrast to the system perspective, in which institutions determine the actors' scope for action, my analysis refutes the structural determination of action and instead attempts to demonstrate the reciprocal influence of action, structures, and the system. I have also attempted to examine the impact of the actors' actions on the processes of structural and systemic change. The starting point of my analysis is therefore not the system but the action of individuals. Individual subjectivity cannot be reduced to the impact of the social. However, it does not pre-exist the social either. It is inseparable from the experiences that produce it.

Contrary to studies that give priority to the need for rationality, my work has emphasized the specific role of women in the process of family and social change, and the weakening of the patriarchal family, essentially, the rejection, especially among young people, of totalizing thought and the neo/patriarchal political order.

I also emphasize the importance of ethnic/religious factors in identity and gender re-constructions. These identity markers, however, are not constructed once and for all. They change in contexts of social transformation. Therefore, the construction of identity should be historicized and contextualized, and identities can be and are contested. But what about the reshaping of gender and ethnicity when "peripheral" underprivileged regions undergo change? Gender shifts occur when hierarchical definitions of masculine and feminine are challenged. Alterations in the gender division of labor, the control of women's sexuality, relationships with authority, and women having significant access to education and an entry into the labor market are key. But ethnicity is not dissolved in social change. Rather, it draws new resources and new forms of expression from it. Far from signifying standardization, the process of social transformation underway in Iran is accompanied by a reformulation of local identities. Transformation also means the renewal of relationships between hierarchy and domination, particularly regarding the definition and attribution of gender, ethnicity, and religion.

I am aware of the relationship between writing and power; about my own positionality as a Persian, foreign-educated, upper-class woman. My position of researcher too was a position of power. The proximity I managed to acquire with my respondents was rooted in their personal need or curiosity, on the one hand, and in the trust I could gain on the other. However, the restitution of the research and the writing was done without the people on whom they are based. In order not to betray them and their trust, I promised myself to reflect their views and share their experiences with the readers of these lines.

Throughout my fieldwork in Iran, I tried not to position myself as an all-knowing authority. On the contrary, I exposed my vulnerabilities, lack of knowledge, and also my thirst to learn from a wide range of women including the educated active middle classes, women's rights activists, the political and cultural elite, and the poor, less-educated, or illiterate often ethnic women. My first encounter with the latter category was in Khak-i Sefid, a poor suburb in northeastern Tehran where a wide range of ethnic migrants and Iranian gypsies called ghorbatis lived.[2] I conducted several interviews and observed different neighborhoods for months. The neighborhood of the ghorbatis was categorized as a dangerous place, known as a hotbed for drug trafficking, and was demolished by municipal authorities some years later. During all these years of research throughout Iran, with the exception of a few individuals who were not talkative, my interviewees accepted to share their experiences, demands, wishes, sufferings, and hopes.

I also met many women's rights activists and feminists, both secular and Islamic, especially in Tehran, many of whom had founded women's magazines and NGOs. A number of other women were members of the Islamic Parliament, business women, etc. In the face of the dominant paradigm of Muslim/Shi'ite, heterosexual men who attempt to render women invisible and to inferiorize women, these feminists or women's rights activists shared the definition of women as a category, homogeneous and unified. Both secular and Muslim feminisms emphasized the singularities and particularities of women in order to make them visible, and to challenge the inferiorization of women and the domination of men. These feminists did not concern themselves, on a theoretical or political level, with internal differences of the "group of women" nor the relations of power which they came across. Especially as their movement was limited to the urban and educated middle classes (from the beginning of the twentieth century), they did not think of strengthening their ties with women from rural areas, the working classes, and ethnic minorities. They refused to see themselves and their experiences and knowledge as situated, socially constructed, marked by ethnicity (Persian), class (educated middle class), gender, or religion (Shi'ite or from Shi'ite origin).[3] This ethnocentrist prejudice that encumbered the feminist majority discourse also implied domination, invisibilization, and victimization of minority women.

Moreover, the expansion of social networks, coupled with the political repression of organized protest activities, has led women's rights activists at the center to abandon face-to-face meetings (especially on the occasion of religious or national holidays or ceremonies, weddings, or births) more suited to the conditions of "ordinary" women. The latter continue to be victimized by those who represent themselves as their saviors, speaking on their behalf instead of producing a space for subalterns to express themselves.[4]

My qualitative surveys of women belonging to various social categories (political and cultural elite, lower and middle class, ethnic, rural, and rural migrants) led me to reject the definition of women as a homogeneous and unified category, and to simultaneously take into account gender and class relations, and later ethnicity and religion. All of which highlight power relations existing among women themselves. As mentioned earlier, parallel to my investigations among middle-class women, my research has also focused on rural migrant women (especially Azaris, Shi'ites) residing in the outskirts of Tehran. This research shows that for this population, ethnicity is increasingly de-territorialized and that the notions of identity construction and multiple belonging have become dominant.[5] This encounter with migrant women of modest means, belonging to non-Persian ethnic groups, was decisive in several respects. First, I was able to observe the strategies implemented by migrant women to survive in the new, often hostile environments—particularly, their ability to negotiate with local decision-makers, and to facilitate the integration and success of their children in this new environment despite their poverty and minority status.[6] Thus, without rejecting the Weberian definition of power, I was able to realize the power that subaltern women possessed: the power to create and nurture, to resist, to survive, to negotiate the problems of everyday life or to bear witness.

In the 1990s, when I started my research, the lack of fieldworks on "ordinary" non-Persian women was striking. Even some years later, the publications on ethnic minorities mainly concern either political parties and movements or, to a lesser extent, Kurdish women's participation in political activities.[7] However, in recent years, more research has been undertaken, especially on Kurdish women, their perceptions about their legal status and social positions. One research conducted in the Kurdish town of Sanandaj shows that despite lack of opportunity associated with both the family and broader society, younger women's growing educational attainment and knowledge of possibilities for change enable them to both articulate grievances and aspire to, and sometimes engage in, collective action for women's rights.[8] The authors argue that "under current circumstances, the external and internal obstacles to Kurdish women's empowerment may appear insurmountable, but the gender consciousness, self-awareness, and inner resilience of many of our research participants suggest otherwise."[9]

Likewise, Fatemeh Karimi's book on Kurdish women political activists has the originality to use their life history. Through their narrative, we learn about their life, education, upbringing, family traditions, and political trajectory. The interviewees argue that women's massive participation in the 1979 revolution and their better access to education triggered Kurdish women's political and military (pishmerga) activities in male-dominated Kurdish parties. Miriam's words sum up the experience of many Kurdish girls and women who were attracted to political activities. A former Komala activist, Miriam, says:

> At that time, the social life of girls like me was, at best, limited to home and school. We were not as free as our brothers to move in the public space. The destiny of women was limited to marriage and motherhood. It was to live another life and escape this routine and monotonous life that I decided to participate in the revolution and then to get closer to the Komala which was considered very revolutionary at the time.[10]

However, research is still lacking on Baluch and Turkmen women who are the main focus of my study.

Methodology

I had prepared my survey questions in France and quickly realized that they sounded awkward to my respondents. They indeed helped to contextualize and adapt my questions, and to gain a further, in-depth understanding of the complexities of Iranian post-revolutionary society in its entirety. They de facto invited me to gradually abandon my existing binary views as a "Westernized" feminist. This gradually led me to grasp the varied methodological and epistemological challenges, allowing me to be attentive to the voices of subaltern women, and to realize their capacity to act, in subtle ways, on their own lives and those of society. In attempting to learn how to speak to the subaltern women, and in investigating their "silences," it became necessary to unlearn the existing masculinist Persian/nationalistic ideological constructions. During my research and encounters with ethnic lower- and middle-class women, I realized that, as Foucault and Deleuze argued, the oppressed, if given the chance, can speak and know their conditions.

However, contrary to the educated middle-class women to whom I always revealed my living and working in Paris, I did not relay where I lived to rural- and lower-class ethnic women. My aim was to avoid further distancing myself from them. They all thought I was a university professor from Tehran. My presence, however, seemed to be seen as a potential vector of their views to the public. They also asked me to report their demands to the government, which I refused arguing that I was doing independent research and was not involved in policymaking. Nonetheless, I assured them that the results of the quantitative survey taken in 2002 would be published by the Statistical Center of Iran and be known to the policymakers. The latter, however, did not pay any attention to the results of our ground-breaking survey in post-revolutionary Iran because they did not match the official discourse. For example, the successive governments had been encouraging temporary marriage as an interim solution to the decline in marriage rate, acting as a response to youth's sexual demands and social problems. Nevertheless, in our survey, from 6,154 boys and girls aged fifteen to twenty-nine who were single and still lived with their parents, 91 percent expressed themselves against temporary marriage.[11] Likewise, the authorities have justified the quasi-absence of women from decision-making political positions under the pretext that women themselves were against women's political involvement. However, our quantitative survey of over 7,600 married women aged fifteen years and over showed that the majority of our respondents were for women's political representation (69 percent in favor of local political positions and 53 percent in favor of national representation).

Our quantitative survey, which was the result of the collaboration between the research group Mondes iranien at CNRS (the French National Center for Research), the French Research Institute in Iran (IFRI), and the Statistical Center of Iran, was conducted in 2002 with a sample of 6,960 urban and rural households in all twenty-eight provinces (later the number of provinces increased to thirty-one). The research sample was composed of 30,714 individuals: 7,633 women fifteen years and older, married at least once, and 6,154 single youths fifteen to twenty-nine years old who lived with their parents—3,437 boys and 2,717 girls. The sampling frame used was adopted from the one resulted from the 1996 National Census of Population and Housing conducted by the Statistical Center of Iran. Each statistical unit is a cluster composed of almost thirty households drawn randomly. A total of 232 urban and rural clusters were thus selected as the sample. The questionnaire contained 150 questions on individual characteristics of household members (age, gender, literacy, level of education, marital status, economic activity, etc.) and household characteristics (revenue and spending, etc.). After several months of discussions with the Statistical Center of Iran, it was admitted to include, for the first time in post-revolutionary Iran, sociological questions and an opinion poll in such a wide survey. Among these questions were marriage and marital life, women's relations with husband and children, awareness of rights, opinion concerning free choice, women's access to work, and women's political responsibilities in both local and national levels. The Statistical Center of Iran trained and deployed throughout the country 200 survey takers for this research. According to general findings of our survey, the average size of the household was 4.4 members, literacy rate of the population six years and over was 81 percent (86.5 percent for men and 76 percent for women), average age at the first marriage was twenty-six for men and twenty-three for women, rate of arranged marriage was 55.6 percent for women and 42 percent for men, and 19.5 percent of mothers were economically active.[12]

My qualitative surveys composed of over 300 open-ended interviews with a wide range of women from different social categories in both rural and urban areas were taken between 1994 and 2008. Approximately one hundred of them belonged to ethnic minorities. The results have both highlighted crucial social, demographic, and cultural changes in Iranian society; a significant increase in women's educational level and its impact on the fertility rate are among them. Following the findings of our national quantitative survey with the Statistical Center of Iran, I also conducted open-ended interviews from 2004 to 2008 in Sistan-Baluchistan province (Zâhedân, Zabol, and several villages), and Sadigheh Sheikhzadeh, my assistant and then a PhD student, interviewed a sample of highly educated women in Iranshahr, Khâsh, and Châhbahâr in

2007–8. My qualitative research also included Golestan province in Northern Iran where many Baluch migrants live. The main reason I focused on these two provinces (plus Hormozgan and Southern Tehran which I do not discuss in this book) was that there was not much existing research on Baluchistan, it being the poorest and the most marginalized Iranian province. The same goes for the Baluch migrants in Northern Iran. Some people in the Organization of Plan and Budget even stated to me that there were no Baluch living in Golestan, and studies conducted by the Azad University had not even included Baluch migrants. My survey comprised of Gorgan, Gonbad Kavoos, and several mixed Turkmen-Persian/Mazadarani villages, Azad Shar, Minoodasht, Galikash, and several Baluch or mixed villages. The themes that I chose to work on include marriage, family, education, children, work, and local political participation, as they are related to the everyday life of ordinary women from ethnic/religious groupings. I also used a number of research in French on gender, ethnicity, nationalism, and religion to offer new sources of knowledge to English speakers.

It should be noted that the Iranian state does not allow the counting of Sunnites or ethnic minorities. Only religious minorities officially recognized by Islam, namely Christians, Jews, and Zoroastrians, can be counted in the census. According to the 2016 census, the country had 23,109 Christians, 130,158 Zoroastrians, and 9,826 Jews.[13] As for the Bahais, a forbidden religion under the Islamic regime, their counting is unlawful. According to our survey, the Sunnites constituted nearly 13 percent of the population, of which 7 percent were native Kurdish speakers, 2.5 percent Baluch, and almost 1 percent Turkmen. Some parts of Hormozgan province in the Persian Gulf, which has a total of 1,920,000 population, are Sunnites. Arab speakers make up 3.5 percent of the population, but only a minority are Sunnites. Finally, the Azeris constituted the largest ethnic minority in the country (23 percent of the population), but they are Shi'ite.

I investigate the impact of post-revolutionary policies on women's demographic, social, and cultural behavior, belonging to ethnic/religious minorities. I also examine how social hierarchy and power relations based on gender, class, ethnicity, and religion operate in Baluchistan province—particularly, areas where the Baluch-Sunnites constitute as the majority of the population but are minorities in terms of power relations, where the human development index is the lowest in Iran. In this province, and through forced subordination, political Shi'ism has tended to regulate the evolution of ethnic/religious minorities through the two technologies of power, namely, discipline and population management or what Michel Foucault called bio-power.[14]

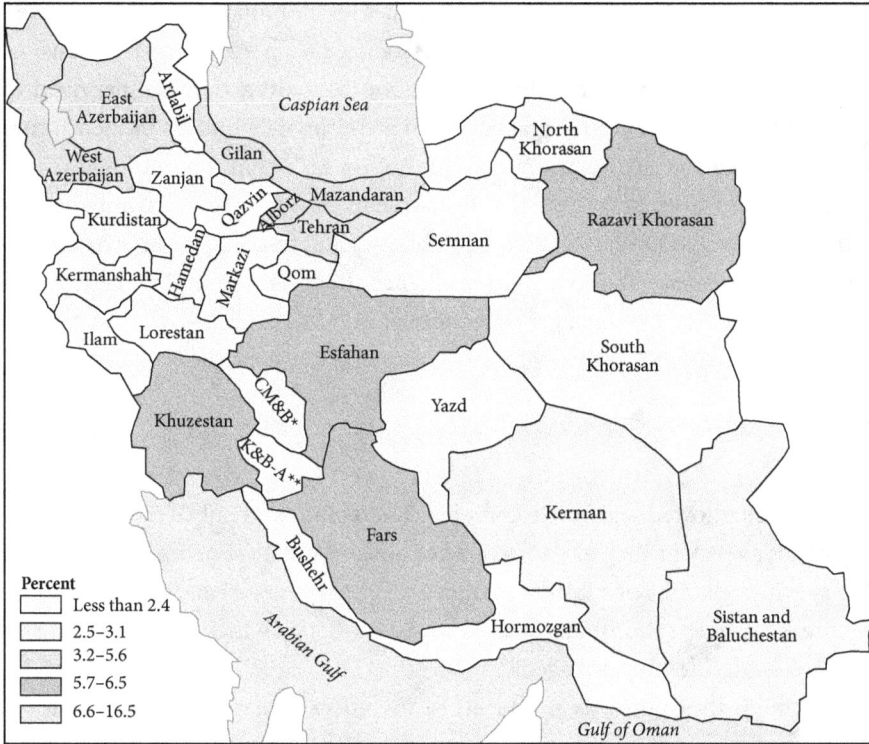

*Chaharmahal and Bakhtiari
**Kohgiluyeh and Boyer-Ahmad

Map 0.1 Relative distribution of population, 1395/2016.

Source: Iran Statistical Year Book, 1398/2019, P. 146.

Marginalization is the regime's response to those who refuse to subordinate to gender, class, ethnic, or religious discriminations that structure the state's policy. On the other hand, I was also interested see whether the intersection of various systems of social hierarchy and domination varied from a Sunnite majority environment to a Shi'ite majority province where Baluch are a minority, both religiously and ethnically. For this purpose, I chose the Golestan province in Northern Iran where fertile lands have attracted many Baluchs for the past several decades and where an important Turkmen population have lived for centuries. Although Turkmen are Sunnite, they do not identify with Baluch migrants. Rather, they side with the Persian/Shi'ite majority to stigmatize Baluch who can thus be considered as an archetype of a pariah.

Despite the diversity of empirically observable situations such as gender, ethnicity, social status, or religious affiliations, popular classes share the fact of being socially and culturally dominated. This domination is characterized by a deficiency in economic resources associated with subaltern positions, or even marginalization in the division of labor. Moreover, they are deprived of valued lifestyles and cultural practices, and are ultimately limited in their future prospects.[15] Olivier Schwartz defined this notion as "a continuum of dominated groups."[16] However, solidarity among popular classes in Iran is impeded by ethnic/religious boundaries that additionally function as social hierarchies. Likewise, inter-class and inter-ethnic alliances between the middle classes and the underprivileged women are either absent or ephemeral.

Agency

As Foucault showed, agency is complex. The paradox of subjectivation is that it situates agency in the very structures of power (and not outside), therefore in the specific relations of subjectivation.[17] The very processes and conditions that secure a subject's subordination are also the means by which he/she becomes a self-conscious identity and agent.[18]

Although the subject is produced as the effect of a subordination, he/she is also capable of a subversive reinvestment allowing him/her to resignify, by producing new contexts, what determines him/her. Thus a subject is both dominated and provided with agency.

Likewise, Saba Mahmood criticizes the individualistic conception of agency, which is thought of according to a binary schema of submission/resistance that naturalizes social ideals of freedom.[19] She admits the existence of agency other than that which amounts to subvert the norms; does not conceptualize agency as a synonym for resistance to relations of domination, but as a capacity for action that specific relations of subordination create and enable.[20] Like Teresa de Lauretis, she believes that individuals are therefore not autonomous from the social.

Iran is a multi-ethnic and multi-religious country with diverse social groups. I expected that the experiences of women belonging to such diversity would not be identical.

My surveys of women belonging to ethnic and religious (Sunnite) minorities revealed the complexity and diversity of their experiences, daily problems, and demands that are sometimes so far removed from those of Tehrani women activists. More importantly, they made me realize that in addition to the gender and class social relations I had explored, it was necessary to consider the ethnic and religious dimensions of these women's identities, potentially even the interaction of various systems of social hierarchy.[21]

I additionally highlight the strategies subaltern women deploy to challenge the patriarchal order in their own subtle ways. For example, by insisting on their daughters' education, or pleading for their marriage at a later age, they essentially fight against the will of the men of their families, often reflective of the traditions emanating from the tribal structures and social customs. Therefore, agency can also be applied to individual transgressions and creations of self-affirmation of these women. They, however, do not deny belonging to these very structures, as they exist as minorities in a predominantly Persian and Shi'ite country. I have thus used the words of N. C. Mathieu "to yield is not to consent" (*céder n'est pas consentir*)[22] to analyze the strategies of these women from ethnic and religious minorities. They may appear as passive victims, unable to muster any opposition to the forces allied against them; or as consenting partners, acquiescent and apparently satisfied with their deferent role; or even as active participants, supporting and sustaining their own inequality; yet when the times are ripe they seize the opportunity to participate in an ongoing series of negotiations, manipulations, and strategies directed toward gaining control of their lives.

In these provinces, ordinary women are joined by those who are often the first generation in their families and communities to be university educated, and who are activists for women's rights. Following Stuart Hall, I argue that these new subjects were excluded because they were subaltern or because they did not belong to the center—emerged or gained, through their own struggles, the means to speak for themselves for the first time. Consequently, they threaten the dominant discourses. As we shall see later, many of these women are working to improve the living conditions of women in their own villages or towns.

In this constant to-ing and fro-ing between theory and practice in the field, I realized the intersectionality of social relations operating at the level of social structures and individuals that interact and feed off each other without being interchangeable or reducible to each other. This presented itself as a theory stemming from the realities of my field, not a fashionable formula stemming from a theory introduced by feminists of color.

These investigations also led me to observe that the revival of ethnic, linguistic, and regional particularisms did not reflect a questioning of the national space and its unity, and the cultural homogenization that the modern state has brought about through mass schooling and urbanization. They instead reflect a fear of ethnic and religious minorities of being relegated to second-class citizenship. Unlike in some countries (such as Turkey) where the dominant state identity is that of a dominant nation, in Iran under Islamic rule, the dominant identity is manifested through a dominant religion (Shi'ism).

My research highlights and analyzes women's agency, showing how power and gender work through the self and the social, but also through emotions and cultural narratives that imply the idea of a resisting agency against the automatism of conservative and Islamist ideologies. It is not a question of reversing the hierarchy, but that of decentering the hegemonic discourse. Not by creating other hegemonies or ethnocentrisms in reverse, but through hybridization, which gives more account of the interactions, interdependencies, and reciprocal construction of subjectivities between the actors. The process of subjectivation or the fields of elaboration of the strategies of self are in interaction with unequal social relations.

Is Objective Knowledge of Society Possible?

Patricia Hill Collins wrote: "I encourage each of you to write, edit, and rewrite your own stories until they ring true for you. Armed with thoughtful interpretations of our lived experiences we can collectively craft new interpretations of our shared realities. Imagine the possibilities for our world if we do so."[23]

Norbert Elias argued that sociology should talk about "what is or has been" and should free itself from social and political ideologies. He wished to transcend as much as possible matters of personal interest or "commitment" in order to describe the "real" world with a "relative distancing."[24] He also argued that "one cannot demand or expect the sociologist to express his [her] convictions about how a society should develop."[25]

However, as Catharine MacKinnon stated, the theorist is not above, or outside, but within the world and the work, where he [she] had been since the beginning. "The theory of 'situated' knowledge is concrete and changeable rather than abstract and totalizing."[26]

Following Sandra Harding, for whom all knowledge is situated, socially constructed, marked by race, class, gender, sexuality, or ethnicity, I attempt to analyze gender in several dimensions and on several levels: gender as a dimension of individual identity is investigated as an interpersonal process of self-awareness and as a dynamic relationship of self to individual and collective identity. Gender is also an organizing principle of social structure. At this level, it is investigated as the foundation of nation, its social institutions ranging from family and kinship structures to the division of labor in social, economic, political, and cultural life. Gender is also at the basis of normative values. It is a system that produces socially reinforced meanings, representations of masculinity, and femininity based on questions of ethnicity, nationality, and religion. These values that provide identity are organized in a binary pattern of oppositions that also act as principles for the distribution of power.[27]

Feminist and gender theories have shown that the role of gender in power relations between men and women is the central principle which structures social life, with social actors also being gendered. Like all social relations, including ethnic ones, gender relations have a material basis. This is expressed through the gendered social division of labor, which has two organizing principles: the principle of separation (there are men's and women's jobs) and the hierarchical principle (a man's job is worth more than a woman's job).[28] These principles can be applied, thanks to a specific process of legitimization: the naturalist ideology that reduces gender to biological sex, and limits social practices to gendered social roles that would refer to the natural destiny of the species. The theorization in terms of the gender division of labor affirms that gendered practices are social constructions, themselves the result of social relations.

We need to focus on the meaning of gender, gendered roles and symbolism, and the ways in which they maintain social order or can promote social change. Placing gender at the center of questioning challenges the disciplinary boundaries and establishes a different perspective on the social world. Gender challenges the Nature/Culture binary opposition that was at the origin of scientific disciplines. It is therefore necessary to rework sociological categories and divisions, to understand women's subjective and everyday experiences, and to identify and analyze the structures and forces that shape these experiences and situations—essentially, to reconceptualize the relationships and relations between individual life experiences and social organization.

As Teresa de Lauretis argued: "To affirm that the social representation of gender affects its subjective construction and that vice versa the subjective representation of gender—or its self representation—affects its social construction opens the possibility of a capacity to act and a self-determination at the subjective level, even individual level of daily micro-political practices. The construction of gender is both the product and the process of representation and self-representation."[29]

In addition to power relations based on social class and gender, working on the articulation between gender, class, ethnicity, and religion allows us to better measure the mechanisms of domination—in this case, a country where Shi'ism became the state religion after the revolution and was grafted onto a state inherited from the Pahlavis, with the principle of defending Persian/Shi'ite identity as the dominant one. Nonetheless, Iranian society is a fragmented society, very different from the one Ayatollah Khomeini, the founder of the Islamic regime, advocated. In the aftermath of the revolution, he continued to advocate the "unity of the ummah" (the community of believers) and "unity of discourse" (*vahdat-i kalameh*), rejecting both individuality and diversity.[30] He even opposed a political system based on a multi-party system, believing that the formation of parties contributed to the fragmentation of society and that it would have harmful consequences on unity.

As mentioned earlier, I perceive ethnicity in a logic of location and boundaries (Persian, Baluch, and Turkmen) but describe it according to age group, community expression, identity construction, and/or multiplicity of belonging.

Stuart Hall distinguished three approaches in the studies on identity. The first, from the Enlightenment period, considers identity as a sense of the self, relatively fixed, and static, that is not permeable to external influences. The second insists on the social construction of reality. The third approach, that I share, is that of an open and ever-changing sense of the self. This approach allows us to grasp the impacts of external pressures on the redefinition and reconstruction of individuals' identities.[31] Forms of subjectivation are made and unmade according to encounters, recompositions of contexts or conjunctural alliances. Refusing to reason about fixed entities makes it possible to put the political subject (and no longer just victims of dominations) back at the center of the analysis by taking into account all its practices, which are ambivalent and often ambiguous.[32]

The Islamic Republic as a Gender Regime

The Islamic Republic of Iran is a gender regime. Sylvia Walby defined gender regime as a series of gendered and interconnected relations and institutions that together constitute a system.[33] Walby argues that the gender regime operates across four institutional domains: polity, economy, civil society, and violence. On the place of the family in gender regime theory, she writes that there are three positions: treating it as an institutional domain; increasing the focus on the family but not as an institutional domain; and dispersing the relevant practices across the four institutional domains. Changing the focus to gender rather than family has been one of the important contributions of gender regime theory to social theory; she notes before concluding that the family should not be treated as an institutional domain.[34] For Valentine Moghadam, patriarchy is enduring, but it takes socially and historically specific forms. She further argued that despite the many country studies on patriarchy, theorization of varieties of patriarchy, or more precisely, the gender regime, has been absent. Moghadam applied Walby's framework to show how institutional changes in the Maghreb signal a gradual shift in the gender regime.[35] Contrary to Walby, she rightfully highlighted the importance of the family as an institutional domain in the Middle East and the Maghreb. She, however, rejected the inclusion of violence as an institutional domain even though recognizing it empirically.

In her earlier works, Moghadam argued that Neopatriarchy entails "two parallel, apparently contradictory developments … (i) the expansion of industrialization, urbanization, proletarianization, and state-sponsored education, which undermines patriarchal family authority; and (ii) the retention of Muslim family law, which legitimates the prerogatives of male family members over female family members." In such contexts, the domestic gender regime prevails.[36]

As discussed in the upcoming chapters, in Iran the family is an institution and, along with laws that attempt to govern and regulate the relationships between men and women, it plays a crucial role in maintaining the power relations between the genders. A gender regime, however, is a social and cultural construct that can be altered, subverted, and deconstructed.

I understand gender as both an individual identity and an organizing principle of social structure, and a cultural and historical product. In my research, I attempted to examine the theoretical and methodological tools analyzing the impacts of gender on the production of knowledge—additionally, the visible and invisible mechanisms of power that influence women's access to responsibilities in social, economic, religious, or political life. I share a resolutely anti-positivist methodology according to which all knowledge is socially constructed and must be understood in the context of the social relationships that produce it. Social scientists like other scientists who influence the process of validating knowledge are inhabited by their own experiences, cultural ideas, and place in intersectional social relations of race, class, gender, sexuality, religion, or nation.

As mentioned earlier, this work attempts to examine the applicability of the intersectional approach to the case of Iran, a multi-ethnic and multi-religious fragmented post-revolutionary society.

Intersectionality: Identity Politics, or a Critical Social Theory of the Non-Elites?

I will discuss Intersectionality as a three-pronged perspective: epistemological (situated knowledge), theoretical (intersectionality of social relations of gender, class, race, ethnicity, religion, etc.), and political (social action against the established unequal social order).

Combahee River Collective, a Black lesbian feminist group founded in 1973, is among the pioneers of intersectional approach in contemporary United States. In 1977, the group issued a manifesto arguing that gender, race, class, and sexuality must be integrated into any feminist analysis of power and domination. They argued that Black women, other Third World women, and working women were involved in the feminist movement from its inception, but their participation suffered both from reactionary forces outside, and from racism and elitism within the feminist movement itself. The Collective also declared that as Black feminists, they were constantly and painfully reminded of how little white women have done to understand and combat their own racism.[37]

Black feminists have shown that systems of gender, class, and racial oppression operate at the individual, social, and structural level of institutions; that dualistic thinking (which emanates from Western metaphysics) is hierarchical thinking that believes in notions of superiority and inferiority as the ideological basis of domination[38]; and that dualistic thinking prevents the conceptualization of complex interactions or reciprocal relationships. They also rejected the positivist approach and, like Sandra Harding, argued that all knowledge is situated. It is socially constructed and must be understood in the context of the social relations that produce it.

Patricia Hill Collins, a leading Black feminist and a sociologist, argued:

Overall, these ties between what one does and what one thinks illustrated by *individual* Black women can also characterize Black women's experiences and ideas as a group. Historically, racial segregation in housing, education and employment fostered group commonalities that encouraged the formation of a group based, collective standpoint. For example, the heavy concentration of US Black women in domestic work coupled with racial segregation in housing and schools meant that the US Black women had common organizational networks that enabled them to share experiences and construct a collective body of wisdom. This collective wisdom of how to survive as US Black women constituted a distinctive Black women's standpoint on gender specific patterns of racial segregation and its accompanying economic penalties.[39]

For Patricia Hill Collins, intersectionality is an analysis claiming that systems of race, social class, gender, sexuality, ethnicity, nation, and age form mutually constructing features of social organization, which shape Black women's experiences and, in turn, are shaped by Black women.[40] From this perspective, the intersectional approach must take into account four domains of power: structural (laws, institutions), disciplinary (administrative and bureaucratic management), hegemonic (ideological naturalization of relations of domination), and interpersonal (everyday interactions informed by various hierarchies). In a more recent definition, Patricia Hill Collins and Sirma Bilge stated: "Intersectionality investigates how intersecting power relations influence social relations across diverse societies as well as individual experiences in everyday life. As an analytic tool, intersectionality views categories of race, class, gender, sexuality, nation, ability, ethnicity, and age-among others-as interrelated and mutually shaping one another. Intersectionality is a way of understanding and explaining complexity in the world, in people, and in human experiences."[41] Patricia Hill Collins argued that social action and experience are important interdependent dimensions of theorizing proposed by subordinate groups.[42] However, she notes, "Within Western social theory, social actions and the experiences they engender are often interpreted as data to be included within existing social theories or bias to be excluded from them. Experience is not a valid way of knowing, and theorizing through social action may not be seen as theorizing at all [...] Intersectionality has been criticized for being too closely associated with the ideas and interests of women, Black people, poor people, and people in subordinated groups. These criticisms work to limit intersectionality's' theoretical possibilities because they constrain important tools for theorizing within resistant knowledge traditions."[43]

For Crenshaw, intersectionality is a supportive concept for the multi-dimensionality of the experiences of Black women. For example, to better identify the various interactions of race and gender in the context of violence against women of color, she develops a Black feminist critique from a book titled *All Women Are White, All the Blacks Are Men, but Some of Us Are Brave*, published in 1982.[44] This is in contrast to the single-axis analysis that neglects the multi-dimensional experiences of Black women. The starting point for Crenshaw's analysis was a complaint filed by five Black women employees of General Motors who had been fired, and had accused their employer's seniority system of perpetrating discrimination against Black women. Black women were not hired before 1964, and those employed after 1970 lost their jobs as a result of the recession because the company fired on the basis of seniority.

The court dismissed the complaint, which was not filed by women or Black men, but by Black women.[45] This implies that only white women experience sexism and Black men experience racism. This one-dimensional framework of discrimination marginalizes Black women within the very movements that proclaim themselves to be Black, but this framework also makes the goal of ending racism and patriarchy even harder to achieve.[46]

Another example Crenshaw presents to demonstrate the multi-dimensionality of Black women's experience is rape. Focusing on rape as manifestation of men's power over women's sexuality tends to overshadow the use of rape as a weapon of racist terror. When Black women were raped by white men, they were not raped as women but as Black women. Their "womanhood" made them vulnerable to racist domination, while their Black skin color denied them protection. This white male power was reinforced by a legal system in which the rape of a Black woman by a white man was simply unthinkable.

According to Crenshaw and other Black feminists, (White) feminists are unaware of how their race functions to mitigate aspects of sexism and how their race privileges them over other women and contributes to their dominant position in the social hierarchy. Definitions of patriarchy often rely on the experiences of White women. As a result, feminist theory remains white, and its potential to expand its analysis by addressing non-privileged women has not been realized.[47]

This is reminiscent of Candace West's observation that women from discriminated social groups with different collective histories and social status have challenged the 1970s [White] feminists' unitary slogan "the personal is political." For example, issues around reproduction and reproductive freedom may take on different meanings for women fighting for abortion rights, and those who have had to fight against forced sterilization.[48]

The multi-dimensionality of women's experience is a fruitful approach for understanding the experiences of women from ethnic and religious minorities in Iran.

The Theoretical Scope of Intersectionality

Intersectionality has been adopted internationally as both a concept and approach within research. But there is no consensus on how to proceed with intersectional analysis. Choo and Ferree[49] distinguish three different understandings of intersectionality that have been used in sociology research to analyze inequalities. These three typologies are given as follows:

First, practices centered around groups. It is about including the perspectives of the marginalized who are subject to various power relations by putting them at the center of the analysis in order to give voices to those who have been excluded.

The second approach is process-centered. It focuses on analytic interactions while taking into account key statistical impacts and "unmarked" categories in a non-additive way. It is often a comparative and contextual analysis of inequalities and examines the impacts of selective interaction between different intersectional dimensions in order to escape a dichotomous approach.

The third approach, which is system-focused, attempts to disentangle specific inequalities of specific institutions: "Economics is often equated with class, family with gender." This approach shows how institutions are historically co-determinants and how systems generate intersectional effects. This is what Sylvia Walby attempts to do in her book *Globalization and Inequalities.*[50]

In *Diaspora, Border, and Transnational Identities*, Avtar Brah[51] mobilizes an intersectional analysis to address issues of migration, diaspora, and borders. She emphasizes multi-axis positionality, arguing that our position in terms of power dynamics depends on different aspects of our identity, but seeing all these aspects does not mean that we are politicized. We need to deconstruct the power relations that create boundaries. Brah explores the intersections of race, gender, class, sexuality, ethnicity, generation, and nationalism in different discourses, practices, and political contexts to study "difference," "diversity," and "community," linking them to analyses of "diaspora," "border," and "location."

Nancy Fraser for her part argues, "Proponents of the identity [...] contend that to belong to a group that is devalued by the dominant culture is to be misrecognized, to suffer a distortion in one's relation to one's self. As a result of repeated encounters with the stigmatizing gaze of a culturally dominant other, the members of disesteemed groups internalize negative self-images and are prevented from developing a healthy cultural identity of their own. In this perspective, the politics of recognition aims to repair internal self-dislocation by contesting the dominant culture's demeaning picture of the group. It proposes that members of misrecognized groups reject such images in favor of new self-representations of their own making, jettisoning internalized, negative identities and joining collectively to produce a self-affirming culture of their own—which, publicly asserted, will gain the respect and esteem of society at large. The result, when successful, is 'recognition': an undistorted relation to oneself."[52] Fraser concluded that "struggles for recognition simultaneously displace struggles for economic justice and promote repressive forms of communitarianism. The solution, however, is an alternative politics of recognition, a *non-identitarian* politics that can remedy misrecognition without encouraging displacement and reification."[53]

Reacting to Nancy Fraser's argument, Nira Yuval Davis argues that the recognition-redistribution dichotomy can be misleading, and that the politics of intersectionality can include and transcend both.[54] For Yuval Davis, intersectional analysis should be a non-additive approach in which social divisions are to be analyzed in both their macro- and micro-dimensions.[55] She believes that identity politics tends to locate people's belonging in a one-dimensional way according to their ethnicity, race, class, gender, etc. The intersectional approach recognizes the multiple identities and belongings of individuals, but also the ways in which different axes and power dynamics constitute them. However, N. Yuval Davis notes, individuals may identify exclusively with one identity category, collectivity or group—women, Blacks, gays—and their social situation is concretely constructed along multiple intersectional categories of social power. On the other hand, social relations are autonomous from each other because the ontological basis of each of these divisions is autonomous, and each gives priority to different spheres of social relations. She argues for the rejection of the naturalization of all constructions of social divisions, and the refusal to give priority to one over the other. She adds that an intersectional approach to stratification requires a mode of analysis that combines case with variable analysis and is sensitive to situated contexts, but does not fall into the trap of relativism that prevents comparative judgment.[56]

Stuart Hall, on the other hand, advocates a model of relative autonomy of the systems of gender, class, and race, i.e., their analytical dissociation.[57]

According to Kathy Davis, the indeterminacy and vagueness of intersectionality are the secret of its success.[58] Intersectionality, she states, addresses the most central and normative concern within feminist studies, namely the recognition of differences within women. For Davis, intersectionality has served some feminists to deconstruct the binary oppositions and universalism inherent in Western philosophical and scientific paradigms. Intersectionality appeared to include a commitment to the situated nature of knowledge, promising to enhance the theorist's reflexivity by allowing her to incorporate her own intersectional position into the production of feminist theory that would be self-critical and accountable.[59]

Sylvia Walby argued that gender and class inequalities do not have the same trajectories of change even though they influence each other. Gender and class inequality regimes adapt to each other but are not mutually constituted.[60]

In her analysis of intersectionality, Leslie McCall makes a distinction between inter-categorical and intra-categorical approaches. Inter-categorical implies a focus on the intersection of different social categories such as race, class, gender affecting particular social behavior, or the redistribution of resources. Intra-categorical studies problematize the meaning and boundaries of the categories themselves, for example, whether Black women are included in the category of woman or the shifting boundaries of who is considered Black in a particular time and place.[61]

As mentioned earlier, intersectionality is also a frame for social action against all-out inequalities. For Patricia Hill Collins, Black feminists and their allies must turn again to the issues that affect Black women's lives on a daily basis to set a new social justice agenda that reaches out to previously neglected groups, especially young Black women workers. Hill Collins believes that "for Black feminism, freedom and social justice are deeply intertwined."[62] She further argued that intersectionality is neither a tool box nor an abstract concept. It is not a demand for identity or a theory which initiates a process of discovering a complex world. Intersectionality can and should have the capacity to theorize social inequalities in a way to make the social change easier.[63]

In her book *Trouble in Gender*, Judith Butler criticizes the etceteras of identity politics that completes the list of attributes [of race, class, gender, sexuality], which, she believes, attempts to incorporate a situated subject and fails to be complete.[64] Advocating the abandonment of categorical thinking, she specified that social movements have nothing to gain from being based on identity, and in particular that feminism can, and must, be based not on the identity of "woman" but on issues that allow it to form alliances with other sources of critique and subversion of norms, other claims for justice and recognition.

My fieldwork in 1994 with a sample of poor rural migrant women from ethnic minority in Khak-i Sefid, a poor neighborhood northeast of Tehran, made me realize that the traditional epistemology was not careful of the multiplicity of women's experiences and intersecting power relations that shape those experiences. Although the bulk of the women were from Azari villages and Shi'ite, their experience of discrimination in Tehran combined their gender, social class, and ethnicity. This experience also gradually led me to acknowledge that I had been unaware of how my family background, social class, educational credentials, and belonging to the ethnic/religious majority privileged me over many women, and contributed to my dominant position in the social hierarchy despite the fate of my family after the revolution. I later asked myself how "ordinary" Sunnite Baluch and Turkmen women experienced the intersection of religion, ethnicity, social class, and gender.

I believe that intersectionality as it has been proposed by some Black feminist theorists and theorists of color can be an alternative to movements based on claims of identity. It is not identity politics, but a critical social theory which is based not on paradigms and epistemologies of traditional knowledge, but on paradigms that emphasize the importance of intersectional oppressions in the formation of the matrix of domination.

Intersectional analysis of social relations of gender, class, ethnicity, and religion that accounts for discrimination in the everyday experiences of ethnic and religious minority women (and men) is a fertile approach when dealing with the question of social inequalities in a class-based, multi-ethnic, and multi-religious country like Iran. In the case of Iran under the Islamic regime, the matrix of domination is structured around a different axis and systems of oppression which interact, feed into, and empower each other. Religion as a power relation and as a marker of identity has been reinforced, and the Shi'ite dimension of Iranian identity emphasized on to the detriment of other components. More importantly, other religious groups, especially Sunnites, are marginalized as second-class citizens. The political system is founded on Shi'ism, and the implemented state policies have consolidated social hierarchy founded on religious/ethnic and gendered identities. I, therefore, advocate a model of relative autonomy of the systems of gender, religion, class, ethnicity, and their analytical dissociation. Intersectionality can be mobilized as an epistemology and a theory that includes ethnic/religious and subaltern women's experiences in the making of social, political, economic knowledge of Iranian women and society, and as a strategy for social justice.

1

Crafting Iranian Nationalism: Intersectionality of Ethnicity, Gender, and Religion

This chapter analyzes the making of Iranian nationalism as an ideology of the modern nation-state. I argue that Iranian nationalism was from the beginning impregnated with the influence of the Western Orietalists and has excluded entire segments of the population because of their ethnic, gender, or religious belongings. A brief contemporary historical review shows that these social relations, however, did not have a unique trajectory of change and should be dissociated analytically. Under the Pahlavis, the social hierarchy was rather based on male Persian identity and belonging to the detriment of other genders and ethnicities. Under the Islamic regime, the Shi'ite dimension of Iranian identity is highlighted to the detriment of other religions, including Sunnism, and women are submitted to men's neo/patriarchal authority. Shi'ism thus overdetermines individuals and tends to legitimize structural relations of power based on gender, ethnicity, religion, or class.

Ethnic Diversity and National Identity

Contrary to the essentialist approach to ethnicity according to which ethnic groups are natural and unchanging, ethnic relations are above all social relations. Economic and political inequalities produce ethnicity, ethnic groups, and ethnic claims. For this very reason, "we need to rethink the notion of ethnicity from the margins, from the dominated."[1]

It is social relations that constitute people in categories and ethnic agents. Ethnic relations structure people's life opportunities, influence their social class standing, condition their practice, and shape their identities. Danielle Juteau argued that ethnic groups are constituted within an unequal social relationship, deny members of other groups access to available societal resources, and thus establish their dominance. Ethnic boundaries are thus shaped while the markers used to define them are chosen. The incessant movement of ethnic boundaries, resulting from changes in the criteria for inclusion and exclusion, leads to subsequent transformations in terms of identification and belonging, the collective "we."[2] According to the subjectivist approach, ethnicity corresponds to individual identity, awareness of belonging, and the agent's identification with an ethnic group. However, ethnic identity is not fixed. It is socially constructed, and collective identity formation becomes part of the conflict itself. For some social scientists, ethnicity refers to the identical characteristics of a group, such as a common origin, historical memories, culture, and connection to a certain geographical entity.[3]

Stuart Hall argues that ethnicity is the necessary place or space from which people speak. It is a very important moment in the birth and development of all the local and marginal movements which have transformed the last twenty years, that moment of the rediscovery of their own ethnicities. "I can't speak of the world but I can speak of my village. I can speak of my neighborhood; I can speak of my community." "The face-to-face communities that are knowable, that are locatable, one can give them a place. One knows what the voices are. One knows what the faces are. The recreation, the reconstruction of imaginary, has destroyed the identities of specific places. So one understands the moment when people reach for those groundings, as it were, and the reach for those groundings is what I call ethnicity."[4]

Contrary to Hall, Elisabeth Cunin stated that ethnicity is usually perceived in a logic of location, in its ties with a specific place that shapes local identities and cultural differences. However, ethnicity is increasingly de-territorialized and inscribed in both national and transnational spaces. Concomitantly, its description as communitarian expression and cultural continuity gives way to an analysis in which the notions of identity construction and multiple belongings are dominant. Ethnicity is not dissolved, but finds new resources and new forms of expression. Appropriation and resource mobilization, both symbolic and material, allow urban and upper and middle classes to appropriate national and transnational identity signs without questioning their own sense of belonging. "If references to hybridization have been mobilized to describe the weakening of identity boundaries and the multiplication of cultural borrowings, the fact remains that globalization also means the renewal of hierarchical relationships and dominance, in particular in the definition and attribution of ethnicity."[5]

Hamid Ahmadi rejects the use of the ethnic group concept for Iran: "Given the historical context of Iran, there are no racial and cultural criteria to distinguish between linguistic and religious groups. Thus the concept of ethnic groups as racial and cultural units is not relevant. The existence of ethnic groups with racial or cultural specificities has its origin in the thinking of scholars rather than in the historical reality of Iran."[6]

However, my observations do not confirm Ahmadi's argument which reflects the viewpoint of the majority. Contrary to ethnic/religious minorities, Persian/Shi'ites as the majority do not think of themselves as belonging to an ethnicity but as universal. Ethnicity reflects a hierarchical view of the relationship between Persians and the rest of the society, the former being the source of the identity traits assigned to the latter. If ethnicity traditionally appears as the result of an identity assignment, which aims to differentiate "us" and "the others" who are supposed to be the only bearers of ethnic identity and attribute, it becomes a resource in the hands of actors who appropriate it and mobilize a category hitherto built from the outside. This endeavor reminds me of the concept of negritude invented by Aimé Césaire to affirm the existence of a people. Negritude, which encompasses ethnic, historical, and cultural characteristics, became an ideology of emancipation.[7]

Economic, cultural, and political stranglehold of Shi'ites/Persians over Sunnites propels a number of the latter to show their "Persian credentials" by separating themselves from other Sunnites. This behavior adopted by some agents/actors/groups in situations of domination is a survival strategy. However, this process of othering reinforces the ethnicized social order that is already set in place. As will be shown, this ethnicized hierarchy is not hermetically sealed, as there is considerable differentiation and fluidity within it. Though, the basic contours of its structure have continued to remain recognizable.

The Iranian modern state has played an active and crucial role in creating ethnic/religious/gender social hierarchy.

In her study of Kurdish women (in Turkey, Syria, Iraq, and Iran), Shahrzad Mojab argues that the state, although uninvited, is prominently, and often violently, present in Kurdistan, a territory without "recognized borders." She further argues that Kurdish women face patriarchal politics of Kurdish nationalist parties, the misogynism of Islamic groups, the political repression of central governments, continuing war, and a largely disintegrated economy and society.[8]

According to Alam Saleh, the Islamic regime appears to adopt two widespread methods designed to numerically marginalize the ethnic groups for the purpose of political control: first, it encourages non-locals to migrate to the ethnic regions and cities; second, it encourages ethnic members to migrate to different parts of the country, away from their ethnic kin. In doing so, the regime denies minority members access to local jobs and deprives them of positions of political power, and plans to redistribute the ethnic population.[9]

He further argues that when ethnic minorities are denied legitimate access to the state's resources and are not capable of achieving their expectations, conflict inevitably becomes the only option for the deprived group to act against the regime and acquire political agency.[10]

It is through the process of primary socialization operating in families from an early age, particularly owing to the influence of mothers, that ethnicity is inscribed in individuals. In addition to the ethnicity acquired through socialization, there is also the ethnicity that is built up in relationship with others enhanced by migration as is the case of Baluch in Golestan province. Ethnic boundaries have two sides, internal and external. These are built simultaneously, in the relationship to others (external dimension) and in the relationship to history and culture (internal dimension). It is in the relationship to others that the culture and history of a group acquire a specific meaning for the actors and give rise to ethnic communalization.[11] Communalization, as the process that leads to the formation of the group, is itself generated by often unequal social relations.

The family is also a place where gender identity is formed. Individual subjectivity, gender, religious, ethnic or otherwise, is indissociable from the experience which produces it. As it shall be seen when I discuss the highly educated Baluch women, micro-political practices made possible by the access of ethnic, rural, and lower-class women to education and professionalization played a crucial role in the intellectual empowerment of ethnic activists. They have challenged the superiority assumed by both their male counterparts and the Persian women from wealthier backgrounds. The static and essentialist construction of these ethnic women is rooted in a perspective representing ethnic minorities through stereotypical and inaccurate images. However, through civic practices, these women have produced meaning which challenged both dominant institutions and local/ethnic traditions—perceived as both powerful and unalterable. They have transformed "I want" into "I have the right," a demand that is negotiable in public space.[12]

Their hybrid identities celebrating the multiplicity of belongings can also be analyzed as a strategy aimed at challenging power relations. Ethnic identity operates within a network of interacting strategies of the groups involved. These strategies are mainly determined by environmental, economic, or political factors. In Iran, despite the revolution, social transformations, including massive urbanization, have altered the organization of society. Ethnic groups and identities have not disappeared; rather, they have altered. Social inequalities and power relations between men and women are not rooted in religion. Religion, however, has often been instrumentalized to reinforce the social hierarchy between classes, ethnicities, and genders. In my study, however, I observed that in some cases, religion, both Shi'ite and Sunnite, was transformed into a natural and hereditary attribute. Those who qualify themselves as guardians of religious hierarchy "established a close connection between purity of blood, endogamous marriage and legitimate birth," as Fiona Wilson argued for the case of Peru.[13]

Ethnic aspects of identity must be studied in relation to non-ethnic aspects as Richard Tapper suggested. "Ethnic identities cannot be studied in isolation but as they are used in hierarchies; ethnic identities have different bases and different connotations, language is often no guide, an individual may claim different 'ethnic' identities, at different times and in different contexts."[14] Ethnic groups stress social reproduction and the concern to carry on the ethnic line. "Women are pressed into acting as the principal, de facto, signifiers of racial and ethnic boundaries."[15] Identities and relations of gender and ethnicity, however, are not immutable. Gender subordination like ethnic oppression is resisted and contested.

Nationalism, Nation-state, and Gender

Nationalism, as an ideological construct, is a modern political phenomenon related to the emergence of the nation-state. Hobsbawm claimed that "nationalism comes before nations. Nations do not make states and nationalisms but the other way round."[16] He also argued for the dual phenomenon of the nation, as it is constructed from above and below. However, according to Mohamad Tavakoli-Targhi:

> The emergence of Iran as a 'geobody' with bounded territory was linked to the global establishment of nation-states and the international demarcation of national boundaries in the 19th century. Territorial enclosure was in part imposed on Iran via the treaties of Golestan (1813), Turkmanchay (1828), Erzrum (1823 and 1847) and Paris (1857). The latter provided the ground for the emergence of Iran's eastern boundaries. But these boundary-formalizing treaties shaped the national body politic and prompted its full anthropomorphization. Territorial enclosure shifted the characterization of Iran from a confederation

of territories to a cohesive entity. [This] marked the transition from an emire to a modern nation-state. The relative fixity of borders provided the ground upon which Iran could be conceived as a unified homeland (vatan) with a distinct character, identity, history and culture.[17]

Tavakoli-Targhi further argued:

A later 19th century abstraction of vatan as home made possible the metaphoric depiction of Iran as the national home and as a site for the cultivation of nationalist sentiments and heart-attachments. The spiritualization of territorial vatan provided the perspectival foundation for the reconfiguration of a cohesive and unified 'national' culture, literature, and history. All viewed as the manifestation of the homeland's soul, spirit, and biography. Once fully anthropomorphalized, vatran became of site of matriotic love, possession, and protection.[18]

Nation-building reformulates social relations in terms of gender, class, and ethnicity. Nira Yuval-Davis underlined four different layers of significance assigned to women in nation-building projects: their capacity to give birth; their assigned role as primary caregivers to children; their representation as the symbols of the nation; and finally their bodies as metonyms for the homeland. She argued that the nation naturalizes gender difference most effectively since national ideologies assign women a reproductive function.[19] Women's role in the national community is first and foremost that of a mother; they are sacralized and understood as a "genetic resource" for the national community. As mothers, they ensure the future of the nation through their reproductive capacity. Since they give birth to future members of the nation, they are also the symbolic guarantors of the community and the honor of the nation. Mothers are then associated with notions of purity, chastity, authenticity, and morality. Maternal female bodies are also used as an allegory of the nation.[20]

Likewise, the most widely shared image of ethnic women refers to the link between women's bodies and their reproductive capacities. Ruth Miller identifies the womb as "the predominant biopolitical space,"[21] where states practice sovereignty.

The nation is gendered, but it is also sexualized. If in the nation's imagination women were above all chaste and loving mothers, femininity has been associated with women's fertility (especially, to give sons to the nation) and men have not escaped their heterosexual and reproductive destiny. Women's responsibility as mothers and wives was to serve the state by serving their families, that is, by teaching their male children to serve the state. Since the purpose of marriage remained procreation, the childless couple was stigmatized. Iranian popular culture referred to a childless couple as "house without light" and infertile women as "burnt eyes." This stigma was even stronger in rural areas:

> After marriage, the bride's entourage eagerly awaited the announcement of her pregnancy, after which she was cherished by her husband, family and in-laws. The father would give his young daughter away for reproduction and he would be discredited if his daughter did not promise a child immediately after the wedding. If the woman continued to be infertile, her husband lost interest in her and, believing that the marriage contract was broken, contracted a second marriage. Children were considered to be the nails that held a woman at home, and women were expected to multiply the bonds that protected them from repudiation. Through his children and especially his sons, the man sought to strengthen the size and prestige of the family.[22]

As for the woman, her social recognition was clearly linked to her sons. "She expects her son to have a strong attachment to her, which in turn serves to counterbalance her husband's superiority in the household. This gives her status and power in a male-dominated society."[23] Queen Farah Diba, the Shah's third wife, who consolidated her marriage and status with the birth of her eldest son Reza in October 1960, a year after her marriage, is an example. The Shah, who had a daughter from his first marriage with Fawzia, the daughter of the Egyptian king Fuad, had to painfully separate from his second wife Soraya, with whom he was in love, due to her infertility. The birth of an heir to the throne when the Shah was considered lacking in virility did not take long to provoke gossip. Queen Farah Diba said, "Rumors were circulating that the Shah was not the father because he could not have sons! Or that I had deliberately given birth in a large hospital in the south of Tehran (the poor part of the city) so that the girl I gave birth to could be exchanged with a boy!"[24]

The control of women and their sexuality is crucial to the process of national and ethnic construction as women are supposed to reproduce the boundaries of national (and ethnic) groups.[25] The language of nationalism chooses women as symbolic depositaries of group identity, describes its objects using the vocabulary of kinship—the motherland (mâm-e mihan), the house (khâneh)—thereby indicating something to which one is "naturally" attached. Iranian modernity, which is the foundation of nationalist ideology, has imposed the gender dichotomy. The nation, politics, and knowledge were associated with the male gender, the homeland with the female gender. As Afsaneh Najmabadi argued, in the modernist-nationalist discourse, the motherland was represented as a suffering body, a vulnerable female figure offering the nationalists the discourse of protecting women and the motherland and defending their honor.[26] Nationalism transformed gender and sexuality and also produced the hetero-normalization of love and sexuality. The woman's body was constituted as the "originary home" of all Iranians. "The Care for "future mothers" as the pedagogues of the nation was linked to the task of caring for the motherland. [...] With the maternalization of body-politic, human agency and responsibility became essential to the preservation and recovery of the motherland."[27] Afsaneh Najmabadi spoke of the erotic mapping of Iran as a body to love, possess, protect, and defend and to die for. She argued that this erotic mapping was essential to the understanding of Iranian nationalism.[28]

Thinking about gender as male/female is a modern imperative made possible through the erasing of other modes of masculinity: *amrad* (young teenager) and *mokhannath* (adult man, object of desire for men). This erasure has been carried out in favor of a heterosexual, virile, hegemonic masculinity. Afsaneh Najmabadi also proposes to read the change in aesthetic sensibilities (disappearance of the female moustache) not as an attempt by Iranian women to resemble European women, but rather as the disappearance of the amrad from the cultural imagination and the erasure of its importance for male sexuality.[29] As the enemies of the motherland were viewed as rapists, the demonstration of zealotry and integrity was viewed as essential to nationalized manhood. Idleness was equated with being woman-like. To mobilize for political action, men were often compared to women, and accounts of women's bravery and self-sacrifice were deployed rhetorically to put men to shame.[30] The concept of honor (nâmous), which had a religious connotation, thus became closely linked to the masculinity of the nation.

The constitutional revolution (1906–11)[31] was marked by the idea of social, ethnic, religious, and linguistic diversity of the nation. This idea disappeared when the nationalist ideology substituted Persianness for Iranianness. This conception denied the ethnic diversity of a state which is the direct heir of an ancient empire.

Inspired by European Orientalism, the intellectual advocates of Western-oriented nationalism attempted to found a new Iranian identity based on the Persian language and on a pre-Islamic past.[32] Orientalism is constructed on the dichotomy between the self (with positive values) and identified with rationality, equality, or liberty, and the other who is identified with irrationality, licentiousness, and exoticism. Conte de Gobineau, for example, held an Aryanist discourse and established a hierarchy between the Semites and the Persians; Persians appropriated and reproduced this hierarchy. "The origin of the Aryan myth is usually associated with Sir William Jone's discovery in 1786 that Greek, Latin, Sanskrit and Persian derived from common roots. The term 'Aryan' itself was coined by the French Orientalist Abraham-Hyacinth Anquetil-Duperron (1731–1806). […] He Europeanized the term ariya, a term he found in the Avesta, fusing it with arioi, the term Herodotus used for Medes […]. The key semantic evolution happened in 1819, when Friedrich Schlegel initiated further Europeanization of Aryan by suggesting that Vedic and Avestan *ariya* are related to German *ehre* (honor) […]. Schlegel altered Aryan from a translation of ariya into a modern racial category, which immediately captured the imagination of his contemporaries."[33] In the course of the nineteenth century, the Aryanist discourse came to permeate the entire corpus of Orientalist writing on Iran and India. Confrontations between races alleged to be irreconcilably different had become a common means to decipher history's riddles in the vein of Gobineau's work.[34]

Orientalism as the colonial ideology also made use of male-dominant discourse and attempted to stabilize the hierarchal social order and "natural" stability of gender categories.

These two elements (Persian language and a pre-Islamic past) made Iranian nationalism an attractive ideology, later endorsed by the Pahlavi dynasty. This new conception of identity leaned on language and territory, in accordance with the dominant model in Europe, especially in France.[35] Secular intellectuals who played a crucial role in the construction of nationalist ideology became the symbolic figures of the modern middle class. They endorsed a narrative of progress that fabricated the universality of European trajectory and according to which Western societies already constituted the future to which others are called to and that they should attain. Through this linear vision, these intellectuals saw the history of their own country as a variation of a meta-narrative called the history of Europe, thereby implying Western cultural, social, political, and technological superiority.[36] They imitated this idealized model, advocated a modernist project based on law, science, and progress, thinking that it would civilize or rather Europeanize the Iranian nation.

Among the intellectuals who contributed to the construction of nationalist ideology were Mirza Fathali Akhundzadeh (1812–78) and Mirza Agha Khan Kermani (1854–96). Their project consisted in substituting nationalism for Islam, whose effect on society they considered disastrous, and in "civilizing" the Iranian nation by Europeanizing it.

Orientalist mechanisms consisted in qualifying as uncivilized/Islamic all the negative aspects of Iranian culture and evacuating them as such.

Intellectuals argued for the new Iran to get rid of its Arab/Islamic ways in order to become more rational, reasonable, and enlightened. Akhundzadeh criticized the inequalities between men and women, and affirmed that Islam was incompatible with modernism and democratic constitutionalism. For these intellectuals who saw the veil as a sign of backwardness and a major obstacle to progress for women, the condition of women served to define the boundaries between the "civilized" world of Europe and the "barbaric" world of Islam. In his writings, Kermani, Akhundzadeh's disciple, "came up with the first mention of term Aryan in modern Iranian writing, [...] and the first to display a good grasp of racialist theories then *en vogue* in Europe. He believed that if one were to observe an Iranian, a Greek, and an Englishman, and then an Ethiopian Sudanese negro [sic] and an Arab, he would clearly be able to judge which one is clean and civilised and which other savage." As to Arabs, Kermani describes them "naked bandits, homeless rat-eaters, vilest humans, most vicious beasts, camel rider thieves, animal-like and even worse than animals."[37]

This racialist discourse was later re-appropriated by nationalist elites such as Hasan Taqizadeh, who published the influential newspaper *Kaveh* in Berlin from 1916 to 1922 and occasionally referred to "pure Iranian race," and the historian and Prime Minister Hasan Pirniya (Moshir al-Dowleh 1871–1935), or the historian Sadeq Reza Zadeh Shafaq (1897–1971).

The construction of a civilized nation-state required the education of women (mothers), making them the educators of (male) citizens and the companions of the men of the nation. The idea of a new configuration of the family as the foundation of the modern nation and the very condition of modernity, centered around the spouses and close to the European model, led intellectuals to claim for the transformation of the marriage from a procreation contract into a contract based on heterosexual love. The family was thus rethought in relation to the national community and no longer in relation to kinship.[38] This reconfiguration of the family was supposed to give new meaning to motherhood. From this point of view, the mother was no longer perceived as a mere reproducer but was above all valued in her new educational and nurturing role. The model of the conjugal family advocated by the modernists found its justification and feasibility in the low rate of polygamy in Iran. According to one estimate, only 2 percent of families were polygamous in late nineteenth century.[39] The harem, an institution peculiar to the rich, had become an important royal and social institution under Nasir al-Din Shah (1848–96), who borrowed from the Russians and the British to cover the expenses of his harem. After his assassination, his son Mozaffar al-Din Shah decided to dissolve the harem, reflecting a change in the perception of marriage by the privileged classes and the approval of its monogamous character in the run-up to the constitutional revolution.[40]

The nation thus took shape in the feminine model of the educated mother. Girls' schools were expected to participate in the regulated emancipation of women and the liberation of men from the burden of household management, enabling men to participate in national politics. "This transformation of woman from a subject of the household to its manager was at once a regulating and an empowering moment although women's education was oriented toward rearing an educated (male) citizenry."[41] On the other hand, women's education was associated with the idea of gender mix or heterosociability, which was nevertheless accompanied by a categorical division of gender roles. The aim of the modernist/nationalists whose project was focused on law, science, and progress was not to free women from religion but from superstition which they argued was enforced through female socialization.

According to nationalist ideology, the respectability and recognition of the men of the nation were measured by the education and upbringing of their wives or daughters and their ability to educate their children. The concept of honor, too, started to change in meaning, although in practice it was still the marker of masculinity. On the other hand, as Kashani-Sabet argued, honor was not only about controlling women's sexuality, but also about controlling their education in an appropriate manner.[42]

Educating women and encouraging them to enter the public space went hand in hand with strict control of women's sexuality but also of their role in society. While nationalists encouraged women's emancipation, they also promoted the values of "modesty" in their behavior and explained that excessive Westernization would lead to the loss of women and the nation as a whole. It is precisely these values of modesty mobilized by nationalists that enabled them to assign women as second-class citizens.

With the construction of the modern state, women were included in the general program of modernization and national development. They obtained the right to education and to work and later gained political rights (1963). However, the implemented reforms did not challenge gender social relations within the family, which was largely ruled until 1967 by a traditionalist model of Islamic laws.

Under the Pahlavi state (1925–79), the model of an ideal woman was that of a modern woman who was a Persian speaker, Westernized, unveiled, educated, and belonging to the urban middle class. However, despite her credentials, she remained modest and accepted the superiority of her male relatives (father, husband, etc.) who themselves obeyed the Shah's authority. The goal of the Pahlavi rulers was not to question gender inequalities but to facilitate regulated access of educated and modern women to the public space and sphere. Sustaining patriarchal authority within the family thus proved indispensable to the strengthening of patriarchal political order personified by the monarch.[43]

Despite this construction of "modesty," some women gained access to public space and salaried jobs, but many women did not benefit from these new dynamics. Indeed, the access of middle-class and upper-class women to revenue earning activities or jobs in the administration consolidated the hierarchies between social classes and ethnicities to the extent that men and women from the subaltern/ethnic groups remained largely excluded from the opportunity to join this new elite through education and professionalization. Thus, national ideologies, backed by the notion of modernity, reformulated the social relations of gender and of class and ethnicity. Indeed, they constructed heteronormative social norms of upper classes or modern educated middle classes structured upon the majority ethnic group.

Correlatively to the idealization of masculinity as the foundation of the modern nation-state, "woman" was idealized as the guardian of both public and private moral order. She was not confined to the family but was assigned to passive roles.

Revolutionary Women: Femininity under Threat

Nationalist movements in which women participated and to which they tremendously contributed[44] have often been described as movements that betray the women's causes that they champion.[45] This betrayal encouraged women political activists to distinguish between these two political projects, with some creating autonomous structures. Feminists and nationalists thus started to approach each other with suspicion, and nationalism is no longer seen by some feminists as a progressive force for change.[46]

In Iran at the beginning of the twentieth century, women's rights or feminist activists had a complex relationship with nationalist struggles because of their minority status. The divergence between feminism and nationalism resulted in the creation of autonomous structures (women's associations, journals, girl's schools).

The gender of the Iranian nation was also articulated around the social movements that led to the founding and consolidation of the nation-state in which women participated: the constitutional revolution (1906–11) and the demands for the transition from an absolutist regime to a parliamentary monarchy, combined with demands related to civic, political, and social rights or citizenship for women. The Tobacco Movement (1891–2) against the Shah's concession to produce, sell, and export tobacco to Major Talbot, a British subject, was the first collective participation of women in a national movement against foreign interference in Iran. Women's participation extended from Tehran to Shiraz or Tabriz, where armed women, led by Zeynab Pasha, rose up and closed the bazaar. Even the women of the Shah's harem gave up their hookah and refused to serve it to the Shah.[47]

It was during the constitutional revolution that Iranians first defined themselves as members of the nation and demanded the building of a national, independent, and constitutional state. Constitutional women founded the Secret Women's Associations (anjoman ha-yi serri) and later the Women's Associations (anjoman ha-yi nesvan) to discuss their social and political rights.[48] They identified with the national/constitutional movement while expressing the demands of women's citizenship. Women who were constitutionalists took to the streets in support of the revolution, with some reportedly taking up arms. According to one foreign observer, "Iranian women were actively involved in the revolution. We have a photo of a group of about 60 armed women in Tabriz. The author also stated that the lifeless bodies of some 20 women constitutionalists had been found."[49]

These women who illustrated their ability to fight and claimed the use of force and the right to violence against absolutism did not correspond to the norms of femininity, characterized by passivity, docility, and dependence on men. Their displacement from femininity was likely to cause the destabilization of men's identities. This included those of revolutionaries, additionally provoking a crisis of masculinity marked by virility, domination, and control over women's activities, bodies, and sexuality. Revolutionary women were thus quickly disarmed by men from their own camps, who asked them to simply support the movement and refrain from physical involvement. In 1909, women constitutionalists demanded political rights for women and staged unsuccessful sit-ins in parliament to pressure MPs.[50] However, they continued to support the parliament, known as the "house of the nation" (khaneh-yi mellat), and to organize against foreign interference by participating in the December 1911 demonstration in Tehran against the Russian ultimatum to close the parliament. The refusal of the majority of the deputies to grant women political rights, which were considered un-Islamic at the time, finally convinced the constitutionalist activists that equal rights could only be achieved through the struggle of the women themselves, and that education was a prerequisite. To this end, they founded girls' schools and women's associations in Tehran, and the provinces and continued to publish women's magazines. The magazine *Danesh* (*Knowledge*) was founded in Tehran in 1910 by Dr. Kahal, a practicing ophthalmologist, and Shekoufeh (Bud) in 1914 by Mozayen ol-Saltaneh, a specialist of education, who established three elementary schools and a vocational school for girls in the capital. But neither modernity nor the constitutional revolution that carried it met the expectations of women activists who demanded social and political inclusion in the national family.[51]

It should be mentioned that the Constitutional Law of 1907 made education for girls and boys compulsory and free until the end of primary school, but the funds to carry out this reform could not be raised. In 1910, there were only forty-seven primary schools for girls with 2,187 pupils.

Women's rights activists took the initiative to establish schools both in Tehran and in several provincial cities. In 1843, Fidelia Fiske (an American missionary) founded a girls boarding school in Urmiyeh that continued to grow under her supervision. Touba Roshdiyeh founded the first school for girls in 1903, Bibi khanom Astarabadi established first school for girls in Rasht in 1905, followed by Azarmidokht Nikravan in 1914, and Roshanak Nodoost Rasht in 1917. Sadiqeh Dowlatabadi, one of Iran's most famous feminists, was also an ardent nationalist and anti-colonial activist. The daughter of a renowned high-ranking cleric in Isfahan, she founded the first school for girls in her hometown in 1917, called the Mother of Schools. These schools were attacked by traditionalist clerics. For example, Seyed Ali Shoushtari issued a religious edict in 1903 that said: "Woe to the country in which girls' schools are founded." However, these initiatives attracted many girls, including those who had previously attended Quranic schools.

In 1918, only two high schools for girls existed: the American Missionary School, established in 1896, and Jeanne d'Arc, a French school founded in 1910.[52]

Women's rights activists also founded women's associations and continued to publish women's magazines, including *Zaban-i zanan* ("Women's Language") in 1919, *Alam-i nesvan* ("Women's Universe") in 1920, *Jahan-i Zanan* ("Women's World") or *Nameh-yi banavan* ("Women's Letter") in 1921, and *Peyk-i Sa'adat-i nesvan* ("The Messenger of Women's Happiness") in 1928. These publications and public addresses by women's rights activists did not please traditionalists. The magazine *Zaban-i zanan* published by Dowlatabadi provoked the anger of religious groups in Isfahan. Threatened and driven underground in her city,

Dowlatabadi was forced into exile in Tehran after an obscurantist group attacked her magazine and cooperative premises. She continued her activities in Tehran by founding other associations. According to Dowlatabadi, her magazine was against Iran's dependence on foreign powers (Russian and British), against the wearing of the veil and for the economic and emotional independence of women, for their education in ethics, literature, and science. She campaigned against British interference in Iranian domestic politics and often intervened publicly on these issues. Although Iran had escaped colonization and had not suffered its destructive impacts because of its strategic location (the Caspian Sea to the north, the Persian Gulf to the south), which was of interest to the two great powers, Britain and Russia, the country was nevertheless their sphere of influence. Dowlatabadi launched a second magazine called *Nameh-yi banavan* ("The Women's Letter"). This magazine, which advocated for women's rights and against the wearing of the veil, was continually threatened.

Nameh-yi Banavan was much like *Taking Care of Home and Children*, edited by Margaret Ashby in New York. Ashby was then president of the International Alliance for Women's Suffrage (IASW) and a friend of Dowlatabadi, who attended the tenth IAWS congress of the IAWS in May 1926 in Paris.[53]

Under Reza Shah's rule, autonomous women's associations were prohibited.

The Nation-state and the Construction of a Hegemonic Masculinity

"Every time men have been forced to give up the physical violence, women's social importance has increased."[54]

In the course of its contemporary history, Iran has witnessed the power-based construction of different normative models of dominant masculinities based on a female/male dichotomy, with heterosexuality as a frame of reference. "The masculine identity is defined as a conquest of the subject by himself. Only masculinity is a praxis, masculine identity is wrested from high struggle against adversity, against the resistance of nature and against that of women, against the divergent interests of men or against their hostility."[55]

Masculinity as a social construction related to a specific experience of being forges a sense of identity and individual, collective right between men within the material relationships that are based in the increasingly globalized family/domestic relations. Masculinity associates men with power and autonomy. As to femininity, it has been correlated with a woman's fertility, their submission and vulnerability, and therefore their need for protection by men and the state that represents hegemonic power. However, as Raewyn Connell argued, masculinities are multiple, socially constructed, and therefore subject to change, and they are experienced locally and globally.[56] But there is a hegemonic masculinity that is promoted as an inspirational model. Weapons as a source of masculine identities linked to power and subordination increase the probability of violence against women. The compulsory unveiling campaign under Reza Shah was an example of the violence imposed on veiled women from religious, traditional families.

The advent of Reza Shah (1925–41), founder of the Pahlavi dynasty (1925–79), who intended to build a modern nation and modernize the country, combined with the emergence of a strong, centralized, and almighty state, strongly hierarchized masculinities. Reza Shah, a former officer of the Cossack brigades who continued to wear a uniform and military boots, constructed and represented a militarized hegemonic model of masculinity associated with power, dictatorship, and violence, but also with sexual vigor and reproductive strength. Let us recall that Reza Shah had eleven children, seven of whom were boys born to four different women.

The Politics of Clothing and the Construction of the Nation-state

"Modernity exposes the woman's body; the more the body is revealed, the more modern the nation. The more that sexuality is spoken, the more modern the culture. Yet, both rich and poor nations, so-called modern and not, suffer domestic violence, rape, and unwanted pregnancies."[57]

Veiling and unveiling are but two sides of the same coin, so that the former becomes an instrument of control over sexuality and the latter an instrument of its exploitation. The unequal power relations between men and women remain unchallenged.

The prohibition of the veil in 1936 and the imposition of new aesthetic codes initiated by Reza Shah, namely, the abandonment of the traditional clothes in favor of the wearing of European clothes for urban women and men, pursued different objectives. They intended to create a new Iranian femininity and to forge modern women and to encourage their presence in the public space, all by subjecting them to the political power. On the one hand, the aim was to subordinate the traditional masculinity of Iranian men. Traditional masculinity is constructed as provider of family needs, assuming control over income and resources as well as women.

The identity of men as providers is likely to legitimize the exclusion of women from work outside the home and, along with men's reproductive capacities, constitutes a major characteristic of masculinity.

For the sovereign, it was a question of reshaping the bodies of (urban) women by subjecting them physically and symbolically to the orders of power. But for the overwhelming majority of women, not wearing the veil meant nudity and the loss of their honor. As for their husbands, fathers, or brothers who, according to traditions, were the guardians of the family's honor (nâmous) and of the women's "modesty," this prohibition was like a castration stripping them of their traditional virility associated with a series of values such as nobility, bravery, and courage. In this sense, the loss of honor added to the existing vulnerability and inability to defend their veiled women, who were violated by police officers who forced the removal of women's veils in public spaces.[58] This campaign of forced unveiling was an added repressive policy that participated in the construction of a model of militarized hegemonic masculinity. The forced sedentarization of tribes called Takht-i Ghapoo (especially the Qashqai and the Bakhtiari), the repression of leaders who refused to submit to the Reza Shah, the imprisonment of nationalists such as Mohammad Mossadeq (the would-be prime minister), and of communists and socialists such as Taqi Arani (who died in prison), and the assassination in prison of intellectuals such as the revolutionary poet Farokhi Yazdi illustrate the silencing of dissident voices. To paraphrase Renan, these violent beginnings which stand at the origins of Iranian modern nation-state have first to be "forgotten" before allegiance to a more unified, homogeneous national identity could begin to be forged. "Omission, and I would even say historical error, are an essential factor in the creation of a nation [...]. Historical investigation sheds light on the facts of violence that happened at the origin of all political formations.[...]. Unity is always brutal."[59]

As we shall see later, important political and military violence has also been exerted on ethnic minorities and political opponents by the Islamic regime in an attempt to construct a modern Shi'ite nation-state.

Despite the forced unveiling of women that stripped men of their traditional authority and submitted them to the state, the power of the state embodied by the powerful king preserved the traditional masculinity. In school books under the title of Shah it was said: "Each family lives in a home. The father is the family's head who works hard to provide his family with all they need. If we consider the

Iranian people as a family, Iran is their home and the Shah is the head of this big family. He is a loving father for all Iranians."[60]

For the modernist intellectuals who inspired and accompanied the political elite at that time, and who acquiesced to unequal gender relations, the main social responsibility and natural role of women were the procreation and education of children. They also thought that women's political participation was in contradiction with their natural characteristics.[61]

Cultural Nationalism and the Nation-state Building

Contemporary nationalism is a force of reaction rather than action, and tends to be more cultural than political.[62] According to Kosaku Yoshino, "Cultural nationalism seeks to regenerate the national community by creating, preserving or strengthening the cultural identity of a people when it is felt to be lacking or threatened. Cultural nationalists see the nation as the product of a unique history and culture and a collective solidarity with unique attributes."[63] For Stuart Hall, the question of identity is crucial and discourse of power creates specific identities because identity is not stable or based on some shared past. In fact, it is constructed within the spheres of history, language, and culture. Avoiding an essentialist view, Hall argued that identities arise from the narrativization of the self, but the necessarily fictional nature of this process in no way undermines its discursive, material, or political effectivity.[64]

Western-oriented nationalism served to enforce the power of Persian men over women, and ethnic and religious minorities. Mahmoud Afshar, a prominent nationalist secular intellectual who had obtained his doctorate in political science in 1919 from the University of Lausanne, was a pioneer of the pan-Iranist movement. In his youth he had been active in the "Young Iran Society" (Anjoman-i Iran-i Javan), a group of nationalist Iranians, most of whom had been educated in European universities. One of the influential members of the group was Reza Khan, who became Shah in 1925. Afshar argued:

> What I mean by the national unity of Iran is a political, cultural and social unity of the people who live within the present day boundaries of Iran. This unity includes two other concepts, namely, the maintenance of political independence and the geographical integrity of Iran. However, achieving national unity means that the Persian language must be established throughout the country, that regional differences in clothing, customs and the like must disappear, and that local chieftains must be eliminated. Kurds, Lors, Qashqa'is, Arabs, Turks,

Turkmens, etc., shall not differ from one another by wearing different clothes or by speaking a different language. In my opinion, until national unity is achieved in Iran the possibility that our political independence and geographical integrity be endangered will always remain.[65]

Reza Shah appealed to uniformity and demanded that Iranians including members of ethnic groups conform their way of life to a new model defined in a Persianized and pro-Western manner. Every nonconforming element was regarded as a sign of backwardness and a possible threat to modernity. But nationalism as an ideological construction is a modern political phenomenon, and as John Breuilly argues, nationalism is about politics and politics is about power and state control.[66] The stake was to create national identities by bringing together membership of the political nation-state and identification with the national culture. Gellner argued "to make culture and polity congruent."[67] A national culture is also a structure of cultural power. The modern Iranian nation under Reza Shah was unified through a violent process of suppression of cultural and political difference.

Anti-colonial and nationalist movements have perpetuated essentialist notions of national culture by adhering to aspects of their own culture incorporated into colonialist stereotypes.

A national culture, as Stuart Hall states, seeks to unify different members in terms of class, gender, or race, into one cultural identity, to represent them all as belonging to the same great national family. But is national identity a unifying identity of this kind which cancels or subsumes cultural difference?[68]

However, in Iran the idea of nation that emerged during the constitutional revolution existed prior to the construction of a modern state by Reza Shah. As a consequence, the legitimacy crisis of the modern, centralized, authoritarian state did not result in the weakening of the nation. In fact, and as mentioned earlier, the idea of nation emerged out of a complex web of internal and external relations in the nineteenth and early twentieth centuries.

A national language is a crucial component of the modern nation-state. The task of making Persian a national language was easy. Modern Persian benefits from rich linguistic materials. It has been an administrative language for the past eleven centuries, is related to European languages, and possesses a very rich literary heritage. Modern Persian language goes back to the ninth century with origins in middle Persian of the Sassanians, who ruled Iran from the third to the seventh century. This has made possible the transmission of cultural Persian heritage, especially through poetry and literature. In the *Book of Kings* (Shâhnâmeh) completed in 1010, Ferdowsi, a great epic poet, tells the legendary history of the kings of Iran, from its origins to the advent of Islam, in order to keep up Iranian pride. He writes in Persian, "purified" from Arabic influence. One understands why the *Book of Kings*, which even many illiterate Iranians know by heart thanks to the storytellers who recited it throughout the centuries in popular cafés, has become the symbol of the permanence of the Iranian nation and national pride for nationalists. The latter have aspired to an ahistorical narrative. They were and still are nostalgic of Iran's pre-Islamic past and despised the "Arab invaders," their language and religion (Islam) which they hold, more than ever, especially under the Islamic regime, responsible for the decline of the Iranian civilization and the ills of the contemporary Iranian society. In addition to Persian as a national language, Iran's history was re-interpreted to serve the present. This classical phenomenon of nationalism had to show the continuity and unity of the nation through the ages, despite oppressions, setbacks, and betrayals. The continuity and unity of Iran were therefore maintained through more than twenty-five centuries of imperial history in order to show the extraordinary endurance of the ancient civilization and the Aryan race (*nezhad-i asil-i âryai*) throughout time. Here again, Iranian nationalism benefited from the works of European Orientalists who posited an Iranian historical continuity, despite the changes that had occurred.

Two periods were clearly distinguished: one was glorified, the other was slandered: the pre-Islamic past was glorified and associated with the grandeur of Persian culture and Zoroastrian religion. In contrast, Islamic culture was qualified as foreign to Iranian traditions and was rejected as such. It was accused of being the cause of ruin during several centuries of foreign domination when the Arab, Turkish, and Mongol conquerors successively controlled the country. The reference to pre-Islamic Iran was useful for several reasons. It allowed for Islam to be credited as the cause of the country's decline and created a counterweight to European influence by stressing the imperial grandeur and the exceptional refinement of the Iranian civilization. Reference to pre-Islamic Iran became a means to emphasize the willingness to renew the glorious epoch in order to obtain the aura. One illustration of this attempt under Reza Shah was the change in the name of the town of Urmiyeh, which became Rezaiyeh. The name of the king was thus identified with the most symbolic place of the Zoroastrian religion.[69] Likewise, Qâim Shahr in northern Iran became Shâhi (related to the Shah). Adoration of the king (shahparasti) was linked to patriotism.

The discovered continuity with pre-Islamic Iran, as developed in the national history, was extended to the current territory of Persia which thereby became the receptacle of the nation. This new relationship to territory was reflected in the blatant way in which the powerful elite proceeded to change the international denomination of Persia by calling the country Iran. A memo, transmitted in 1934 by the Ministry of Foreign Affairs to embassies and international organizations, said that "Iran was the birth country and the land of the Aryans. It is therefore natural that we take advantage of this name, especially in these days when great nations in the world start looking at the Aryan race in such a way that indicates the grandeur of the race and of the civilization of ancient Iran."[70] Kashani-Sabet also argued that the production of knowledge around race and identity produced by colonial actors and institutions was appropriated by the Iranian state and developed to include an Aryanist discourse that sought to maintain social hierarchies and divisions.[71]

However, it seems to me that the Aryanist discourse and racism target foreigners, especially "Arab" and other invaders rather than non-Persian ethnicities inside Iran. As Gilroy argued:

> We increasingly face a racism which avoids being recognized as such because it is able to line up 'race' with nationhood, patriotism and nationalism. A racism which has taken a necessary distance from crude ideas of biological inferiority and superiority now seeks to present an imaginary definition of the nation as a unified cultural community. It constructs and defends an image of national culture—homogeneous in its whiteness yet precarious and perpetually vulnerable to attack from enemies within and without [...] This is a racism that answers the social and political turbulence of crisis and crisis management by the recovery of national greatness in the imagination. Its dream-like construction of our sceptered isle as an ethnically purified one provides special comfort against the ravages of [national] decline.[72]

The French anthropologist Didier Fassin argues: "We can speak of racism when we are dealing with a relationship to others whose difference is both reified and radicalised: reified meaning that there are traits defined as an essence of otherness; radicalised presupposes an over-determination of these traits in relation to any other possible form of characterization."[73]

For the French philosopher Étienne Balibar, racism is a "total social phenomenon," which "is inscribed in practices (forms of violence, contempt intolerance, humiliation, exploitation), in discourses and representations that are all intellectual elaborations of the prophylaxis or segregation (the need to purify the social body, to preserve the identity of the "self," of "us," from all promiscuity, from all interweaving, from all invasion), and which are articulated around the stigma of otherness (name, skin color, religious practices)."[74] In France, he argues, the categories of "indigenous" and then "immigrant" gradually replaced the notion of race in order to disaggregate class mobilizations. It is now "culture" or "ethnicity" that overdetermines individuals and legitimizes structural relations of domination. He also asserts that current racism, which he calls "neo-racism," is "a racism whose dominant theme is not biological heredity, but the irreducibility of cultural differences; a racism which, at first sight, does not postulate the superiority of certain groups or peoples over others, but 'only' the harmfulness of the erasure of borders, the incompatibility of lifestyles and traditions." Balibar argues that this process causes a general displacement, through which a "theory of ethnic relations" is developed, whereby culture—and cultural difference—is made as the "natural environment" of the human being. Balibar's perspective is very wary of the notion of "culture" as ambiguous.[75] His argument seems closer to the case of ethnic/religious minorities in Iran where cultural/religious difference between some ethnic-religious minorities and Persian-Shi'ites is often used to mark an essentialized hierarchy or what can be called *cultural racialization*. Under the Islamic regime, and we shall discuss later, the expansion of education (in Persian) throughout Iran has contributed to the hegemony of the Persian language. Therefore, ethnicization or cultural racialization is based on religious difference rather than linguistic one. However, the hegemony of Persian language has not led to the erasure of non/Persian languages. Recurrent demands for these languages to be taught at universities, especially in non-Persian majority provinces such as Kurdistan and Azarbaijan, have been renewed under the Islamic regime.

Under the Pahlavis, aspirations to uniformity invited all members of ethnic groups to conform their way of life to a new model defined in a Persianized and pro-Western manner. Each nonconforming element was regarded as a sign of backwardness and a possible threat to the modern nation and territorial integrity. In the beginning, nationalist intellectuals did not have a crucial impact on the Iranian society; only the empowering social classes were affected by their normative expectations. But with the extension of modernization and industrialization policies under Mohammad Reza Shah (1941–79), different ethnic minorities became increasingly affected by the exclusive tendencies of Westernized nationalism and its drive to uniformity.[76]

The modernization project had two characteristics: nationalism and secularism. For some specialists, the main components of Iranian national identity in modern Iranian discourse were Persian language, the Aryan race, a shared history, patriotism and adoration of the Shah. Homogenizing identity tended to erase linguistic, ethnic, cultural differences and replace them with a uniform language, culture, literature, art, and ethnicity.[77] Iranian nationalism of the early twentieth century was marked by archaism and referred to the glorious past in order to create patriotic sentiments and national pride.

But is there a single definition of national identity? Ernest Renan defined nation as the cult of ancestors, the willingness of being together, having done important things together and the willingness to continue.[78] However, this old nation that Renan defined no longer exists. This view, with which some still live today, is relevant to a dated definition of national identity. But does a bond still exist between the past and the future? National identity is not formed once and for all. In France, for example, "the republican identity came after feudal, monarchical and revolutionary identities. The crisis of French national identity for example started in the aftermath of the First World War."[79] It was further deepened when France lost Algeria in 1962, and when some years later the state power, as a major dimension of national consciousness, was weakened. The old national identity was further weakened with the disintegration of all forms of authority (family, church, political parties, etc.), especially following the May 1968 revolution.

As Firat Oruc argued, nation-state formation in the Middle East has posed significant challenges to pluralism. Efforts to standardize and create a particular national identity have led to the suppression of differences for the sake of the "ideal citizen." National belonging has imposed internal homogeneity as a non-negotiable imperative at the expense of difference.[80] He further argues that the concept of pluralism refers to the inherent coexistence of multiple community formations (religious, ethnic, legal, civic, etc.) in a given social site. Sites designate a range of heterogeneous domains and platforms of collective action and engagement. Sites of pluralism encompass all the material areas where individuals and groups perform, claim, regulate, and contest power relations within polities and communities. Pluralism calls for an engaged commitment to recognize and understand other across perceived or claimed lines of difference.[81] Oruc mobilized what James Scott calls "public" and "hidden" transcripts,[82] and argued: "Marginalized and subordinate communities often find themselves in a position of employing a dual discourse of conformity (public) and defiance (hidden) in their relation with their dominant counterparts."[83]

The construction of the nation-state under Reza Shah was a collective undertaking of a group of individuals whose aim was to both unify the country around a common cultural, social, and economic denominator and to secure political sovereignty. This required territorial consolidation, centralization and expansion of public administration, monopolization of the means of coercion, and the elimination of political rivals (especially powerful tribal leaders through repression by Reza Shah, and big landowners by his son through the land reforms). However, political modernization or the integration of the population in the political system, expansion of their rights, and the intensification of their obligations remained absent from societal projects conducted by the authoritarian-modernizing state.

Prior to the February 1921 coup that brought into power Reza Khan, regional movements existed in parts of Iran. Many intellectuals regarded these movements as threats to territorial integrity, and the formation of a nation-state with a modern centralized structure. The democratic movement of Khiabani in Tabriz, the Kurdish movement of Isma'il Agha, and the Jangal movement in Gilan did not find support among the intellectuals of the capital. The Gilan uprising, consisted of peasants, workers, bazaaris, and clerics, was the most important and widespread of these movements.[84] Later under Mohammad Reza Shah, the Republics of Azarbaijan and Kurdistan were both crushed. The Democratic Party of Azarbaijan (Firqah-i Demokrat) was created in north-western province of Azarbaijan toward the end of the Second World War when the Red Army was stationed in northern and north-western Iran. Its leaders were pro-soviets who demanded the independence of Azarbaijan from Iran. With the support of the Red Army the Firqah created an independent state which lasted one year. Following the negotiation with Prime Minister Qavam, the Red Army withdrew from Azarbaijan. The Iranian army took control of the major cities of this province, the azari independent movement collapsed, and the movement was repressed. Some of its leaders fled to former Soviet Union. The Kurdish Republic shared the same fate. In January 1946, the Kurdish Republic of Mahâbâd was established by the Kurdistan Democratic Party of Iran. It was supported by the Soviets but when the Red Army withdrew from Iran, the Iranian army took control of the region and the Kurdish Republic collapsed in December 1946 followed by the disintegration of the Kurdistan Democratic Party of Iran.

The main idea behind the formation of a strong national army and the national system of conscription was to centralize and empower the state and to modify the relationship between the individual and the state. "The individual who was recruited to the army to defend the nation would no longer be motivated by ethnic considerations."[85]

In addition to a strong national army, the modern nation-state also needed the expansion of modern education. Reza Shah had acquiesced in the nationalism of the intellectuals, and "had read modern, liberal virtues into pre-Islamic Iran."[86] The intellectuals, who, like Ahmad Kasravi, considered ethnic and language diversity a source of conflict,[87] advocated cultural and linguistic uniformity, the restructuring of provinces, and the application of a uniform system of nomenclature, so that the ethnic, linguistic, and cultural diversity of the provinces would disappear. The unification of the educational system started in the mid-1920s when a uniform syllabus was prepared for both the public and the private elementary and secondary schools. Reza Shah believed that in order to promote nationhood, a common national language was both necessary and urgent. In 1928, standard textbooks for all regions were introduced, and the use of Persian became compulsory in all schools to counteract ethnic and linguistic diversity.[88] Under his rule, the number of modern primary schools jumped from 432 in 1921 to 2,407 in 1941, and the number of modern secondary schools climbed from 33 to 321 during the same period. The number of elementary and secondary students (boys and girls) increased from 44,819 to 315,355 during the same period. The ratio of [urban] female students to total students rose from 16.9 to 28.[89] However, this policy did not apply to rural and tribal regions where the majority of the population lived under both Reza Shah (80 percent) and the Shah (53 percent in 1976).

Reform and expansion of bureaucracy, creation of a civil status, creation of a national bank, and uniformity of dress also strongly participated in the formation of a nation-state.[90]

This type of nation-state building unsuccessfully aimed at cultural and linguistic uniformity of a multi-ethnic Iran, which was supposed to promote allegiance to the new regime. Thus, Persian became compulsory in the administration and educational institutions. In 1923 the use of other languages in public institutions was forbidden. This measure intended to erase ethnic identities in favor of Persianity.

The status that the Persian language acquired under Reza Shah as the official language and its exclusive use in the public administration and the educational system associated with the expansion of education has had a tremendous impact on the identity construction of urbanized new generations of males from non-Persian origins. Hall looks at the role of language in culture and the production of meanings. As a representational system, language uses signs and symbols to construct meanings. These representations produce culture, which help people not only communicate but also interpret the world in generally related ways. Hall notes that cultural meanings are not just created as part of our imagination, but have concrete effects and help organize social practices. Therefore, he moves away from Ernest Gellner's notions of "high" culture—to mean "good" culture—versus popular culture, which is often seen as mass "low" culture.[91] Instead, Hall is interested in all forms of representations that convey meanings and illustrate what is distinctive about "the way of life" of any given group. Meanings are produced when we express ourselves, be it via language, the things we consume, or the stories we tell.[92]

Iran as a modern nation-state is in fact a cultural hybrid. Essentialist nationalist/Islamist ways of thinking, however, understand cultures as definitely distinct and separate from each other, concealing the fact that cultural boundaries are constructed by human being.

As Homi Bhabha pointed out, a characteristic of colonial discourse is its dependence on the concept of "fixity." "Fixity" as a sign of historical, cultural, and racial differences in the discourse of colonialism, he argued, is a paradoxical mode of representation, as it implies rigidity and immutable order as well as disorder, degeneration, and demonic repetition.

Just as the stereotype is the main discursive strategy of colonialism, a form of knowledge and identification that vacillates between what is always "in place," already known, and what must be anxiously repeated without ever being proven in discourse.[93]

Although I do not equate the discursive strategy of the dominant groups in Iran with that of colonialists, stereotypes being the major discursive strategy of fixity, objectification is paramount.

For example, the laziness of Shirazis, the greed and cunning of Isfahanis, the naiveté and zealotry of Azari men, the idleness of Rashti men, the simple-mindedness of Loris, the slothfulness of Kermanis, the brutality of the "Bedouin" Arabs, the "essential violence" of Baluch men, etc., often also portrayed as drug traffickers who cannot be trusted. It should be added that some of these stereotypes concern groups of Persian/Shi'ites who are not from Tehran. "Phrases such as 'I know them, that's the way they are', show the maximum objectification successfully achieved."[94]

Following Homi Bhabha, it can be argued that this process of ambivalence, central to the stereotype, constructs a theory of nationalist discourse. For it is the force of ambivalence that gives this discourse its credibility; ensuring its repeatability in changing historical and discursive conjunctures informs its strategies of individuation and marginalization, produces the probable truth and predictability that, for the stereotype, must always be in excess of what can be empirically proven or logically constructed. As mentioned earlier, the fixity is also employed by some ethnic minorities against others, for example, Turkmen against Baluch in Golestan. Along with the Persian/Mazandaranis, the Turkmen portrayed Baluch men as thieves, wrongdoers, criminals, money launderers.

The influence of orientalist discourse on the nationalist discourse is still strong. To paraphrase Edward Said, "The tense they employ is the timeless eternal."[95] In Iran under the Islamic regime, Shi'ism as the political ideology of the state and the official religion has made other religions, in our case Sunnism, a key signifier of difference, subject to discrimination and authoritarian form of control. Moreover, religion is associated with culture to present an imaginary definition of the Iranian nation as a unified cultural-religious (Shi'ite) community.

Classification of cultures is indeed a political project. The state's promotion of a new national identity is remarkably crystallized in the architectural creations of the nation-state building period under Reza Shah. The architectural style of public buildings was modeled on modern European buildings, though they had slightly modified facades with touches of pre-Islamic (mainly Achemenian and Sassanian) motifs, demonstrating the rediscovered continuity with a pre-Islamic past.

Reza Shah's reforms conducted to construct the nation-state contributed tremendously to the development of the modern middle class whose members became officers of the national army or state employees. They conceived and constructed the nationalist ideology and conducted the nationalist project. At their advent, members of the emerging modern middle class were overwhelmingly members of the aristocracy, gentry, and other groups from the upper classes. Under Reza Shah, with the expansion of both education and administration, the modern middle class started to include the sons of the merchants and the clergy who abandoned religious schools in favor of newly created secular schools as well as the Tehran University. The number of male students in religious schools decreased sharply from 5,532 in 1929/30 to 784 in 1941/2.[96] Even a significant number of sons of prominent clergy who studied at religious schools abandoned the *madresa* and went to secular schools. After graduation, they joined the administration or sought employment in secular public schools.

Modernity and Modesty: The Ambivalence of the New Iranian Woman

In the 1920s and 1930s, women's rights activists, including the Patriotic Women's Society of Iran (jamiyyat-i nesvan-i vatankhah-iran), continued to share the perspective that if the new woman is first and foremost a modern manager of the home, a loving mother and wife, she must first educate herself and acquire knowledge and science before she can claim political involvement or demand that the government grant women political rights. This association, which has worked hard to obtain civil and social rights for women, was founded in 1922 by the intellectual Mohtaram Eskandari, a Qajar nobility and principal of a girls' school in Tehran. Mastoureh Afshar was the president of the society after the death of its founder in 1924.[97] The Society of Patriotic Women of Iran published a magazine of the same name. The interventions of the delegation of Iranian women's rights activists from the Patriotic Women's Society of Iran at the Second Congress of Eastern Women held in Tehran in November 1932 were in the same direction. The latter nevertheless demanded equal pay for the same work with the same qualifications as men and access for women to higher education.[98]

Reza Shah's reforms largely met the expectations of these activists, with the abolition in 1936 of religious courts presided over by religious judges ruling on inheritance or divorce, and the acceleration of schooling for girls in urban areas so that by the end of the 1930s, girls made up nearly a third of primary and secondary school students. In addition, the founding of Tehran University (the first in Iran) in 1936, which gave women access to higher education and certain jobs, especially in teaching and administration, helped to professionalize them.

However, the implementation of the reforms did not change gender relations within the family. The civil code promulgated in 1933 was largely based on Islamic laws: repudiation, polygamy, and temporary marriage remained in force, and marital unions between a Muslim woman and a non-Muslim man was prohibited. The aim of the authorities was not to eradicate gender inequalities but to facilitate the regulated access of educated and "modern" women to the public space. From this perspective, femininity was clearly associated with modesty and the inferiority of women. Women were asked to be "modern" but "modest" and continued to be valued exclusively in their maternal role. According to the traditional model of marriage, the woman, represented as an object of desire, is taken by a man. The Persian term for marriage is zan gereftan (literally translated as taking a wife). For Queen Fawzia, the most important responsibility of women was to raise well-educated children. Women's magazines published portraits of educated and active women who refused to abandon their family duties. Shams ol-Molouk Mosahab, the first women to hold a PhD in Persian literature and a future senator, declared her domestic life more important than her career, and motherhood inseparable from education.[99]

Women were finally granted the right to vote and stand for election in 1963 as part of Mohammad Reza Shah's (1941–79) land reforms. In addition to this right, young unmarried women were later required to serve in the Army of Knowledge and Health or take part in military service. The granting of political rights to women provoked an outcry among the clergy, including Ayatollah Khomeini, the future leader of the 1979 revolution. However, as the elections were not free, this right did not lead to significant participation of women (or men for that matter) in political activities.

The Family Protection Law, adopted in 1967 and amended in the 1970s, embodied the new model of the modern but modest woman. It also gradually transformed the traditional family, which was marked by a strong gender and age hierarchy. Among other things, the law limited men's unilateral right to divorce and polygamy, raised the minimum legal age for girls' marriage from thirteen to fifteen and then to eighteen. However, the state did not remove the legal and social function of religion, and the laws remained close to the Islamic model. Repudiation was abolished and divorce became judicial, but polygamy was not abolished, it was only regulated, and temporary marriage continued to exist. Women obtained the right to divorce and custody of children after divorce, but parental authority remained with the father and paternal grandfather. Inheritance law remained based on Islamic laws (the woman inherits half of the man's share). Moreover, women still needed their husband's permission to leave the country.

In the 1930s and 1940s under Reza Shah, new interpretations of Islam had emerged and a group of religious thinkers, who had abandoned their ecclesiastical dress and who did not reject modernism, attempted to modernize religion without interfering with politics. Mohammad Taghi Shari'ati, Ali Shariati's father in Mashhad, Ali Akbar Hakamizadeh, and Shari'at Sangeladji in Qom were among the most prominent of these religious thinkers. Under Mohammad Reza Shah, Ali Shari'ati attempted to both modernize and politicize Islam. These endeavors had created both a cultural and political alternative to Westernization policies of the Shah and had gained strong bases in the society. Mohammad Reza Shah, like his father, tried to justify his policies by appealing to a combination of Western acculturation and the pre-Islamic past. The official line tended to deny that Iran belonged to the Islamic civilization and attempted to erase fourteen centuries of Iran's Islamic history although the Shah made pilgrimages to Mecca and Imam Reza's shrine in Mashhad, among others. To mark the separation from the Islamic world, the Shah ordered the organization of Persepolis ceremonies for the 2,500th anniversary of the Iranian monarchy in 1971 and later changed the calendar accordingly. Feelings of humiliation and outrage were shared by a wide range of people, who witnessed their history being manipulated by the Shah. Instead of diminishing the importance of Islam, this extravaganza increased its cultural and political importance. Even secular intellectuals clamored for the return to the hegira calendar. Cultural alienation of the majority of Iranians led to cultural resistance and ultimately an enforced Islamist counter-culture.

The Shah's state was called into question by the process of consolidation and integration of the nation-state. The traditional model of power was challenged by aspirations for citizenship brought about by social, economic, and cultural change in urban areas.

While the state embodied the monopoly of power generating homogenization, it also generated significant demands for the retreat of power.

Authoritarian modernization and state secularization which did not recognize freedom of expression and thought alienated the modern middle class. In particular, secular intellectuals, both men and women, and provoked their opposition against the Westernized elite. State monopoly over cultural and political discourse led the more radical intellectuals to downplay Western political values. A number of them even advocated a "purified oriental identity" against an "infected occidental identity."[100] Jalâl Al-i Ahmad (1923–69), a former communist activist (Toudeh Party) from a clerical family, published a book entitled *Westoxication* that gained tremendous popularity among the educated middle class. He contributed to the revival of Islamic culture by denouncing Westernization and Westernized intellectuals whom he accused of imitating the West. He is cherished under the Islamic regime.

During the 1979 Revolution, secular and religious actors shared a definition of national identity that was founded on both Iranianness and Islamity. But in the aftermath of the revolution, the Shi'ite dimension of Iranian identity was emphasized to the detriment of other dimensions, and other religious groups, especially the Sunnites. The political system is founded on Shi'ism as the political ideology of the state apparatus, and the implemented state policies consolidated social hierarchy founded on religious and gendered social relations. Islam served as a mobilizing ideology during the Revolution but, in its aftermath, it was appropriated by new leaders. The Islamic Republic founded its legitimacy partially on Islam, partially on the public will. But the Islamist power elite also attempted to draw parallels between central myths of Shi'ism (especially the martyrdom of Imam Hossein, the third Imam) and the present time. This is written in the preamble of the Constitution: "In the course of its revolutionary accomplishment, our nation has purified itself from the impure dust and mold. It cleansed itself from imported ideologies. It has returned to authentic Islamic doctrinal positions and world views. At the present, the nation intends to construct its own exemplary society according to Islamic criteria."

As for the religious actors, their demands had been shaped within the models and vocabulary of a modern political domain. They did not advocate the return to the golden age of Islam and they had been influenced by the egalitarian discourse and the political engagement of left-wing secular actors.[101]

Under the Pahlavis, modernization policies concerned, in particular, urban areas. Rural areas where the majority of the population, including non-Persian/Shi'tes, lived still suffered from lack of schools, health facilities, roads, electricity, etc. Under Reza Shah, until the 1940, only one-fifth of the population lived in urban areas.

The urban population grew sharply between 1956 and 1976, especially as a result of rural exodus. Employment opportunities attracted the rural population to large cities, especially Tehran, in search of work and better life conditions. Women who lived in ethnic/Sunnite provinces were largely left out of the rapid social changes that occurred in the late 1960s and 1970s in large Persian dominated towns. According to the results of my fieldwork, back in those years, gender relations among the Baluch and Turkmen women were not influenced by statutory changes introduced by the Family Pretection Law of 1967 or the Shah's grant of political rights to women in 1963.

Female literacy rates for the age groups six to sixty-five increased from 18 in 1966 to 36 percent in 1976. During the same period, the average literacy rate for

Table 1.1 A note on the population of Iran.

Year	In thousands	Urban population as percentage of total population
1930	2.64	20.9
1940	3.20	21.9

Souce: Julien Bharier, "A Note on the Population of Iran 1900–66" in *Population Studies*, Vol. XXII, N°2, July 1968, P. 275.

Table 1.2 Urban population of Iran 1956–76.

Year	In thousands	Urban population as percentage of total population
1956	5.954	31.4
1966	9.794	38.0
1976	15.854	47.0

Source: Statistical Year Book, Tehran, Statistical Center of Iran. 1976.

the age groups six to twenty-four increased from 28 percent in 1966 to 51 percent in 1976. As we shall see later with the data of our sample, the literacy rates for Turkmen and Baluch and other minority women grew sharply, especially after the revolution. The expansion of education and even higher education along with urbanization after the revolution led many traditional Sunnite families to agree to send their daughters to school and some even to university as educated Baluch women declared. However, gender relations among Baluch and Turkmen have not been altered radically and male domination is still paramount.

According to the 2016 National Census of the Population and Housing, 40 percent of the Iranian population lived in towns of over 200,000 inhabitants, 25 percent in towns with over 1 million people, and 19 percent of the population lived in greater Tehran. Likewise, since 2000, the population of rural areas has been declining in absolute terms. In 2016, only 25 percent of the population was rural.

Revolutionary and Muslim Femininity

The model of the modern, Westernized, and modest woman advocated by the imperial regime did not suit the educated young Shi'ite women from traditional and religious families who, in the 1960s and 1970s, sought out a religious but modern female model. Several thousands of women were attracted to the teachings of Ali Shari'ati who, between 1967 and 1972, lectured at Hosseiniyeh Ershad, a religious institute then located north of the capital. Shari'ati (who died in 1977) was a religious intellectual who studied sociology in France and developed a politicized and modern version of Islam. He aimed to transform religion into an ideology of liberation, denounced the Shah's policies of cultural Westernization and, following Frantz Fanon, advocated cultural introspection. He also opposed the monopoly of religion by the clergy, which he accused of having alienated Iranian youth from Islam. In his book *Fatemeh Is Fatemeh*, which became extremely popular among educated urban religious women, Shari'ati reconstructed the classical female models of Shi'ism through a revolutionary approach to the personalities of Fatemeh (the daughter of the Prophet and wife of Imam Ali, the first Shi'a Imam) and Zeynab (his daughter, and sister of Imam Hossein). While he emphasized their piety and virtue, he especially valued their courage and determination, their fight against injustice, and their political activities against oppression. However, Shari'ati's new interpretation of religion did not challenge gender power relations or male superiority. Young religious and urban women reappropriated this female model propagated by Shari'ati to participate in the 1979 revolution. Khomeini, for his part, adhered to this new representation of the Muslim woman. He was also influenced by the increased oppositional activities of young secular educated women in the 1970s. Many of them, often students or high school teachers, had opted for an armed struggle against the Shah's regime. Almost all of them were executed in prison or killed in clashes with the coercive forces. As his statements from his exile in Najaf show, the involvement of women, often secular and leftist, in oppositional activities had a profound impact on the future leader of the revolution who had primarily seen women as mothers and wives.[102]

Shortly after the victory of the revolution, the Family Protection Law was retracted and a new law based on a traditionalist interpretation of Islam was enacted, imposing a series of regressions on women's rights. The veil, the first sign of the construction of the Islamic regime and its guarantor, became compulsory. According to the new rulers, it symbolized the pure blood of the martyrs and the honor of the Shi'ite nation that the state claimed to preserve. Slogans and emblems such as "We did not give our blood for women to walk around naked (unveiled)" or "My sister, your veil is your honor" illustrated this assimilation claimed by Islamists. The political dimension of "purification" was reflected in the discourse of the state, which demanded unquestioning obedience to the power of the "pure" and "representatives of the innocent saints." Thousands of modern working women who refused to submit to the demands of the Islamists were dismissed or forced into early retirement, while others went into exile. This new veiled Islamist femininity that symbolized modesty reinforced the beliefs of Islamist men in their new virility.

Official Discourse under the Islamic Republic and Revival of Ethnic and Religious Identities

Eric Hobsbawm argued that nationalism, nationhood, and ethnicity are dual phenomena social processes that are constructed essentially from above yet cannot be understood unless also analyzed from below.[103]

Ahmad Kasravi (1890–1946), one of the most prominent Iranian nationalist intellectuals, belonged to the Azari or Azarbaijani ethnic group, the second largest after the Persians. However, he produced a solid research work on the ancient Azari language and origin of the Azarbaijani people. Arguing that ancient Azari language had been closely related to Persian language and that the influx of Turkic words began only with the Seljuk invasion (1038), Kasravi believed that the true national language of Iranian Azarbaijan was closely related to Persian.[104] Therefore, he advocated the linguistic assimilation of Persian and Azarbaijan, which symbolized a revival of an ancient tradition. His innovative thesis was in tune with an educational preoccupation of the time. Taqi Arani, a leading communist intellectual, posited the intersection of education and politics by arguing: "If compulsory primary education is not possible all over Iran, it must be implemented in Azarbaijan at any cost, not only for education but also for political reasons."[105]

The Islamic Republic as an authoritarian regime pretends to tolerate the diversity of social, ethnic, or religious groups (officially recognized by Islam, i.e., Judaism, Christianity, Zoroastrianism). Article nineteenth of its Constitution stipulates that all Iranians, regardless of ethnicity or tribe, are equal before the law. And that color, race, language, or other similar characteristics shall not be a source of discrimination.[106] In reality, however, ethnic-religious minorities are discriminated against.

The amendment to the twelfth Article of the Constitution stipulates that in regions where the followers of each of the religions compose the majority of the population, local regulations would be set according to these religions, in the limits of the councils' power (city, village, etc.), and should be respectful to the rights of the followers of other religions.[107] Nonetheless, in Baluchistan and Golestan I observed ethnic discrimination, and both educated and uneducated Baluch and Turkmen complained of discrimination they suffered. For example, although the number of educated Turkmen men is quite high, the jobs especially with decision-making authority in the local administration in Golestan, even in Turkmen majority towns such as Gonbad Kavoos, were handed to Persians. Likewise, educated Baluch complained of all kinds of discriminations ranging from financial to administrative and religious. In Zâhedân, for example, where the majority of the population is Sunnite, they had only a few mosques. The most important is Makki mosque. The state discriminations have led the Sunnites to widely share the desire of wanting to come out of the shadows. The Makki mosque, funded by the worshippers, illustrates this aspiration.

> The Makki Grand Mosque is undergoing a lot of changes. There are dormitories, schools, a library, a cafeteria, and even a small pleasant patio. From the inside, it almost gives the feeling of being in an enclosed space. A religious dignitary declared that they are working hard to expand this mosque, building a second prayer hall that will be able to accommodate even more worshippers. At the same time he said they are raising funds to help the poor.[108]

The religious frame of reference functions as a possible support for the mobilization of minorities in a Weberian perspective. This process reminds us of how the enslaved people in the American South relied on Christianity—a religion that was supposed to ensure their conformity and docility—to reject the very essence of slavery by projecting their rights and values as human beings.[109] If the religious frame of reference can lead to racialized assignment and ethnicization, it sometimes activates forms of ordinary mobilization of resistance or individual and collective resilience.

In some areas limited and controlled by the dominant social system, there is a revival of ethnic and religious identities and local and regional authorities. According to a university student in Iranshahr and a member of the editorial board of the literary-cultural journal *Estoon* (a Baluch word which means Thunder), the Makki mosque has a student's affair office and organizes cultural classes and meetings with Sunnite clerics and tries to unite students and clergy. He declared that most Sunnite students have their religious beliefs. During my fieldwork, the Sunnites I encountered said that the majority of the mosques built by state authorities were Shi'ite and that Sunnites could hardly obtain authorizations to build additional mosques. Therefore, Sunnite worshippers had to pray either in the streets or in places other than mosques. In Zâhedân, the mosques organized religious ceremonies, but only men could go to the mosque. The women attended ceremonies in the homes in their neighborhood. In recent years, the Makki mosque has opened areas for women worshippers.

The Article 15 of the Constitution of the Islamic Republic stipulates: "The use of local and tribal languages in the press and mass media and for the teaching of the literature of these languages in schools is authorized alongside Persian." Under the reformist President Mohammad Khatami (1997–2005), nationalism was redefined by several criteria, including the Persian language, Iran's ancient history and Shi'ite Islam, and ethnic and religious minorities remained largely excluded from the political community. "The two universities in Zâhedân together have more than ten thousand students from all over the country. The development of these universities has been done at a forced march in recent years, allowing, among other things, to 'Iranize' the region with the arrival of educated youth and far from the Baluch problems."[110]

As a study of school text books shows: "The perception of belonging is clearly hierarchical. Ethnic belonging is placed at the bottom, followed by national belonging, which is itself subject to religious affiliation. Thus the ethnic question becomes a strictly national matter within the Ummat [community of believers]

Figure 1.1 Makki Mosque, Zâhedân, Iran (Wikimedia Commons).

which alone constitutes a whole transnational world."[111] The supra-national character of Islamic ideology makes the reference to Iranianness as a national and cultural identity to be imbued with Islam. According to this discourse, Iran, the land of our forefathers, is an Islamic homeland. Nationality must submit to Islam, ethnicity has a double allegiance both to the nation-state and to the ummat. "We Muslims are equal brothers; region, language or accent, race or color cannot divide us." This study of text books shows: "The Turkmens are only presented by the evocation of their seniority on the national space. The cultural distance with them translates into the non-fluency of Persian. The Baluch language is mentioned as a local language that has undergone many foreign influences." Among the lacunar ethnic groups, the most marginal place goes to the Baluch. They and Turkmen are the only two Sunnite ethnic groups for which the text book does not provide any support for national identification. Both are put at a distance except that the ethnic culture of the Turkmen is rewarding and that of the Baluch is strange. Belonging to the Sunnite minority, not being of Iranian origin, or having been subjected to a non-valued brewing or being assimilated to invading ethnic groups of the past are marginalizing factors. They are added to socio-economic and cultural factors linked to the space occupied, as well as to the demographic weight of the relevant ethnic groups, in order to achieve successful integration or conflictual integration or even marginalization.[112]

The expansion of education has led to the hegemony of the Persian language, especially among younger generations. "The rapid progress of schooling in the cities but also in the villages finally imposed Persian as the lingua franca. The weak demographic dynamism of ethnic Persian regions is thus largely offset by the expansion of Persian culture and language. Becoming a city dweller means first of all speaking Persian."[113]

In our nationwide survey taken in 2002, 55.5 percent of the respondents were familiar with at least one local or ethnic language and 45.5 percent only spoke Persian. When local and ethnic languages are of "stifled aspirations," Persian becomes a language of liberating "secret missives." For example, a number of young Turkmen girls studying at school and are therefore fluent in Persian told me that they talk with each other in Persian in front of their illiterate mothers when they do not want them to understand their secret talks. But it did not appear to me that their use of the Persian language was a sign of superiority of Persian over other languages or ethnicities. Likewise, speaking the ethnic language in public did not qualify as a political act. Speaking it at home or teaching it to one's children certainly contributes to their identity construction, but educated young people of non-Persian origins who have been to school use both Persian, as a privileged support of the national identity, and their ethnic language as a privileged support of ethnic identity in their daily lives. Thus, both languages have become an integral part of their multidimensional identities.

State broadcasting now has programs in regional languages, including in Baluch and Turkmen. In 2004, however, one of the demands of older Turkmen whom I encountered in Gonbad Kavoos and the adjacent areas was to watch the same national programs (including soap operas) broadcasted on national television but in Turkmen language. I asked them why they didn't watch the television programs of the Republic of Turkmenistan which they could capture without any need for antennas. They replied: "Because we are Iranian and we want to follow what goes on in our country but in our own language." Likewise, Turkmens showed interest in their country's news and cultural productions that could be reached through watching TV programs. They did not watch television programs from Turkmenistan and showed no interest in what was going on the other side of the border either. In Gonbad Kavoos, for example, children watched national TV and illiterate Turkmen mothers who did not speak Persian were aware of the news through their children who spoke Persian.

Zeynab and Sahar, two young Turkmen girls, said: "We watch the programs of our TV [Iranian TV]. Among us Turkmen, our mothers do not watch much TV for the lack of time. They do housework and handicrafts. During the day, they have no time, and in the evening they are too tired. It's mostly the children who watch. We, for example, watch the news until midnight."

Oghoul, a Turkmen mother who did not speak Persian, said her daughter listens to the radio, including foreign radios that broadcast in Persian, and then she tells her mother everything she has heard. But for the news, everyone watches. So Oghoul knew what was going on in the country, either from her children or from her husband.

Sahar and Zeynab sometimes speak Persian to each other, especially when they want to tell secrets in front of others who are not fluent in Persian. Sahar said: "You have to speak Persian. Persian is spoken everywhere in Iran. I don't know if Persian is also spoken abroad but here Persian is necessary." Likewise, Zeynab emphasized:

> Here [Iran] is our homeland and we must speak Persian. In school you have to speak Persian, in university too (in Gonbad there was the Payam-i Noor University). Many Turkmen women from the generations of parents who did not speak Persian because they did not go to school, finally went to Nehzat (literacy courses for adults) and learned Persian. Young people speak more and more in Persian, especially when there is a mixed meeting of Persians and Turkmen. At school, in this district, not only are the children Turkmen, the teachers are also Turkmen, but they teach in Persian. In the courtyard, during recess, the children speak to each other both in Persian and in Turkmen.

In Khak-i Sefid as well as Bagher Shahr in Shahr Rey South of Tehran, azari migrants whom I interviewed spoke azari, their mother tongue, when children were absent but turned into Persian in presence of their children. When I asked the reason, they explained to me that they did not want their children to pick azari accent because their school mates might make fun of them. Their strategy was to obtain social mobility for their children through education and integration in Tehran's environment, far from their home villages to which they did not intend to move back. Every element that might go against that strategy was rejected, including the teaching of the azari language to their children.

Under the Islamic regime, among the foundations of the newly constructed heterogeneous nationalism, the Persian language appeared as the most permanent one. In 1988, when Ali Khamenei, the current leader, was president of the Republic, he made a speech entitled "The Splendor of the Persian Language and the Need to Protect It." In the speech, which was inconceivable a few years earlier, he acknowledged the national language to be the most important and original element of cultural identity of all nations, and declared that Persian was "the language of the true revolutionary Islam." He even compared Arabic to Persian and argued for the expressive superiority of Persian over Arabic asking himself whether Hafez (the great Iranian poet of the fourteenth century) was translatable into Arabic.

Following his election in 1997, President Mohammad Khatami declared that "the distinguished Iranian nation had a great Islamic and national heritage."[114] He stressed the double heritage to propose a redefinition of Iranian nationalism that would take into account elements that had been excluded by Westernized nationalism and Islamist revolutionary ideology. On an international level, he reproduced the same conception by proposing to develop a "dialogue among civilizations." In his view, international relations should no longer be interpreted through distorted religious or imperialist views but through culture. In this discourse, Iran is said to belong to a civilization defined by several criteria, including the Persian language, Iran's ancient history, and Shi'ite Islam.

The redefinition of nationalism suggested by former President Khatami, however, led to the reintegration of Westernized nationalism's exclusivist tendency, especially with regard to ethnic groups.[115] More importantly, it did not go against a political system that is founded on Shi'ism as the political ideology of the state apparatus, or state policies that consolidate social hierarchy founded on religious and gendered identities.[116]

Under President Ahmadinejad (2005–13), who owed his election to Shi'ite vote, and to the Leader's support, ethnic, religious, and gender discrimination and exclusion increased tremendously. Social hierarchy founded on ethnic, religious, and gender identities was accentuated by state policies that were based on religious criteria with Shi'ism as the condition of access to economic, cultural, social, and political resources, including in provinces where the majority of the population is Sunnite (i.e., Baluchistan and Kurdistan). Under Ahmadinejad, the High Council of Cultural revolution approved a rule in 2007, according to which the management of Sunnite theology schools was placed under the supervision of Ayatollah Khamenei's representatives. The Sunnite clerical authorities protested vehemently this project arguing that the planning of Sunnite religious education in theology schools is the duty of Sunnite religious authorities, not the Shi'tes. Molavi Abdolhamid, the highest Sunnite religious authority in Iran and the Imam of Friday prayer in Zâhedân (the capital city of Baluchistan) known as a moderate, declared that religious beliefs are the red line of Sunnites and no individual, group, or state should pass this red line. He also warned the authorities against politicization of religion or making the religion state-centered.[117]

During the presidential campaign in 2013, President Rohani's discourse attracted discriminated ethnic and religious minorities, especially Sunnites. Molavi Abdolhamid qualified President Rohani as extremely capable and cultured and declared having appreciated the attention he has given to religious and ethnic minorities. "The participation of Sunnites in these elections was very important and everywhere in the country they have voted almost exclusively for Rohani. During the last eight years [under Ahmadinejad's presidency] Sunnites suffered very high pressures. If the moderation advocated by Rohani is realized and intelligent policies are applied, Sunnites and Shi'ites can easily live and work together."[118] He further added: "Sunnites voted massively for Rohani because of his science and know-how, his dual clerical and university training, his capacities and his positions during electoral debates. Rohani's slogans during the electoral campaign, namely deliberation and hope, played a decisive role in the Sunnite vote, although the Sunnite had also highly supported president Khatami and Rafsanjani."[119]

Several hundred thousand Iranians of the Sunni faith live and work in Tehran, without ever having obtained permission to build their own mosques. In Tehran, one of the main Sunni places of prayer was destroyed by the intelligence services while President Rohani was on an official visit to Kurdistan. Rohani never appointed a Sunni minister to his government. Baluchistan remains the poorest province in the country, where some of the population has no choice but to smuggle and traffic to survive. Shahindokht Molaverdi, then Rohani's vice president for women's affairs, announced on February 23, 2016, with regret and bitterness that all the men in a village in Baluchistan who were involved in drug trafficking had been executed. The announcement caused an uproar among judicial officials who accused her of siding with drug smugglers.[120]

In her study of Baluchistan, Sadigheh Sheikhzadeh claimed that by marginalizing the Baluchistan region and refusing to offer modern facilities, the Baluch population had no other choice but to bypass the Islamic regime and turn to traditional Baluch structures for their social, cultural, juridical, and political needs. She argued that through its policies, the Islamic regime has thus postponed the completion of the political construction project of modern state in Iran, and has excluded and oppressed the Baluch who could have taken part in this project. The result, she believes, is that the process of the formation of the nation-state has remained unfinished.[121]

As Alam Saleh mentioned: "Ethnic and national issues cannot be excluded from the state's polity and the linking of ethnic identity to national security remains a major priority in terms of ensuring the security of the state [...]. Intranational ethnic tensions pose a greater security challenge to Iran's national security than those presented by regional and global military threats."[122] He contended that the "ethnic problem" does necessarily emerge due to Iran's multi-ethnic composition, but through the increasingly politicized nature of ethnic issues in the country. It is the product of the state's policies that have consistently securitized ethnic issues.

Unlike Saleh, Ahmadi highlighted the role of regional and international factors in the politicization of ethnic issues in Iran and argued that political participation is likely to play a crucial role in weakening ethnic belongings and politicization of linguistic and religious differences.[123] To overcome ethnic crisis in Iran as a multinational entity, Ali al-Taie suggested to replace nation, which he considered too narrow, with society which, by definition, is a more inclusive and extended concept. He also proposed that cultural pluralism be recognized effectively and a multilingual policy be implemented through the teaching of various Kurdish, Turkish, Baluch, etc., languages along with Persian at schools all over the country.[124]

The claims of minority groups are relevant to inequalities in the distribution of economic, political, and cultural power, and represent real social issues. It should be recalled that ethnic and religious minorities as well as the youth, women, and intellectuals significantly participated in the election of Khatami (and to a lesser extent Rohani), and through their votes demanded their inclusion in the national political community. However, these hopes were shattered. Under both Khatami and Rohani, the State policies consolidated social hierarchies based on ethnic, religious, and gender identities. Rohani's government only set few measures that were not remedies, but rather disguised the ethnic/religious question. Despite his electoral promises, and the vote of the Baluch, Kurds, or Turkmen in his favor, he did not appoint any personalities from religious minorities, especially Sunnite, to the government. However, in accordance with his promise concerning the recognition of the cultural rights of ethnic minorities, his government authorized the teaching of the Kurdish language at university in Kurdistan. This initiative was qualified as "opportunistic" by some, but welcomed by groups who advocated, unsuccessfully, the extension of the measure to all languages from primary school onward. It should be emphasized that the Iranian state does not authorize the counting of minorities. To circumvent this shortcoming, and in order to have an estimation of the number of non-Persian population, we asked the question of local and ethnic languages in our survey.

Nevertheless, the country has many elected women municipal councilors and women mayors, including in Golestan and Baluchistan (for example, Saniyah Balouchzehi in Sarbâz). In an unprecedented move of great symbolic importance, Rohani appointed two women as city governors (Ma'soumeh Parandvâr in Hamoun and Homeira Rigui in Qasr-i Qand) in the province of Sistan-Baluchistan. Homeira Rigui, born in 1976, was later appointed ambassador to Brunei.

Under the Islamic regime, nationalism and Shi'ism have steadily strengthened and reinforced the masculinity of the men of the Shi'ite nation and its corollary, Shi'ite femininity. The hostility toward Iran by Arab countries, mostly Sunnites, and the regional policy of the Islamic regime, described as expansionist by its Arab neighbors, have strengthened ties between nationalism and Shi'ism in Iran. Religious ceremonies, especially the commemoration of the martyrdom of Imam Hossein, are crucial moments in the representation and reconstruction of hegemonic Islamist masculinity.

For Islamist-nationalist ideology, the concept of honor (nâmous) symbolized by and in the Islamic veil has become closely linked to the masculinity of the Islamic state. The Iraq-Iran war, which further militarized masculinity, had a crucial impact on individual and collective subjectivities and on gender relations and the gender fabric, the extent of which remains to be demonstrated.[125] Like Imam Hossein, the martyrs of the war symbolized the sacralized masculinity. This construction of masculinity based on a dichotomous vision forged, during the war, a femininity whose main components are asceticism, sacrifice, and purity.

Under the Islamic regime, the model of an ideal woman is that of an urban middle class, Shi'ite, veiled, educated but modest woman: a good mother and wife. She endorses the model prescribed by the Islamic state, accepts her husband's superiority who obeys the almighty Islamic state, especially its leader. In both monarchical and Islamic "republican" models, women belonging to religious and ethnic minorities, especially Sunnites, are excluded from the state-initiated construction of modern women, based either on Persianity under the Pahlavis or on Shi'ism under the Islamic regime.

Since the advent of the modern nation-state under Reza Shah in the 1920s, the Persian language has appeared as the most permanent foundation of nationalism and its drive to uniformity. Under the Pahlavis, Westernized nationalism intended to erase ethnic identities in favor of Persianity and later Iran's separation from the Islamic world with the organization, in 1971, of Persepolis ceremonies for the 2,500th anniversary of the Iranian monarchy, and the change in Calendar accordingly.

Under the Islamic regime, Islamist/nationalism has intended to crush non-Shi'ite religious identities. As will be seen in the upcoming chapters, the expansion of education in recent decade has led to the hegemony of the Persian language. However, aspirations of religious/ethnic minorities to be included in the national political community have been shattered due to the all-out discrimination mainly based on religion that have impeded the completion of the nation-state building project.

Map 1.1 Map of Iran.

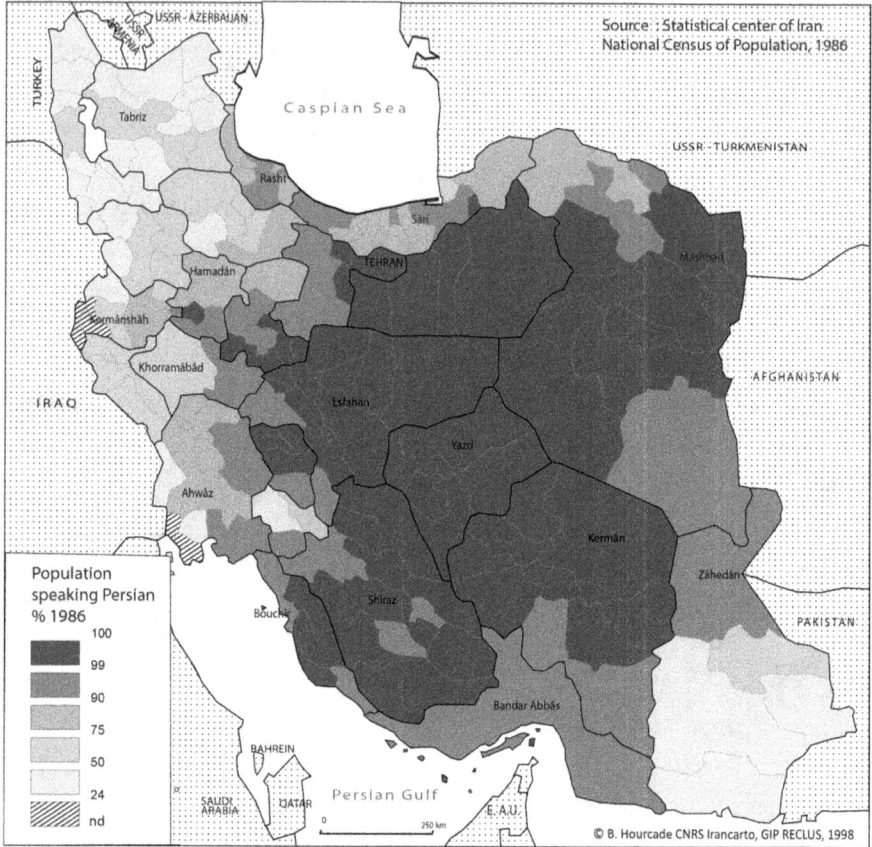

Map 1.2 Population declaring speaking Persian in 1986, by district (*shahrestan*).

(From B. Hourcade et al. *Atlas d'Iran,* Paris, Documentation française, 1998. by courtesy CNRS, Centre de recherche sur le monde iranien, Paris.)

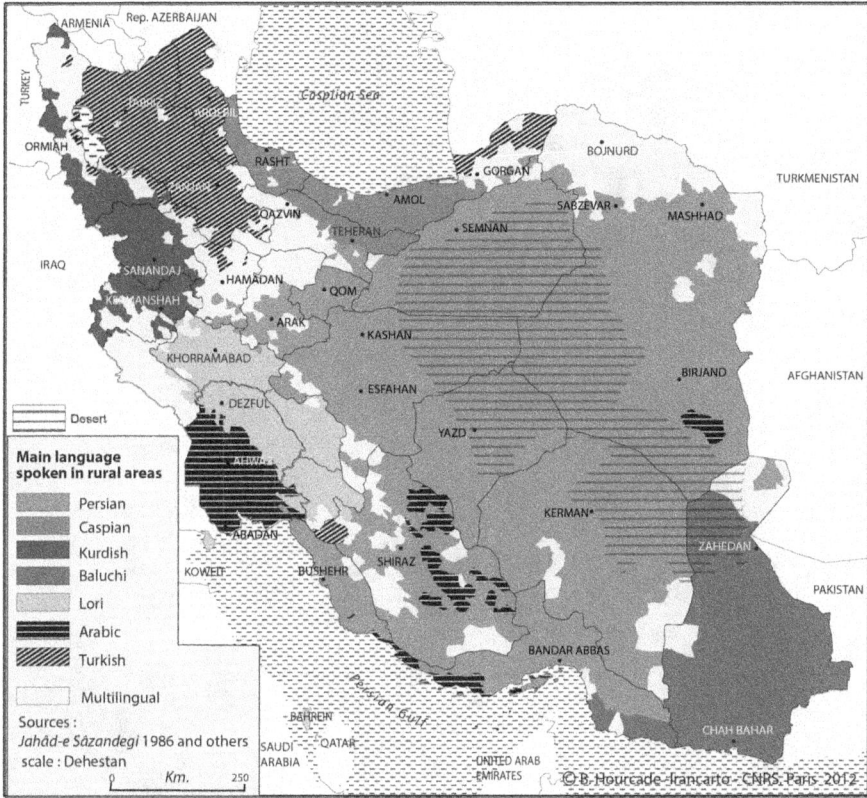

Map 1.3 Languages spoken in rural areas in 1986, by rural district (*dehestân*).

(From B. Hourcade, "Main languages spoken in rural Iran." https://irancarto.cnrs.fr. by courtesy CNRS, Centre de recherche sur le monde iranien, Paris.)

2

Baluchistan

Map 2.1 Map of Baluchistan Province.

As mentioned earlier, in addition to Persian/Shi'ite majority provinces such as Tehran, Isfahan, and Hormozgan, I also chose to conduct my fieldwork among non-Persian, non-Shi'ite population in Sistan-Baluchistan, a Sunnite Baluch majority province and Golestan where Turkmen Sunnites compose over 45 percent of the population in some towns and where many migrant Baluch are settled. In order to grasp the social, cultural, and religious differences, I also interviewed Persian-Shi'ite population in these provinces. After a brief presentation of these two provinces, I will present and discuss the results of our quantitative and qualitative surveys taken in 2002, 2004, and 2007–8 which have been completed with the latest available data.

Sistan-Baluchistan is the second largest, the only rural majority province, and holds the record for absolute poverty. It has common borders with Pakistan and Afghanistan. The history of the Baluch goes back to several thousand years ago, they protected the Iranian borders against foreign invaders, and their chieftains had a military function. Under the Shah, the impoverished economy of the Baluch regions forced the Baluch men to work in the Persian Gulf countries. After the revolution, poverty and high unemployment rates led some Baluch men and youth to risk involvement in both drug- and oil-trafficking activities. Instead of dealing with grievances and demands, the Islamic state's response has been a security policy.

In this region, classic patriarchy has its origins in the tribal and agnatic structures that have formed the basis of social organization and the anthropological structures of kinship associated with it. Despite social change, the continuity of a tribal social system and the state policies contribute to the persistence of religious problems between Shi'ites and Sunnites, and traditions like polygamy, a high number of children (especially sons) per father, and gender inequalities.

Although I had started my field works in Iran's poor suburbs of Tehran where many disadvantaged ethnic migrants live, I had never been so touched by the disarray of a number of women in Baluchistan. When I returned to Tehran, I spoke with several women's rights activists and even a Nobel Prize winner about what I had seen and encountered. None of them reacted; they all looked at me in a strange way letting me know that they already encountered many problems to deal with in the capital. One of them who worked with Zahra Shojai, the then head of Women's Affairs Office, suggested that I write a report to President Khatami! I refused telling her that I did not work for the government and that it was the president's responsibility to find out about what went on in the country. My pain lasted for a long time to the point that I could not even transcribe the registered tapes of my interviews with women without crying my eyes out. Yet, they are also courageous ordinary women who tried to change things from within their families, targeting the so-called traditions that prevented their daughters to continue education after primary school and struggled against early marriages.

However, the subtle struggle of "ordinary" women has not been recognized and taken seriously, including by many researchers, mainly because strategies they deploy and their repertoire of action are very different from the ones mobilized by women's rights activists in large towns. For example, they do not show their discontent publicly, even less by demonstrating in the streets, or making the veil a major issue.

The province of Sistan-Baluchistan is over 187,000 km² and has almost 1,000 km of common borders with Pakistan and Afghanistan. Zâhedân is its capital. "The Eastern border was drawn by the Border Commission assigned under the Goldsmith Plan in September 1871, and has separated parts of Baluchistan from Iran. Baluchistan has the lowest level of development among all Iranian provinces [...] in spite of huge maritime, mineral and agronomic resources. And in spite of the borderline location which offers trade and employment opportunities."[1]

Various Baluch tribes are scattered in Iran, Pakistan, and Afghanistan.

Some of the members of the largest Iranian Baluch clan the Notizayi or Shahbakhsh-live in Quetta City, in Pakistan. Barahouyis are a large population and also have connections in Pakistan. The Iranian tribe Barakzay lives in Saravan, Zabol and Iranshahr and Nimrooz in Afghanistan. Another sizeable group is Rigui, living in Pakistan, the Shahnavazi live in the border areas. Some Baluch people have dual citizenship of both Iran and Pakistan. Some men have several wives in Iran, Afghanistan and Pakistan.[2]

The Making of Zâhedân as a Chieftown

At the beginning of the First World War, the British government, in order to supply its troops stationed in Iran with food and ammunition, undertook the construction of a railway from Quetta, a city in the Indian Empire, now in Pakistan, to the intersection near Zâhedân. Thus, the insignificant caravan town became a city, which had to be protected militarily. As soon as Reza Khan took power in 1921, he also stationed brigades there. Zâhedân became an important strategic center, so close to the border. It also had to be organized administratively.[3] Its commercial dynamism increased further during the Second World War and following the partition of India and Pakistan. While the city ceased to have regular relations with the Union of India, trade with West Pakistan increased and Sikhs who had previously come here periodically on business also came and settled in the area. Similarly, Muslims who had fled the central and southern provinces of India that were now part of the Indian Union, and who were unable to settle in the already-overcrowded Karachi or other cities in Pakistan due to the scale of the exodus, sought asylum in Zâhedân and the surrounding area. They found a welcome, if not warm, then at least understanding in this foreign and yet very poor land, and were added to the core group of recently settled Baluch.

This group of exiles later obtained Iranian nationality. Some, more cultured, settled in Tehran, where the knowledge of Urdu among them was then highly appreciated in various offices, including those of the radio, television, and press.[4]

Zâhedân experienced rapid population growth. Its population increased from 17,495 in 1956 to 549,000 in 2001 and 586,000 in 2016[5] and approximately 639,000 today. Extraterritorial trade has been a basis for population growth in the region, and many people are engaged in informal business including shopkeepers, peddlers, and drug business.[6]

When I was in Baluchistan, parts of Zâhedân looked like an occupied territory. We could see Pâsdârân and Basidj militias everywhere. The best buildings in town were occupied by them. I had the feeling that there was a curfew in the evening after dark. We were told not to go outside of our residence unless a driver and a bodyguard accompanied us under the pretext that the town was not safe for non-locals.

Zâhedân is located 40 kilometers from the point where the Iranian, Pakistani, and Afghan borders meet. The porosity of the borders with these stirring neighbors has made this region one of the world's major drug-trafficking highways. I recall a day we went to Zâbol for our research, and on the way back to Zâhedân as it was getting dark our car broke down. Our local guides panicked and asked us to hide so that we would not be seen. There were no military or Pâsdârân at sight. Fortunately, the car was repaired quickly and we could return to Zâhedân safe. Later I was told that as night fell, drug traffickers were taking over the roads, and that because they were armed with heavy artillery, the security forces could not deal with them effectively. In fact, more than 4,000 of them had already been killed by the traffickers. So the instruction was confinement at home during the night.

In Baluchistan, gender segregation and division were still paramount. For example, in Zâhedân, the men's bazaar is not mixed, and women do not have the right to shop in this men-only bazaar. However, our driver who turned out to be unaware of this rule dropped us there without warning us. I entered the bazaar with two other female colleagues to do some shopping for our male relatives. Everybody stared at us; then toward the middle of the bazar we saw a Baluch man with quite an impressive mustache sitting on a chair, surrounded by men. When we passed by him he looked at us with contempt and said something angrily in Baluch which we did not understand and did not pay attention to. Then we entered a shop to buy men's clothes. The shopkeeper, a young and polite Baluch man, asked us to leave the bazar immediately. He told us that the mustached man was a criminal wanted by the police. He even showed us his picture as wanted in a local newspaper. He had killed someone but the police would not dare enter the bazar, the young shopkeeper stated. We found out that he had just threatened to cut our throats if we didn't leave the bazar immediately. Frightened to death we ran away as quickly as possible. Once in the street, we looked around. No police were in sight. Everything was calm! We rushed to a taxi and asked the driver to take us to women's bazaar. He was stunned to hear that we had ventured in the men's bazaar. He finally dropped us in front of a bazaar promising us that it was safe for us. We breathed a sigh of relief when we noticed women inside. It was actually a gender mixed one. There I saw several women selling the Baluch embroideries sewed onto dresses, and several women who were accompanied by their husbands who walked in the front and their wives in the back. They shopped for their wives who nonetheless did not talk to the male shopkeepers herself. Her husband did it for her. But there were also Baluch women alone or together in a small group, including one of my interviewees who was there to buy materials she needed for her sewing activity.

A Brief History of Baluchistan: Origins, Culture, Identity

According to Brian Spooner, the name Baluch is of unknown etymology. As a tribal appellation, it can be traced back into the pre-Islamic period, but the society in which it now applies appears to have formed mainly in the eighteenth century as a function of a number of historical factors in at least two different and relatively unrelated political histories.

He further mentioned that the Baluch structure reached its final form in the eighteenth century. The decline of the Moghols had left a power vacuum in the area. In 1666–7 as part of the local maneuvering to fill it, a group of Brahui tribesmen were able to expel their representative from Kalat and establish themselves. In the 1740s, Nader Shah's treatment of the Brahui reinforced the idea of the political identity of the area. This identity was always represented as Baluch not Brahui. The intervention of Mohammad Shah from the West, and the British from the East toward the middle of the nineteenth century set the seal on the hierarchical model of society that had developed as a function of the interactions of the nomads and the settled communities. Although there had been periodic intrusions and interference in Baluchistan throughout the medieval period—the most recent (before Nader Shah) had been the Qizilbash under the Safavids in the early seventeenth century—there appears to have been no large-scale investment by foreign power of the establishment of long-term administration, or incorporation of the area into any larger political unit from before the Seljuq period until the British began to interfere openly toward the middle of the nineteenth century. Spooner further argued that the intervention initiated by Nader Shah in the 1740s may have been unique in the Islamic period: it galvanized the balance of power in the area, given the newly risen Brahui Khans of Kalat the ability to establish themselves. Later their position was stabilized and maintained by the British. The latter status of the Khans of Kalat was an important factor in the development of the idea that the Baluch were one people, despite the fact that they spoke Brahui and recruited their administration from among Persian-speaking Dehwar peasants. The idea of unity took on new significance as a result of the nationalist policies of the governments in Iran and Pakistan since the Second World War. Baluchistan has been introduced as a refuge area; Barth used the term shatter zone.[7]

However, Spooner argued that Baluch society as we know it ethnographically appears to be a product of the Qajar period. Although the Baluch arrived in what is now known as Baluchistan long before the Qajars came to power, many of the characteristic and distinctive forms of Baluch social life today can be traced to the effects of Qajar influence and, to some extent, of direct Qajar intervention. Although the Qajar period saw the formal division of Baluchistan among Iran, Afghanistan, and India, the area remains culturally homogeneous today. The structure, he emphasizes, is the product of the combination of two factors: (1) tribalism which may be characterized as an emphasis on kinship and descent as organizing principles, in the absence of significant resources or other capital on which to base economic and political relationships; (2) small scattered agricultural settlements that provided a relatively stable but local basis of power for political leaders. "Most of the agricultural populations of the area, although they speak of themselves in tribal terms, are in fact not tribally organized. They are concerned not with genealogies and group boundaries but with networks of kin and other personal relations which they extend as far as they can in all directions."[8]

Before the Baluch became the dominant ethnic group in the latter Middle Ages, the area was divided into two separate named districts: the higher, colder, northern, northwestern areas called Sarhad (the borderland, of Sistan to the north) and the lower, warmer, southern areas were called Makran.

> Within Makran, the cost was always somewhat distinct, populated by people known as Med [...], oriented towards the sea, and dependent on fishing and trading from small ports. In Baluchistan, nomadic tribes are typically small, especially in the mountains that constituted the greatest proportion of the area. Their territorial boundaries often appear to be defined more by topographic limits to pastures than by social or political dynamics, or by any relationship to genealogically derived social boundaries. Since at least the beginning of last century [19th] there has been continual migration in search of more ample resources.[9]

In Baluchistan, although I observed Sarhadis who live mostly at the northern borders, and their poverty-driven life conditions and many with drug addiction, I could not interview them. The people I met and interviewed were from settled tribes in urban or rural areas, not nomadic. Many looked down on Sarhadis whom they qualified as uncivilized, poor, even thieves. However, this qualification is not relevant to the reality of Sarhadis and shows the disregard of urban Baluch middle class toward them. Salzman had pointed out that: "Lacking the division of social strata and economic classes among themselves, the Sarhadi tribesmen were basically egalitarian. The lineage system favored equality."[10] In this regard, the Sarhadi tribes were similar to the Yomut Turkmen.[11]

For Fredrik Barth, Baluchistan seems to have come into being historically as a cultural borderland—as an indirect result of population movements and political upheaval in neighboring areas during the medieval period. Barth argued that the cultural border between Baluch and Pashtuns in Northeast Baluchistan (Pakistan) has moved slowly and intermittently Northward at the expense of the Pashtuns, without any associated movement of population. Groups known to have been formerly Pashtuns and Pashtun speaking were, when Barth was there in 1960, Baluch speaking and fully accepted by themselves and others as Baluch. According to Barth, a century or so prior to the intrusion of the British the anarchy that prevailed in the area generated a complex history of local conquest and succession in which certain structural features of the tribal organization of the competing groups became overwhelmingly significant. "From such processes of fragmentation and mobility a vast pool of personnel results-persons and groups seeking social identity and membership in viable communities."[12] The structural difference between Pashtun and Baluch society facilitating this one-way assimilation is the difference between egalitarianism and hierarchy. In both cultures, the patrilineal principle determines political rights in the tribe and rights of access to resources; honor is defended obsessively against any person with whom equality is claimed, and honor involves obligation toward dependents, including clients and guests. However, Pashtun identity depends on membership in a council of equals, a group of brothers. "Baluch tribal organization, though derived from the same concepts, is not based on the particular mechanism of the egalitarian council. Though defense of honor among equals is important, it thus does not become built into the political system as a major tactical consideration. A model for the Baluch political system is the relationship between a father and his sons."[13]

My own observations show that despite the array of changes which have occurred in the past sixty years since Barth's research, this model of relationship between fathers and sons still persists in the social system of Iranian Baluchistan, and greatly contributes to the persistence of polygamy and a high number of children (especially sons) per father. The sons are both considered as old age insurance and as central in enforcing power relations with other clans.

Baluch identity is also a linguistic identity. As Spooner argued, a linguistic idiom might spread because it is the language in which a particular adaptive type of communication has developed. The spread of linguistic idioms might facilitate the diffusion of the associated social forms.[14] Although the Persian language has been widely diffused through school in the past several decades, it has not erased the Baluch language or the associated social forms. However, the Baluch, like the rest of the Iranian population, are in the process of social change that is likely to affect, in the long run, the Baluch social model. In Baluchistan like in Golestan, Baluch and Turkmen complained that the national television programs were not platforms for the local population to air their demands or to present and cherish their history and culture. It was rather a propaganda device of a central government that despised the rich cultural heritage of these peoples. "Even Sistani (Persian-Shi'ites) intellectuals, poets, writers and researchers refuse to write about the very ancient history of Baluch in this region. Why shouldn't we have a Chair of Baluch language and literature at the university like in Kurdistan and Azarbaidjan?"[15]

In addition to language, and as Salzman argued, clothes have social functions as well. They mark off, through similarity and difference, membership in common or different social categories. Baluch clothes signaled Baluch ethnicity. Those Baluch working in urban setting (for example, in Zâhedân, in offices and shops) sometimes adopted Persian clothes, just as they used the Persian language. On the other hand, members of other Iranian ethnic groups virtually never wore Baluch clothes. "Within the community of Baluch, characteristics of clothes could signal membership in status groups."[16]

Indeed, clothes are vectors and external signs of identity. The educated middle-class Baluch women I met did not wear Baluch clothes at home. They wore clothes like Persians, differentiating themselves from uneducated Baluch women of lower-class origins. In doing so, they attempted to share the common denominators with Persian educated middle-class women, especially a higher education diploma and professionalization. Adult males wore mainly white Baluch clothes and chose dark colors for receptions or gatherings. In Baluchistan the standard for clothes was largely determined by social group membership. Room for personal expression was very limited.[17] Gender and age were also marked by clothes. Children wear more loud colors, young women more colored tissues and embroideries, middle-aged women less colored embroideries, and older women usually prefer gray or black pants, dresses, and veils. "While the standard of dress is collectively rather that individually determined, collective opinion is affected by exposure to other forms of dress and the arrival of new materials, and thus local fashion changes could be seen in the adoption of external modes and in the shifts in the internal standard that could be considered local fashion."[18]

According to Hamid Ahmadi, the Baluch are from Aryan origins and prior to the Islamization of Iran following the Arab invasion, most Baluch were Zoroastrians. Originally, the Baluch lived in eastern and southeastern Iran. Under the Seljuqids and Monghols they began to migrate toward Sindh and Punjab in today's Pakistan. Baluch are divided between Iran (second largest Baluch population), Pakistan (where 40 percent of them live), and Afghanistan. He also argued that religious differences between Sunnite and Shi'ite groups have played a more important role in ethnic political mobilization than linguistic or cultural specificities. The political and intellectual elite, he emphasized, have played the crucial role in shaping ethnic identities. In contemporary Iran, he maintained, the Baluch elite have been made of the educated sons of the chieftains, some of who were educated in Western universities. However, Ahmadi argued that in Baluchistan the formation of urban educated middle classes has been slow, and the leadership of political activities has remained in the hands of the traditional elite (chieftains).[19]

Mahmood Zand-Moghadam, one of the notable specialists on Baluchistan, author of a four-volume book in Persian titled *The Baluch Story*, cultivated an interest in Baluchistan and began conducting research in the province from the early 1960s.[20] He argues that the Baluch language is one of the Iranian languages from Middle Pahlavi origins. The dominant assumption is that the Baluch lived in northeastern Iran (some say in Gilan due to similarities with local languages in Anzali) and migrated to Baluchistan during the Sassanian period (who ruled the Iranian world between 224 and 651). In Achemenian inscriptions (*katibeh*) and later during Parthian and Sassanid Empires, Baluchistan was called Maka, which later became Makoorân. Baluch are known to have always protected the Iranian borders against foreign invaders even during the Moghol invasion. For this very reason, the Baluch chieftains are called commanders (sardârs). Contrary to other tribes elsewhere in Iran where their chieftains owned a significant amount of land, livestock, and wealth, the Baluch tribes and their chieftains had a military function.[21]

Zand Moghadam also argued that under the Cold War and to prevent the left's influence and to better control the region, the Shah's state accelerated the modernization of the Iranian Baluchistan. New roads were constructed and paved, new airports were built and the number of flights from and toward Baluchistan increased. The province, which is 1,600 kilometers far from Tehran, became no more than two hours flight.

Baluchistan gained more importance following Daoud's coup against Zahir Shah in Afghanistan. The King's cousin and former prime minister, Daoud, organized a coup in 1973 while Zahir Shah was on a visit to Rome, and proclaimed a republic. Daoud was toppled by a Soviet-supported communist coup in 1978. The rise of the leftist pro-Soviet ideologies in Afghan, Pakistani, and Iranian Baluchistans came to be considered as a serious threat by the US and its Pro-American allies in the region. Baluchistan thus acquired a strategic importance.[22]

Isolation, Poverty, Migration

For Brun, Geissler, and Bel, in the early to mid-1970s, Baluchistan was marked by isolation, poverty, and outward migration. "The reconnaissance missions that we conducted on behalf of the Plan Organization in 1972 and 1973 revealed to us a zone really stricken by several years of drought. The agricultural and public health surveys carried out in the following years confirmed the precariousness of the living conditions of the majority of the peasants and nomads. For lack of fodder, the latter had lost or sold at a low price half or two-thirds of their goats. The sorghum had dried up on the ground and the rice fields had yielded nothing but straw. When the rains returned in November 1973, the farmers had no seed or plow bulls, which had been sold off during the famine and taken to slaughterhouses in nearby cities. Those who were able to do so crossed the border into Pakistan illegally and bought cheap bags of wheat and rice to feed their families, who had been rationed for months."

According to these authors, "the meals were extremely monotonous, consisting, depending on the area, of rice or sorghum bread, wheat and barley, accompanied by a sauce that rarely contained meat or dried fish. The diets were characterized by an almost total absence of meat, fruits, and vegetables, excluding dates and wild edible plants. Milk was lacking due to periods of drought and the disappearance of the herds, and the traditional exchange of foodstuffs had considerably diminished because no one had anything to exchange with the neighboring regions."[23] They further argued: "Prisoner of its isolation, its poverty and its traditions, Iranian Baluchistan constitutes for the oil Emirates of the Persian Gulf a reservoir of cheap and nearby labor. Clinging to what corresponds to the western half of the ancient Makran, on the edge of the Iranian plateau, in a region naturally turned towards the Strait of Hormoz and the Gulf of Oman, this population has been reduced to deep poverty by successive droughts which have affected the harvests of the last few years. Natural population growth forced the Baluch to look for work outside the country. The proximity, the similarity of climates and the scale of salaries pushed them more towards the Emirates than towards the interior of Iran where the term 'Baluch' is a contemptuous insult."[24] The three authors further stated that those who go to Oman, Qatar, Dubai generally find work without difficulty, either in construction sites (laborers, drivers, carpenters, etc.) or as servants, guards, or gardeners.

The available statistics are very imprecise on the extent of the migration, but an example is the coastal area corresponding to Shahrestan of Châh-Bahâr and south of Iranshahr, where, in 1973, out of a population of 87,750, the number of absentee emigrants was estimated at 30,000 people, mostly young men. This is practically the only one in Iran where there was a decrease in the population from 1956 to 1966. Those who have the best jobs stay years without coming back, fearing to lose their place and to ruin themselves on the occasion of a visit to the family, as they have to be generous with gifts. The laborers and housekeepers return more easily when a good rainy season or a good harvest to participate in agricultural work. The financial capital that could have benefited the farmers is thus diverted to external commercial channels. The hard-earned money in the Emirates goes back to the Japanese motorcycle and radio dealers in Tehran or Karachi.[25]

Marginalization and poverty of the Baluch people made Baluchistan a fertile land for the activities of oppositional groups. The Baluchistan Liberation Front was created in 1964 to unsuccessfully advocate the independence of Baluchistan. Later, in 1980, in the aftermath of the revolution, Amanollah Barakzayi created a group called Pishmarg Baluch. With several other Baluch chieftains, he later created the Baluch United Front against the Islamic regime and was close to monarchists. In the 1990s, another group was created called The People's Front for the Liberation of Baluch, with active participation by members of the Narouyi tribe.[26] Ahmadi further argues that following the revolution, some Marxist non-Baluch groups from Fadaiyan and Peykar organizations and some Baluch middle-class elites co-founded Democratic Organization of Baluch People and demanded autonomy for Baluchistan. The scope of their activities, however, was overshadowed by that of Baluch chieftains.[27]

Molavis

Until the late 1960s, the Baluch clergy usually obtained their degrees of interpretation (ijtihad) either from the Kurdish Sunnite clergy or from the Saudi religious authorities, some of whom had wahabite inclinations. The Shah of Iran wanted to cut off these ties with strangers and helped the Baluch clerics in the formation of their own theology schools in Baluchistan, to mainly gain independence from foreigners. The ministry of education recognized the degree of Sunnite students, who completed their theology studies, as a BA degree, thus making it possible for those who volunteered to become high school teachers.[28]

The religious problems that we witness today started after the revolution when the constitution of the Islamic Republic promulgated the government of a Shi'ite jurisconsult (velayat-i fagih) and that Shi'ite minority in Sistan-Baluchistan province started to construct extravagant Shi'ite mosques. The Baluch in turn began building their own mosques. "Before the revolution, Sunnites and Shi'ites prayed in the same mosques together although their traditions are different. But nowadays they won't enter each other's mosques."[29]

In the early 1980s Spooner argued that the changing economic and political context has made the individual potentially independent of the tribal group, and undermined the status of the chieftains.[30] However, it appears that the weakening of the *Sardârs* in post-revolutionary Iran has not led to the individualization of the Baluch. It has rather strengthened the Molavis and their position of power among the Baluch. Some like Molavi Abdolhamid are outspoken and advocate the religious and linguistic identity of the Baluch and air the demands of the Baluch population against discriminations of the state and local Shi'ite authorities. The strengthening of the Molavis was also a result of the actions undertaken in the immediate aftermath of the revolution by non-Baluch groups such as Fadaiyan Khalq and Peykar who waged an ideological war against the Baluch chieftains. They influenced the educated Baluch youth who founded their cultural groups modeled after political-cultural Arab or Turkmen groups themselves influenced by leftist organizations. The Baluch religious community opposed Marxist groups who propagated anti-religious thoughts in Baluchistan. Molavi Abdolaziz, the then highest religious authority in Baluchistan, founded the Union of Muslims to fight against them. "The leftist groups whose ideology did not correspond to the realities of Baluch society and the local mode of life faded away while the Molavis' authority and influence gathered momentum. Especially since the Shi'ite clergy had acquired much authority and power after the revolution."[31] According to Zand Moghadam, Abdolaziz supported the Islamic regime but following the increasing influence of Shi'ite clergy and the promulgation of the constitution with the principle of the government of a jurisconsult Abdolaziz gradually lost the support of other Molavis who migrated to Pakistan.[32]

Zand Moghadam also declared that during the rise of Taliban to power in 1996, around one thousand Iranian Baluch left the country to join the Taliban and later al-Qaida. However, with the fall of the Taliban in 2001, fundamentalist wahabite aspirations decreased considerably in Baluchistan. He stated that the time had come for the Islamic government to heal the wounds and to proceed to national reconciliation, but no initiatives have so far been undertaken by the government. Baluch complained that the national television broadcasts the news of Friday prayer with only some hundred participants but refuse to do the same for the Sunnite Friday prayers with much more participants. Zand Moghadam stressed: "It is urgent to end religious discriminations against Sunnites. Why shouldn't a Sunnite become a judge? Why shouldn't Sunnite Baluch be overwhelmingly appointed as governors, administrators, etc.?"[33]

Structural Change

The process of social change was initiated by structural changes that have occurred in Baluchistan, however, gradually since the 1970s.

Expansion of Education

The first boys school called Ahmadiyyeh was founded in 1910 in the Sistan region. Almost fifteen years later the first boy's schools were created in Baluchistan: especially in Khâsh, Sarâvan, and Iranshar by the army. The first pupils were from upper-class origins, sons of the chieftains. Mahmood Zand-Moghadam recalls that in the 1960s, when he was conducting research in Iranshahr, there were only three Bachelors.[34] Access to public education for women was made possible much later.

The educated middle class in Baluchistan began to increase following the establishment of universities and institutes of higher education in Baluchistan from 1972 onward. Following the revolution and during the first post-revolutionary decade, an increase in the number of schools was quite gradual. From 1988 to 1997, there was a sharp increase, and from then onward the increase remains steady. During the second period, the number of school girls grew sharply. Teachers training schools for women motivated girls to pursue education and seek jobs in girls' schools. Also girls' schools were founded in rural areas. In 2003, 132,000 or 44.4 percent of the total pupils were girls in the Sunnite majority Baluchistan. They comprised 67,000 or 46 percent of pupils in the Persian majority Sistan.[35] The literacy rate of Baluch married women was estimated at only 41 percent, and 53 percent of child deliveries in this province still take place in homes by untrained traditional midwives.[36]

According to the 2016 National Census of the Population and Housing (the last census), its population was 2,775,014 and its literacy rate was 76 percent. The share of the province to the total population of the country was 3.47 and the average annual growth rate was 1.8 (against 1.2 for the country).[37] In Baluchistan, the average literacy rate was 84 percent in urban areas, and 68 percent in rural areas. The average literacy rate in the country was 91 percent of all men and 84 percent of all women. In urban areas, the rate was 93.5 and 88 percent, respectively. Total literacy rate of the ten to forty-nine years in the country was 94.7 percent. The average household size for the country is 3.3; for Baluchistan it is 3.9.[38] Likewise, in 2016, 60 percent of the Iranian population was under thirty-four. Only 9 percent of the population was sixty and over. In Sistan-Baluchistan, 38 percent of the population was aged zero to fourteen, the highest ratio in the country. Sistan-Baluchistan is the only rural majority province with 51 percent of its population still residing in rural areas. It is also one of the rare provinces with a positive annual growth rate.

Table 2.1 Population estimation by gender in urban and rural areas by 1,000 persons.

Year and province	Total country	Male	Female	Urban areas both genders	Male/ female	Rural areas both genders	Male	Female
1398/2020	83,075	42,018	41,057	62,367	31,539/ 30,828	20,708	10,478	10,229
Sistan & Baluchistan	2,978	1,502	1,476	1,516	765/751	1,462	738	725

Source: Iran Statistical Yearbook, 1398/2020, P. 131.

Table 2.2 Population by religion and province, 2016 census of the population and housing.

Province	Total	Muslim	Christian	Zoroastrian	Jew	Other	Not stated
Total country	79,926,270	79,598,054	23,109	130,158	9,826	40,551	124,572
Sistan & Baluchistan	2,775,014	2,766,139	473	4,155	40	553	3,654

Source: Iran Statistical Yearbook, 1398/2020. Statistical Center of Iran, P. 156.

Table 2.3 Number of literate population and literacy rate among population aged six and over in Urban and Rural areas by sex and province, by 1,000—1396/2016.

Urban areas literate

Province	Population 6 & over both genders/ male/female	Literate Both genders	Male	Female	Literacy rate both genders	Male	Female
Total country	53,208/ 26,791/ 26,416	48,305	25,048	23,257	90.8	93.5	88.0
Sistan & Baluchistan	1121/ 570 551	943	503	440	84.2	88.4	79.8

In an interview with one of Iran's reformist newspapers *Sharq*, published on September 7, 2021, Molavi Abdolhamid made declarations on women's education and social activities: "In this province before the revolution only some specific families sent their girls to school and Baluch women did not participate in the elections either ... Following the Islamic revolution some Ulema reached the

Table 2.4 Number of literate population and literacy rate among population aged six and over in Urban and Rural areas by sex and province, by 1,000—1396/2016.

Rural areas literate

Province	Population 6 & over both genders/ male/female	Literate both genders	Male	Female	Literacy rate both genders	Male	Female
Total country	18,255/ 9,353/8,902	14,334	7,849	6485	78.5	84	73
Sistan & Baluchistan	1,157/ 577 ,580	789	428	362	68.2	74.2	62.3

Source: Iran Statistical Yearbook, 2020, P. 651.

Table 2.5 B.A. Students at higher education institutes by gender and province 1398–9/2020–1.

Academic year	Total both genders	Male	Female
2020–21	3182989	1638746	1544243
Sistan& Baluchistan	82613	43507	39106

Source: Iran Statistical Yearbook, 1398/2020. Statistical Center of Iran, P. 485.

conclusion that they should bring women in and published religious edicts that women should vote and go to university and study. We established dorms for women here who come to study from remote parts of the province and cannot afford to pay for their housing ... Women are now present in social activities."

An increase in the number of schools and of the student population, the numerical growth of the educated population, the increase in modern communication networks, radio, television, internet, telephone, smartphones, the formation of NGOs, the establishment of civil institutions such as city and village councils have all led to a rise in social and political awareness. All these factors have brought about change in traditional perceptions. New values thus emerged such as education and modern knowhow, individual independence from tribal, ethnic, and family affiliations. Women thus gradually began to leave the home to receive an education. Some have continued their studies at university, some work in the administration, others are teachers at schools, university professors, medical doctors, social activists, NGO founders, and members, and some have been elected in different village and city councils.

According to the owner of a computer service company, the internet arrived in Baluchistan at the beginning of the year 2000, but the penetration rate was quite low in comparison to central parts of the country. A dentist who also owns a computer service company declared that in Khâsh around 2,000 people used internet, 70 percent of who are Baluch and many are students. Moreover, many sites held by the Baluch Diasporic community are filtered, and the Sunnite sites both in Persian and Arabic are controlled and filtered as well.[39]

Non-governmental organizations seem to have provided both Baluch men and women with various social and cultural activities. In 2008, over 150 NGOs had been registered in Sistan-Baluchistan province. Several of them were charity organizations, some were women's NGOs, and several others were dedicated to cultural activities. Ahang-i Baluch in Iranshar was one of them. Most members were aged sixteen to twenty-eight, and they concentrated their activities on organizing Baluch music festivals, cultural debates, theatre plays, etc. It also published a journal called *Seday i Ghalam* (The Sound of Pen).

The Youth Association of Voice of Justice (Anjoman-i javânân sedayi idalat) was another NGO founded in 2003 in Zâhedân by young men and women and claimed 3,000 members. A woman student member of the NGO declared: "Most members are from the local student population. They are from several ethnic backgrounds: Baluch, Persian, Turkmen, Kurd, Azari Turks, etc. Our NGO is not ethnic or religious. One of our activities for example was the organization of a conference on February 9, 2004 titled 'Our Iran' to protest against the National Geographic that had called the Persian Gulf Arabian Gulf. We invited local government authorities to attend the conference but none of them came and did not even value our initiative. They don't even accept our love of Iran and seem to be unhappy about it."

However, the access young Baluch have to higher education has not diminished ethnic discrimination. "In the early 1960s nearly all teachers in Sistan-Baluchistan province were from the neighboring provinces of Khorasan and Kerman."[40] Despite the current availability of thousands of university-educated Baluch, "more or less the same situation persists in many areas such as Châhbahâr, where in 2014 non locals constituted 80% of the educational staff."[41]

Expansion of Poverty

In the 1990s and 2000s, a long drought paralyzed the Sistan-Baluchistan province and the desert expanded to cover the cultivated lands. Livestock disappeared either due to drought or were drawn during the flood. To make a living, many poor Baluch had no other choice but to survive through drug, food, or oil smuggling. Many have been imprisoned on drug charges and their families plunged into even more poverty as a result of losing a wage earner. I saw many mourning Baluch women in Zâhedân whose men (fathers, husbands, sons) had been killed by the military forces on drug or oil smuggling charges to and from Afghanistan and Pakistan, or were executed in prison. At the gas stations, I noticed many adolescents aged twelve and older who obtained their 20 liters subsidized gas ratio per day and per family which they then smuggled to Pakistan. When I asked them why they were not at school, they replied that they were their families' breadwinners and that because there were no other job opportunities they had to sell the gas which was then smuggled to Pakistan. On the roads, I noticed several burnt trucks that were used to smuggle gas to Pakistan and had been destroyed by the Iranian military.

"Oil smuggling increased in Baluchistan, especially under Ahmadinejad during the oil boom. Authorities estimated that between 3 to 10 million liters of oil products were traded every day in 2013, they also claimed that 67% of Sistan-Baluchistan vehicles are exclusively engaged in this business."[42]

According to UNODC World Drug Report, Iran accounted for 74 percent of the world's opium seizures and 25 percent of the World's heroin and morphine seizures in 2012. The widespread drug trafficking in the region has spread stereotypes about Baluchistan as a lawless land rendering the word "Baluch" synonymous with "drug dealer."[43]

The socio-political impact has been dire too as it has led to the further securitization of Sistan-Baluchistan.

For some economists, under the Islamic regime, the overall distribution of government expenditures shifted toward lower income groups, especially through expenditures on infrastructure—roads, electricity, clean water, schools, and rural health clinics. Salehi-Isfahani argued that the outcome of these policies on the poor has reflected in the narrowing of the gaps in education and fertility between urban and rural areas and in the rapid decline in overall poverty in the last two decades.[44] He concluded: "There is no doubt therefore that average living standards are much higher in Iran today than what many unhappy middle-class Iranians believe existed in the 'golden' era before the Revolution."[45]

For others, however, poverty rate has gone up in recent years leading to further class divisions. According to the findings of the Islamic Parliament's Research Center, of a population of 80 million Iranians in 2016, more than 13.3 million (3.44 million families) or 17 percent of the total population lived below the poverty line. On average, these families have four members. Of the total number of the poor in Iran, 10.7 million live in urban areas. This number comes to 18.33 percent of Iran's total urban population. Concerning poverty in rural areas, in 2016 more than 2.617 million villagers, or around 737,000 families, lived below the poverty line according to the Research Center's study. The average size of a rural poor family is 3.6, a little smaller than the average urban family. In short, at least 13 percent of Iranian villagers live below the poverty line—almost one in every eight villagers.[46] As a result of American sanctions against Iran's oil and gas exports, the number of poor families has increased. The Islamic Parliament's Research Center's study shows that the country's per capita income has decreased by 34 percent from 2011 to 2019. According to the study, despite the increase in household nominal income, the purchasing power of households decreased by about one-third compared to 2011. There are no recent reliable figures about poverty in Iran, but Parviz Fatah, the former director of the very conservative Imam's Relief Committee, founded in 1979 to assist the most vulnerable families, declared in 2017 that 10–12 million people lived below the poverty line.[47] This was before the severe economic downturn began due to new American sanctions that started in 2018. The worsening of the economic situation in recent years has increased the number of poor Iranians. According to Hossein Raghfar, a well-known Iranian economist, in 2018 (prior to the American sanctions), 33 percent of the country's population or 26 million Iranians lived in absolute poverty, and 6 percent were starving.[48]

The number of individuals in poverty has increased steadily. The Ministry of Cooperation, Labor and Social Well-being declared in August 2021 that 36 million Iranians (or 43 percent of the total population) were poor and that 10 million more people were below the poverty line in comparison to last year.[49]

Yet, poverty affects women more than men—particularly over 3 million women heads of households. The feminization of poverty has become so alarming that Parviz Fatah, aired concern about this situation: "We need to pay special and serious attention to the issue of women's poverty. More than one million seven hundred thousand families are under the protection of the Committee, of which one million are headed by women. The organization model of our Committee is male-dominated, while poverty has become female in the country."[50]

According to recent research, the percentage of female headed households has increased sharply from 8.4 in 1996 to 12.7 in 2016. Sistan-Baluchistan with 18.4 percent has the highest percentage of employed women heads of households.[51]

Absolute Poverty in Baluchistan

Sistan-Baluchistan is the second largest province in Iran and holds the record for absolute poverty in the country. In 2016, around 45 percent of its population lived below the absolute poverty line. This implies that people could not afford to feed themselves an average of 2,100 calories a day, which is the minimum necessary for subsistence according to the parliament Research Center. It is estimated that in 2016, 1,232,275 people were living in poverty in the province, which equates to 269,341 households. The average household size was 4.6, around 0.7 percent larger than the overall average at the provincial level. In other words, poor families tended to be bigger than those with more money.[52]

Hamid Reza Rakhshani, general director of Education in Sistan-Baluchistan, declared that in 2021–2 when the Covid-19 pandemic hit the country, 461,000 pupils enrolled in urban areas of the province and 110,000 (or ¼) could not afford to buy tablet or smart phones to follow online courses. Likewise, the former minister of education had declared that 21 percent of the total pupils in the country had to drop out of school because of poverty and a lack of access to electronic devices. The two poorest provinces are Sistan-Baluchistan and Kohgilouyeh and Boyer Ahmad.[53]

The impoverished economy of the Baluch regions and high unemployment rates have forced some Baluch to risk involvement in trafficking activities.

I share the following account which corresponds to what I witnessed in Zâhedân as well.

> Zâhedân's city center is not a drug-trafficking hotbed, although its inhabitants are amused to confess that 'you can always find what you're looking for.' Alcohol, narcotics, and also car parts, clothes … The center's bazaars are a tangle of huge tote bag shops: thousands of rags, counterfeit goods and the latest outfits 'fallen off the truck; enough to disorientate the visitor, in a region where 90% of the population wears traditional Baluch clothing. Appliances, air conditioners, and other fans flood the market; the economy of the entire city seems to be based on smuggling. The outlying districts, however, do not all have water or electricity, and have become lawless zones, ravaged by drugs.[54]

Baluch as Sunnites and non-Persian/Shi'ites are stigmatized and discriminated against by the majority. Indeed, negative popular stereotypes have remained strong and public policy of the Islamic state has contributed tremendously to these mass images.

Molavi Abdolhamid declared:

We supported the reformists for 24 years. We voted for Mr. Khatami because we thought he would initiate some political openings and changes ... I met with Mr. Khatami several times and gave him reports of discriminations against Sunnites but he did nothing. The same happened with Mr. Rohani [...] They both said they wanted to implement change but had received some phone calls and were not authorized to appoint Sunnites. We are disillusioned with the reformers ... They did not accept to take the risk and appoint Sunnites to high positions. This discrimination and inequalities were very difficult for us ... Now conservatives asked us [Sunnites] to try them and promised to appoint Sunnites to important positions. We voted for Mr. Raissi who sent several envoys to Zâhedân. But he did not appoint any Sunnites as minister either. Well, when we decide to vote for a candidate, we do not ask for authorization, why is [Raissi] asking for authorization?[55]

Women Social Activists as Role Models

It is necessary to grasp the meaning, the subjectivities and the practices deployed by women in an environment structured by and around men. In Baluchistan, as elsewhere in Iran, middle-class parents have been more open minded than those from tribal upper classes. Nasrin's father was among them. A single thirty-nine-year-old gynecologist at the Iranshahr Hospital, Nasrin studied at the universities of Mashhad and Zâhedân and has worked in Sarâvân (southern Baluchistan) for two years. Her mother was illiterate but her father was an educated man and a state employee, and encouraged her to study. "When my father sent me to school, my grandfather disagreed and wanted to take me with him to prevent me from going to school. But both of my parents were supportive of me. In 1988, when I was admitted to Mashhad university [1300 kilometers north of Iranshahr], my parents did not oppose me studying so far away from home. I was among the first generation of Baluch women who did not want to study to become a school teacher but wished to specialize in other scientific branches. From 1986 onward, Baluch young women started to specialize in gynecology." Nasrin argued that in tribal Baluchistan, most of the educated women belong to middle classes. The lower classes don't have the financial and cultural means to allow their girls to study, while the upper classes (tribal chieftains) are opposed to their daughters' high education thinking that study is for ordinary people.

"Back in my teen years, when I looked around me, all women were in inferior position. I started to believe strongly that the only solution to get myself a better condition was to study far from home." Nasrin is very critical of Baluch tribal traditions, especially early and arranged marriage. "I speak Baluch to my Baluch patients and try to help women understand their bodies. They trust me and talk to me about their private sexual problems."

Likewise, Saideh, a thirty-three-year-old woman who was born in Bampur, became a role model for the women in her family and her social environment: "When I started to drive a car, my entire family was against. But I persisted. Now it has become common for women to drive here." Saideh is still very cautious in her attitude and behavior. "Although I live on my own with my children, I always inform my parents and brothers about my whereabouts. I'm aware that if I commit an error, it would be detrimental to my sisters and other women in my family."

Saideh who now works for the Welfare Organization has been involved in social and political activities. It is interesting to note that even an open-minded individual like Saideh prefers her daughter to get married to a relative and disapproves of marrying Persian/Shi'ites for religious reasons.

Another young female role model is Ziba Azizi, a social activist and teacher born in 1984 in the village of Azizabad in Qasr Qand (literally the Sugar Palace), Baluchistan province. Throughout her life, she has been bold in the face of institutionalized gender discrimination and opposition to education from all those around her, including her mother. As the eldest child in her family, Ziba was barely allowed to study, and only on the condition that, like the rest of the girls in the village, she would learn all the household chores, from making bread and food to childbearing.[56] She has four sisters and three younger brothers. During all the years she studied in elementary school, she had to walk to school, then at home she helped her mother, and then at night, she did her homework. In her interview with Maryam Dehkordi, she aid: "I didn't even have a book in the first months when I went to school," she said. "Despite all the shortcomings and suffering, I studied with enthusiasm, and now I am a teacher for other girls, for whom I hope there will be a better future."

Ziba Azizi continued her studies and obtained an MA in sociology from Bojnoord University. She then married and has a son. Ziba wants to teach him gender equality. In 2018, she won the title of the fourth creative rural woman in the world by the United Nations World Women's Foundation (WWSF). She has worked very hard to educate and inform families, especially rural women and girls of the area. One of her most important actions in the Qasr Qand region has been to try to prevent child marriage. She has managed to attract funds from local donors, and finance educational and cultural projects in the region.

It is important to note that over the years, she has never received any support from government officials and institutions in Iran. "Women's paths have been opened. They can say 'no' to their suitor or choose education over a forced marriage. They can go to other cities to further their education. They can live happier and obtain their rights." She gave an example of her efforts to prevent child marriage:

> One day, one of my pupils told me that she had a suitor and that her father wanted to marry her. I found out that her father was poor and unemployed and had accepted to marry her little girl for financial reasons. With the help of my friends, I took out loans for her father and found him a job so that he would have no excuses, and I managed to prevent my student from getting married at a young age. Sometimes I had to argue with families for days and weeks to achieve this goal. There were even several times when I was threatened by the families of children who were about to get married, but I did not give up.

Ziba also worked to enhance women's financial autonomy in her village.

"In Baluchistan, we all learn needlework since childhood. I managed to attract the attention of local benefactors to set up sewing workshops in the village. Then we could sell the result in other cities. This also helped women's employment." With the women of the village, she mixed traditional sewing with innovation and by changing the colors presented their art in a modern style, acceptable throughout Iran. She registered a brand called Nora and presented the work of rural women across Iran with this brand.

Another initiative of Ziba Azizi was to set up an "Iranian house" in the area. In 2016, the house was established in collaboration with the famous charity NGO Imam Ali, the aim being to provide educational items to poor pupils in Qasr Qand.

The successful experience of establishing an Iranian house prompted Ziba Azizi to establish a "house of science" in the area. The need for a rehabilitation, psychological, and social center in the region was strongly felt, she said: "The House of Science provides equal educational opportunities for our daughters and sons, children who usually live on the outskirts of cities, usually devoid of identity cards, whose parents are drug addicts or who have left them on the streets."[57]

Sima is one of the rare women who is an artist, a painter in Baluchistan. Women are the key subjects of her paintings. She has also participated in several exhibitions in Châhbahâr. Sima lived in Pakistan and was not fluent in Persian. She participated in literacy courses for adults to learn Persian and later obtained her high school diploma. Her aim was to pursue art at the university. On the difference between the situation of Baluch women in Iran and Pakistan, Sima said: "In both countries limitations are imposed on Baluch women. In Iran, however, Baluch women are much more emancipated. Although here men are more conservative than their Pakistani counterparts, women are more smart. They have learnt how to use available means, like education for example, to seek better situation for themselves."[58]

The model of gender, religious, and ethnic power relations founded on either Persianity or Shi'ism is increasingly challenged by aspirations for full citizenship rights of both marginalized men and women brought about by social, economic, and cultural change.

Figure 2.1 A Baluch girl in a poor neighborhood in Zâhedân in traditional Baluch cloths. Picture taken in 2004 by Azadeh Kian.

Figure 2.2 Baluch children in a poor neighborhood of Zâhedân. Picture taken in 2004 by Azadeh Kian.

Figure 2.3 A Baluch man, Shahr-i Soukhteh. Picture taken in 2004 by Azadeh Kian.

Figure 2.4 A woman in Keykha village in Sistan, victim of drought, standing before a traditional wood-fired bread oven. Picture taken in 2004 by Azadeh Kian.

Figure 2.5 A poor Persian Shi'ite family in Zâhedân. Picture taken in 2004 by Azadeh Kian.

Figure 2.6 A Persian Shi'ite lower-middle-class family in Zâhedân. Picture taken in 2004 by Azadeh Kian.

Figure 2.7 Children of a Persian middle-class family in Zâhedân. Picture taken in 2004 by Azadeh Kian.

3

Golestan

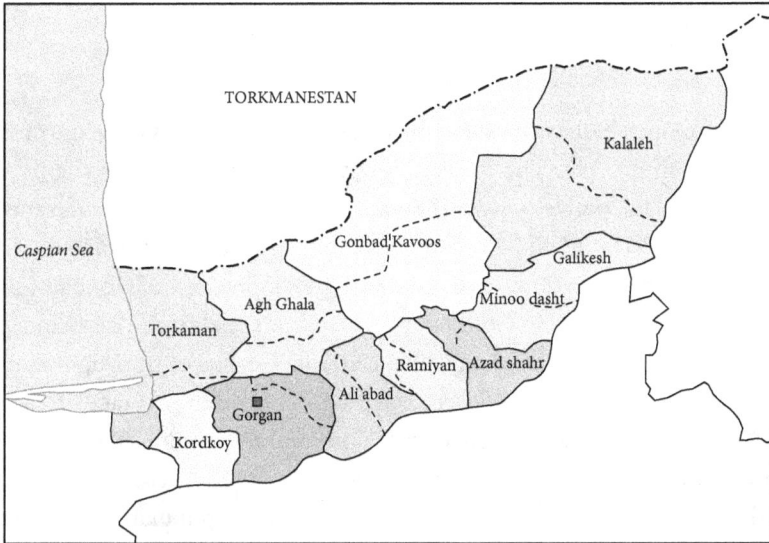

Map 3.1 Map of Golestan province.
Map by Ali Zifan, Wikimedia Commons.

Golestan province has the second lowest percentage of urban dwellers in the country. It has a mixed population of local Persian Shi'ites, Turkmen Sunnites, and Baluch Sunnites and a number of other ethnicities such as Azaris (Shi'ites) or Kurds (manily Sunnites). The settlement of Turkmen in northern Iran goes back to tenth century, and their raids of the nineteenth century to kidnap Persian girls and use them in slave trade had crucial political consequences. In recent decades, the memory of the Gonbad Kavoos wars between Turkmen groups and the Islamic state in 1979 and 1980 has become a marker for Turkmen who have a strong sense of their cultural identity. Their traditions, including consanguineous marriage and women's inferior status, have survived but are increasingly challenged by the educated young generation. The local Persian/Shi'ites respect Turkmen but are reluctant of intermarriage. The Baluch migration in Golestan dates back to a century ago and more migrants settled there recently due to draught in Baluchistan. They have integrated the norms of the Persian/Shi'ite majority. Their women are much more emancipated than their counterparts in Baluchistan, and are taken as role models by them. The Baluch migrants, however, are stigmatized and discriminated against by the authorities, the local Persians and the Turkmen.

Socio-demographic Characteristics

Golestan province in the northeastern part of Iran was split off from the province of Mâzandarân in 1997. The Persian/Mazandarani inhabitants of the province call themselves the natives (mahali) and consider others as ethnic migrants.

Its size is 20,367 km² and Gorgân is its capital. Its population increased from 25,380 in 1956 to 350,676 in 2016. Likewise, the population of Gonbad Kâvoos, the major Turkmen town in Golestan province, increased from 18,347 in 1956 to 151,910 in 2016. According to the 2016 National Census of the Population and Housing, the population of Golestan was 1,868,819 and the average literacy rate was 82 percent: 88 percent for men and 77 percent for women. The share of the province to the total population of the country was 2.34 percent. The average household size for Golestan is 3.4,[1] and 27 percent of its population was between zero and fourteen. The annual growth rate in Golestan is only 0.03.

Table 3.1 Population estimation by gender in urban and rural areas by 1,000 persons.

Year and province	Total country	Male	Female	Urban areas both genders	Male/ female	Rural areas both genders	Male	Female
1398/2020	83075	42018	41057	62367	31539/ 30828	20708	10478	10229
Golestan	1951	978	973	1078	541/538	872	437	435

Source: Iran Statistical Yearbook, 1398/2020, P. 131.

Table 3.2 Population by religion and province, 2016 census of the population and housing.

Province	Total	Muslim	Christian	Zoroastrian	Jew	Other	Not states
Total country	79,926,270	79,598,054	23,109	130,158	9,826	40,551	124,572
Golestan	1868,819	1865,881	128	1,526	15	1,007	262

Source: Iran Statistical Yearbook, 1398/2020. Statistical Center of Iran, P. 156.

Table 3.3 Number of literate population and literacy rate among population aged six and over in Urban and Rural areas by sex and province, by 1,000—1396/2016.

Urban areas

Province	Population 6 & over both genders/ male /female	Literate both genders	Male	Female	Literacy rateboth genders	Male	Female
Total country	5,3208/ 2,6791/ 2,6416	48,305	25,048	23,257	90.8	93.5	88.0
Golestan	889/ 443/ 446	804	416	388	90.4	93.8	87.0

Table 3.4 Number of literate population and literacy rate among population aged six and over in Urban and Rural areas by sex and province, by 1,000—1396/2016.

Rural areas

Province	Population 6 & over both genders /male/female	Literate both genders	Male	Female	Literacy rate both genders	Male	Female
Total country	1,8255/ 9,353/8,902	14,334	7849	6485	78.5	84	73
Golestan	751/ 378/ 373	608	328	280	81.0	86.8	75.1

Source: Iran Statistical Yearbook, 2020, P. 651.

Table 3.5 B.A. Students at higher education institutes by gender and province 1398–9/2020–1.

Academic year	Total both genders	Male	Female
2020–1	3,182,989	1,638,746	1,544,243
Golestan	63,117	31,740	31,377

Source: Iran Statistical Yearbook, 1398/2020. Statistical Center of Iran, P. 485.

Poverty in Golestan

One in three residents of Golestan (35 percent) lives below the absolute poverty line. This equates to 650,000 people, or 180,000 families. The rate of unemployment in Golestan is 12.3 percent, according to the latest figures from 2018. This is slightly higher than the national average. However, only 37.1 percent of working-age residents have jobs, and 17 percent of those who are employed do not work full time. According to the Statistical Center of Iran, the inflation rate in Golestan province was higher than the national average in November 2018. In that month, inflation was 51 percent higher than it had been two years earlier. While nationwide food prices rose an average of 68 percent in that period, in Golestan they rose by 75 percent. This is despite the fact that the province has some of the richest agricultural lands in Iran.

Golestan has the second lowest percentage of urban dwellers in Iran (53 percent), after the province of Sistan-Baluchistan. However, two in five of these residents, or 400,000 people, live below the absolute poverty line. Poverty in rural Golestan is less extreme than in the province's towns and cities. This is not because the villages are flourishing, but because their cost of living—especially housing—is lower. Of the 870,000 villagers in Golestan, 235,000 (27 percent) lived below the poverty line in 2016, according to the Iranian Parliament Research Center.[2]

Turkmen Population

The majority of Iran's Turkmen population live in Khorasan, Mazandaran, and Golestan provinces. The dispersal of the Turkmens in three Persian majority provinces decreases their chance to elect their own representatives to the parliament. The number of Iranian Turkmens was estimated at 550,000 before the revolution.[3] If this estimate is close to reality, then the current number of Turkmens can be estimated at around 1,500,000 because the Iranian population has increased by 2.5 times since the revolution.

The Turkmen people of Iran have a strong sense of their cultural identity, which is clearly perceived by their Persian-speaking neighbors. The latter have heard of the Turkmen raids of the nineteenth century, when the opposition between Shi'ites and Sunnites was used as a religious pretext for Turkmens to kidnap Persians and Persian women and use them in slave trade. Aware of their warlike past and proud of their tribal ancestry, the Turkmen people have retained a certain superiority complex within the Turkish-speaking community itself, to which they adhere only secondarily, for linguistic reasons. Their religious status as Sunnites sets them socially apart from the other Turkic speakers of Iran, almost all of whom are Shi'ites. "Cut off from the Soviet Turkmens, they live in relative cultural isolation."[4]

The memory of the Turkmen Sahra wars or Gonbad Kavoos wars in 1979 and 1980 remains very vivid to the point that all Turkmen aged forty and over I met or interviewed used this date as a marker to talk about the important events in their lives, for example, their wedding date, the birth of their children, or the construction of their house.

Although during the first year of the Iraq-Iran war, mobilization concerned mainly western and southwestern Iran adjacent to Iraq and partially occupied by the Iraqi army, people from all over Iran were mobilized later to take part in the war. Men were sent to the front either as volunteer militias (Basidjis) or as soldiers serving their compulsory two-year military service. Among them some were from ethnic and religious minorities. Several were killed, others were wounded. Turkmen men who participated in the war and were wounded said they have never received any assistance from the government. Direct participation of ethnic women from other parts of the country, however, seems to have been marginal compared to Khuzistan, Kurdistan, or Ilam as illustrated in Mateo Mohammad Farzaneh's research.[5] As one woman volunteer from Southern Iran declared to him: "I did not go to war, the war came to me."[6] According to Farzaneh who interviewed various women volunteers: "All the women from Khorramshahr and Abadan exhibited in the most nonreligious form their sincere love of their home cities and the need to protect their nation[…]."[7] This clearly was not the case of women who lived far from the front. Moreover, two domestic wars were waged against ethnic militant groups: one in Turkmen Sahra (also called Gonbad wars) and the other in Kurdistan. They both ended with hundreds of ethnic people dead or wounded. For Turkmen, the memory of this war has remained even more important than the Iraq-Iran war.

Following the February 1979 revolution, a group of Turkmen created Turkmen People's Cultural and Political Center and gained the support of leftist political groups, especially the Organization of People's Fadayi Guerrillas. The first war was put into motion in March 26, 1979, in the context of Turkmen people's oppression and exploitation which went back to pre-revolutionary Iran. One of the demands aired by the group was the redistribution to Turkmen peasants of lands in the vast and fertile plains that had been owned by the Pahlavis and their affiliates.[8] The Shi'ite militias were brought in from Mashhad by the government and deployed in the city of Gonbad Kavoos. A guerrilla war took place during which one hundred Turkmens died in the battle. A short ceasefire was established between the central government and the Turkmen and Fadaiyan coalition. It, however, did not last long. The Second Gonbad war broke out in February 1980 when a march was organized in the city to commemorate the 1971 Siahkal operation.[9] The Siahkal operation had been carried out in the context of security preparations for the celebrations of 2,500 years of the monarchy in Iran beginning October 20, 1971. "To create the calm necessary of the event, SAVAK [the Shah's secret service] had launched a crackdown on all opposition. The head of internal security of SAVAK had declared in a televised talk that Iran was an island of stability and that nothing moved without the knowledge of Iranian security." Over a month after this televised talk, a small group of guerrilla attacked a Gendermerie post in Siahkal in Gilan province. The operation was a reaction to the arrest of several guerrilla activists in February 1971. Although the Siahkal operation was neither accurate nor successful, it shattered the image of "island of stability" and ridiculed Iranian security.[10]

The commemoration of the Siahkal legend almost a decade later was not appreciated by the central post-revolutionary government. The army responded with heavy artillery and at the same time "Four pro-Fadayi Turkmen leaders who had been negotiating with government representatives on the issue of land and peasant councils were kidnapped at a checkpoint. Their bodies were found a week later. The war ended the movement of pro Fadayi Turkmen peasants."[11]

As William Samii noted, the Islamic State is aware of minority grievances and demands. Instead of dealing with them, it blames its difficulties to foreign scapegoats.[12]

The Origins of Turkmen and Turkmen Dynasties in Iran: A Brief Overview

This chapter will present a brief history of Turkmen to both historicize and contextualize the study. Power relationships can be better understood if they are placed in the long history of the politico-religious context of the society.

The settlement of the Turkmen of Iran in the northeastern region dates back to the tenth century and was consolidated in the eleventh century during the rule of the Seljuqs, also of Oghuz origin, who spread Islam in its Sunnite form. The Turkmen people did not retain the system of twenty-two Oghuz tribes[13] but, subject to political changes and new historical and demographic conditions, organized themselves on new bases.[14]

Following the fall of Ilkhanides (1256–1335),[15] western parts of the Empire (Iraq, Azarbaïdjan, eastern Anatolia) became dominated by three tribal groups: Jalayerids from Moghol origins, Qara Qoyunlu (Black Sheep), and Aq Qoyunlu (White Sheep), which were two Turkmen semi-nomad confederations with unknown origins. Throughout the fifteenth century, these two dynasties attempted to dominate western Iran.

The Qara Qoyunlu (1380–1468) were pushed toward eastern Anatolia by Moghol invasions. The governing family was probably from the Iva clan of the Oghuz; their headquarters were at the north of Van and Urmiyeh lakes. They extended their authority on Azarbaijan and eastern parts of Anatolia. Religious affiliation to the Qara Qoyunlu is said to have been staunch Shi'ism although the more contemporary sources give a more moderate picture. Shi'ism, however, appears as the dominant religion of Turkmen of this region, a tendency that was reinforced following the mounting of Safavids to power.[16] The concentration of the Turkmen accelerated the already-engaged process of the dominance of Turkish languages in Azarbaijan.

In reference to the confederation of Aq Qoyunlus (1378–1508), they are also from Oghuz people, the ruling family belonging to Bayandur clan. They were centered in Diyarbakir in eastern Anatolia. Under the rule of Uzun Hasan (the Tall Hasan 1453–78), the dynasty was at its height and its power was renowned internationally. The capital city was moved from Diyarbakir to Tabriz that had been the capital of the Qara Qoyunlu. Tabriz thus regained its prestige. Italian merchants and ambassadors narrated the beauty and splendor of the city. Aq Qoyunlus were ardent Sunnites but their force was undermined by Shi'ite propaganda in favor of the Safavids.

Turkmen Safavids

In 1499, Ismail, who later founded the Safavid dynasty, gathered Turkmen fanatics called the Qizilbash (Red Heads) because of their red caps. Ismail crushed Aq Qoyunlu Alvand and seized Tabriz in 1501 where he declared himself Shah. He imposed Twelver Shi'ism as the state religion.[17] Shi'ism thus became the official religion under the Safavid dynasty (1502–1722). The Safavid kings included the Shi'ite ulama in the political power, who in return recognized the legitimacy of this dynasty. During this period, the ulama also obtained religious titles and increased the number of religious treaties written. Safavids thus appeared as the leaders of a confederation of Turkmen tribes in eastern Anatolia. This confederation was strengthened by a radical version of Shi'ite Islam, which had drawn the tribesmen into religious/military brotherhoods.

> The Safavid rise to and precarious hold on power depended on their relationship with Turkmen tribal chiefs originally from Anatolia and Syria. These new tribes were reconfigured around a mystical devotion to the Safavid Shahs. The members of this fighting brotherhoods known as Qizilbash accorded their leader Ismail quasi divine status. As representatives of individual tribes they were rewarded with positions of power in return for military support and loyalty. Later, newly converted slaves were appointed to occupy key military and administrative posts supplanting the Qizilbash elite.[18]

Within a few years they took the rest of western Persia, and Fars and Khorasan, but were prevented from breaking back into their old homelands in Anatolia when an Ottoman army defeated Ismail at the battle of Chaldorân in 1514. This failure limited the new regime to borders corresponding closely to those of Ancient Persia.[19] Before the Safavid conquest, the Persian territories were slightly more disposed to Shi'ism than any other part of the Islamic world, apart from centers of strong Shi'ite beliefs like the shrine cities of Qom and Mashhad. Sunnite Muslims were probably in a majority, and outside Persia there were large numbers of Shi'ites in Anatolia, Lebanon, and elsewhere. "The Safavids imported Shi'a scholars from Arabia and Lebanon, and enforced Shi'a religious practice in mosques and schools. Sunni theologians left Persia for more favorable lands."[20]

Nader Shah Afshar, who ruled Iran from 1736 to 1747, was from Afshar Qizilbash background. The Qereqlu Afshars to who Nader Shah's father belonged were a semi-nomadic Turkmen tribe settled in Khorasan. Nader was born at Dastgerd, a fortified village, northwest of Mashhad. The Afshars had been moved there in earlier centuries from the western part of Persia—partly to divide over-mighty tribal confederations that may have threatened revolt, partly to help defend an exposed frontier region. Fierce Turkmen nomads on horseback often mounted raids into the region from the steppe lands beyond to the North and East, carrying off slaves and animals for sale in the towns and cities along the old silk road of Central Asia. According to one story, Nader and his mother were carried off in to slavery by Turkmen raiders when he was still young.[21] Because the Turkmen were Sunnite Muslims and their Persian victims were Shi'ite, religious scruples about making slaves of the hapless Persians did not apply. Their way of life based on pastoralism and riding had scarcely changed since prehistory. Fear of Turkmen slavers would have been ever present in the background of Nader's childhood.[22] Nader's mother tongue was a dialect of a language group spoken by the Turkic tribes of Iran and Central Asia. He would quickly have learned Persian, the language of "high culture" and the cities, as he grew older. But the Turkic language was always his preferred everyday speech, unless he was dealing with someone who only spoke Persian; Nader learned later to read and write in Persian. Nomadic and semi-nomadic pastoralists made up about one-third of the population of Persia in the early eighteenth century, amounting to at least 3 million people.[23]

"The last Turkmen migration toward Iranian regions started without interruption with Russians' conquest of Central Asia [between 1839–1895] until the hermetic enclosure of borders following the retreat of the soviet army from Iran in 1946."[24] As mentioned earlier, prior to the Russian conquest of Central Asia, Iran had lost the Caucasus territories to Russia following two wars that ended in two treaties: the Golestan treaty of 1813 and the Turkmenchay treaty of 1828. Yomouts and Goclans were the two major Turkmen tribes that migrated to Iran. Yomouts comprise over 50 percent of Iranian Turkmen. They are a majority at Gonbad Kavoos and many live in Gorgan. As to Goclans, they are numerous in Bojnoord (in Khorasan). Until 1928, Yomut pastoralists crossed the Iran-Soviet borders during their seasonal migrations but the Soviet border was effectively sealed to nomadic movement in 1930, and the Iranian government under Reza Shah pursued forced sedentarization. Yomuts are particularly active in agriculture, more so after the 1960s when agricultural machinery was introduced and more emphasis was set on cash crops.[25]

Turkmen are settled and are especially active in agricultural activities and herding. In rural areas I visited in Golestan province, Turkmen and Persian alike mainly cultivated wheat and barley.

Shortly after the Second World War, various local merchants, both Turkmen and non-Turkmen, who had accumulated fortunes during the war by taking advantage of the rapid rise in the price of grain, leased large tracts of crown land and began to cultivate them with machinery imported by the government. Such operations proved profitable, and a number of men of wealth and influence from Tehran began similar large-scale operations in the Gorgan plain. Turkmen entrepreneurs of this sort employed other Turkmen as wage laborers in these operations, while non Turkmen capitalists imported labor from the poor regions of southeastern Iran, the Zabul region of Sistan, and Baluchistan. The result was an increase in population density south of the Gorgan. The process of agricultural development was accelerated in 1955 when the government began selling crown land to ordinary Turkmen tribesmen in two hectare plots of irrigated land or 10 hectare plots of dry land (which was prelude to the 1963 agrarian reform). These Turkmen had been tenants on crown land up to this point, in most cases occupying the same region they and their immediate ancestors had occupied before 1925.[26]

The Tale of Ghoochan Girls: From Family Honor to National Honor

Turkmen are respected, feared, and stigmatized by the Persians. The reason for the fear and respect lies in their history; stigmatization has a more recent caused issue related to their Sunnite religion.

In "The Tale of Ghoochan Girls," Afsaneh Najmabadi tells the story of Persian girls who were kidnapped by Turkmen tribes in 1905. The sale of Ghoochan girls to the Turkmen and the capture of the Bashghanloo women by the Turkmen (both Yamut and Goclan) took place in 1905 under the Qajars when Asef al Dowleh was governor of Khorasan and his son, governor of Ghoochan and Sâlâr Mofakham, ruled Bojnoord. The governorate of Khorasan was then financially and politically very rewarding,[27] and it was said that the governor of Khorasan was like a monarch. In addition to the arable lands, Mashhad was the center of pilgrimage and trade with its extravagant awqafs (religious endowments). The governors ruled these regions autocratically and forced the peasants to pay high taxes. Those who did not have the financial means sold their daughters to Armenians and Turkmen to gather enough money to pay their taxes. It was said that the Turkmen took the girls to Ashkhabad and sold them to Armenian merchants who then forced them to become either slaves or singers and dancers in cafés. Some were seen working in cafés in Tbilisi. According to some reports the figure of girls was estimated to be around one thousand. Both those who were sold and those who were captives were kept anonymous and were called "the Ghoochan Girls."[28] The northern and eastern regions of Khorasan had become the center of tension between the Russians, the British, and the Iranians. The Russian occupation of the northern and western parts of the Caspian had caused concern to the British. The defeat of the Qajars made visible the political and military weakness of this state. On the other hand, on an economic level, Russian control of these regions had led to greater security, improved agricultural activities, and increased trade and commerce with Russia. The inhabitants were satisfied with the presence of the Russian army. The caravan route between Tehran and Mashhad, which had previously been under constant threat from Turkmen raids, had become much safer.[29]

In people's narratives, the story of Ghoochan girls was at the heart of their anger against the governors of Khorasan and the central government. It ultimately played an important role in the constitutional revolution.

Following the Constitutional revolution and during the first Parliament, the requests to return the Ghoochan girls back to Iran was one of the important issues discussed, although the government remained silent. The members of the Parliament retaliated by proposing a motion of no confidence against the government whose members were handpicked by the Shah. Finally, in 1907 a commission was created at the ministry of justice to investigate the selling of Ghoochan girls and the capture of Bashghanloo girls. Two weeks later Sâlâr Mofakham, the governor of Bojnoord, was found guilty. He was removed from his post and condemned to pay a fine and to make efforts to return the girls back home.[30] The tale of the Ghoochan girls was known to everyone and became a national narrative. In the political language of that time, the loss of land (to Russians and the British) and loss of national honor were related. So was the articulation between the Turkmen raids and the government's inability to defend Iran's territorial sovereignty, especially against the Russians and the loss of northern territories to Russia. Women became a symbol of the homeland in the political thought of the constitutionalists. The combination of selling girls with the hostility between Shi'ites and Sunnites, with the tension between tribes and rural population, the differences between Persians and Turks, with taking by force girls to the other side of the borders and selling them to Armenians (non-Muslims), transformed the Ghoochan girls to Iranian girls and from what was the family honor to the national honor.[31]

The Survival of Turkmen Traditions

Hobsbawm and Ranger argued:

> Traditions which appear or claim to be old are often quite recent in origin and sometimes invented[...] Invented tradition is taken to mean a set of practices, normally governed by overtly or tacitly accepted rules and of a ritual or symbolic nature, which seek to inculcate certain values and norms of behavior by repetition, which automatically implies continuity with the past. In fact, where possible, they normally attempt to establish continuity with a suitable historic past [...]. All invented traditions use history as a legitimator of action and cement of group cohesion. It becomes the actual symbol of struggle [...] [32]

Although my sample was composed of urban and rural settled Turkmen, many of their pastoral traditions that William Irons discussed had survived, one of which is monogamy.

> The primary factor militating against polygyny is the high bridal payment required for a polygynous union. The bridewealth for a married man seeking an additional wife is generally three times the amount the same girl would fetch if she were to marry a previously unmarried man. Such a bridal payment is difficult for most families to gather together, and makes little sense in terms of the development cycle of domestic households. The capital a man would need to acquire a second wife for himself could be used instead to acquire brides for three of his sons. Only exceptionally affluent fathers would consider such a luxury.[33]

These traditions are still alive, and my interviewees gave the same financial reasons to analyze the absence of polygamy among Turkmens. This tradition which encourages monogamy, however, has not altered the unequal gender relations within families.

"The fate of a household is ultimately determined by its male members [...]. Men are the heads of households, and as such, are the property holders of the Turkman society [...] Turkmen are quick to point out that although wives are essential to the growth of a family, they can be replaced." Irons also maintained: "The majority of households follow the ideal pattern of nuclear families breaking off from patrilocal extended families."[34] Irons writes that women only play subordinate roles, have inferior status, and are not supposed to be in contact with men beyond the sphere of kinship.

Turkmen women's lack of insistence to take their inheritance is another tradition that has lasted. Irons noted that when a daughter of a deceased man refuses to grant her share of her father's estate to her brothers, a complete rupture of all social relations results. A woman who holds to Islamic law [daughters inherit half the share of their brothers but they inherit the land as well] cuts herself off completely from her agnates. In case of serious mistreatment by her husband, a woman can only turn to her brothers, father, and more distant male agnates for assistance; being completely cut off from them is therefore a serious matter. A woman who does not give her patrimony to her brothers also faces the possibility that if she were widowed, her brothers would insist on reclaiming her and, if possible, marrying her off elsewhere. Such a procedure would separate her from her children who, if they were no longer nursing, would usually remain with their agnates. It is rare for a woman to insist on taking her inheritance, and when a woman does, it is usually a result of strong coercion from her husband. As a result of this tradition and as Irons emphasized, "Most Turkmen women own very little property. When a woman marries, her father usually gives her a small dowry, consisting of clothing, jewelry, carpets and household utensils. Wealthy men also give their daughters a dowry in livestock, usually either a camel or a cow."[35]

During my research, I observed that elder women pull their Turkmen head scarf over their face in front of their parents in law (both father and mother in law) and older men in the family and did not speak to them as a sign of respect. Irons had the same observations: "The wife avoids all those in her husband's household senior to her husband, including guests, by veiling her face and not speaking to them. When such senior individuals are present she avoids her husband as well in the same way."[36] This tradition, however, is observed less among the younger and the more educated women. In urban areas, married women wear a small hat beneath their Turkmen head scarf when they are out in the public space to signify that they are married (see Figure 3.1).

Likewise, Irons writes that after the wedding the bride is considered to have undergone a permanent change in status, from that of unmarried girl to that of married women. "On the morning after the wedding, women of the groom's family, younger than the bride, pull her tresses backwards where they will henceforth be worn in the manner of a married woman rather than in front of her shoulders in a manner of an unmarried girl."[37]

Irons reported: "Turkmen claim that they do not allow for divorce. This is a matter of custom rather than religion." He also mentioned: "Husbands have considerable authority over their wives and the right to use corporal punishment to enforce their authority."[38] In my research, I did not see or hear of any conjugal violence but women respected their husband's authority. Likewise, divorce

Figure 3.1 Picture of Turkmen women in Ashooradeh. Copyright Hamid Hajihusseini.

continues to be stigmatized among Baluch and Turkmen, and in our quantitative and qualitative surveys we had few divorced women. I provide tables on the rate of marriage and divorce in the chapter "Impact of Structural Transformations." They concern each province but do not specify the ethnicity or religion of the married or divorced people. However, divorce is no longer stigmatized in many other regions of the country such as Tehran, Mazandaran, and Alborz where, today, there is one divorce per two marriages.[39]

Active Women as Role Models

Zoleikha Adeli, called "Golbahâr" (spring flower), is an example of a successful role model. She is a Turkmen who has made famous the Turkmen carpets of the villages of Golestan beyond the Iranian borders. On her Instagram page, she introduces herself as "Handmade Turkmen carpet maker and Gabbeh, CEO of Golnegar Turkmen Cooperative Company, advisor to the ladies of Bandar Turkmen and the best entrepreneur in the country." On all her Instagram pictures, she appears wearing traditional Turkmen clothes, long and colored scarves with long and colored robes. She is an entrepreneur who has received honors for establishing carpet cooperatives and forming various forces to produce Turkmen rugs in Iran.

Her workplace is decorated with statues, plaques, and pendants handmade from Turkmen rugs. In her interview with Maryam Dehkordi, she declared: "My father was a cultured man and had a very friendly relationship with his children," she says. "So was my mother. For example, when I came back from school, I would tell them everything. They listened to me like a friend. In such an atmosphere, I went to university. I studied business administration, then carpet design and knitting at the University of Applied Sciences."[40] She learned rug design and knitting first from her mother, then in college, but the study of this field led her to decide to create a rug cooperative in 2003 based on what she had learnt during childhood and teenage years and her experience in studying and teaching later. "I was twenty-three when I got married. Back then, studying for girls was not considered as important as it is now." Zoleikha and her husband have a girl and a boy. Zoleikha said that her husband was her companion like her parents. She also developed a free professional school. Zoleikha Adeli and her family had countless problems at the beginning of their career. Her cooperative is now recognized every year as the best cooperative in the field of carpets, and she was elected as the head of the "Women Entrepreneurship Commission of Golestan Province." Today she is also a member of the board of directors of the entrepreneurs of Golestan province. The successful entrepreneur is now looking to set up a center called Turkmen Banu to operate in three sectors of clothing, handicrafts, and traditional cuisine: "I intend to support female-headed households in this center, in particular." Zoleikha Adeli has a recommendation for Iranian women. She believes that everyone should take the first steps to do anything from where they are rooted: "You don't need to leave your city or village to make big steps. You can do great things where you are." In spite of her success, she recalls the discriminations to which the minorities are subjected. "It's a good thing to listen to the heartache and words of people who share their roots with you."[41]

Baluch Migration in Golestan Province

I had first conducted fieldwork in Gorgan and Gonbad Kavoos and several villages and small towns with a sample of Turkmen and Mazandarani/Persians. Later, I decided to do research on Baluch migrants, many of whom lived in Minoodasht region. In April 2008, Sadigheh Sheikhzadeh and I arrived at Gorgan airport. We took a taxi to Minoodasht, 90 kilometers away. We were alone on the road. The driver looked at us from time to time in his rearview mirror. Suddenly he said: "Let me put a tape for you that will cheer ou up." Then we heard the speech of a man who explained in detail the sexual intercourse of a man and a woman, presumably how a husband should satisfy sexually his wife. At first I couldn't believe my ears. I looked at Sadigheh and found her very embarrassed. To no avail, we asked the driver to stop the tape. He instead turned up the volume. I had to yell at him and threaten him with calling the police. He stopped the tape, and in revenge he drove like a madman. Finally, we arrived at our destination—a rather large three-story hotel near Minoodasht that had had its time of splendor. The garden was abandoned but renovations were underway inside the hotel. We asked for a room with two beds. The first one was dirty, so we asked and obtained another one. The room was on the second floor, reserved for families. The windows overlooked the fields that spread out to infinity. Around eleven o'clock in the evening and before going to bed, I wanted to have a herbal tea. The telephone in our room did not work. So I decided to go downstairs to ask the night watchman, a nice and polite young man, for some hot water. When I came back, I found a note under the door of our room that said: "We like you. Please call us." The author of the note had left a cell phone number. The hotel was plunged in total silence, amplifying my fear. I was stunned. Sadigheh was once again uncomfortable, feeling responsible for my safety. We quickly decided to go and find the night watchman, the only person we had met all evening. We found him on the stairs. He was coming up with the tray of hot water and cups. I asked him to come back down and then, once downstairs, I explained to him, in a jerky way, what was happening. He proposed to go upstairs with us and dial the cell number on the note. A phone rang in a room just across ours. He knocked at their door. There were three young men in the room. Leaving the men, we went downstairs again. Tears were streaming down my face. The place was totally foreign to me. I had no bearings and didn't know what to do. The night watchman called the owners of the hotel—a mature couple. I could barely talk. While shaking and crying, I handed them the infamous note and demanded that they call the police. They begged me not to involve the police in this because it would have negative consequence for the hotel. They then read the note and looked at me, puzzled. They couldn't understand why I was doing such a big deal out of a note. They asked whether the men had harassed us. I answered no but the point is why did they dare to even make us such a proposal. Sadigheh who had been trying to calm me down declared: "Dr. Kian the owners are right. This is nothing compared to what we women experience in this country." Finally, I agreed to leave the police out of the story only if the owners expelled the men from the hotel right away. They acquiesced. I later found out why they were scared to call the police: men alone were not authorized to stay at the same floor that was reserved for women and families.

The major issue, however, was that some people found it strange that two women were traveling alone with no man looking after them. Doing research did not mean much to them. I, however, was welcomed by my interviewees, both women and men, who did not hesitate to share their experiences, hardships, and hopes.

To start my research in the villages, I needed a reliable car and a driver. The owners of the hotel proposed a man in his late fifties who used his car to transport passengers. Following a meeting with him, I hired him. He turned out to be a retired revolutionary Guard (Pâsdârân), who had participated in Iraq-Iran war and had been wounded (janbâz). His three children were university students and his retirement pension was not enough to make the family's ends meet. Because he had been wounded during the war, he could not find a job and used his car to earn an extra money. During my research in Iran, I also met a number of Pâsdârâns still in duty who became construction painters, drivers, etc., during weekends. This alone showed that contrary to the common belief, all revolutionary Guards did not benefit from the wealth of their institution.

Baluch in Golestan: Between Integration and Stigmatization

According to the economist Khosrow Naraghi, an important Baluch migration movement started in the 1960s toward the cotton fields of Gorgan and Dasht Gorgan [Gorgan Plain], which were very labor intensive, and whose extension was the result of the agrarian reform. "Open to the intensive exploitation of capitalist type, the northern regions drained the Baluch peasantry."[42]

Indeed, as my research too revealed, some members of the Baluch community migrated to the area that became the Golestan province several decades ago, some others came there more recently from the 1980s onward, especially because of drought in Baluchistan.

In the aftermath of the revolution, following the Gonbad wars, the land of big landowners was confiscated by the state. In Golestan, those who had not been affiliated with the Shah's regime could keep 75 acres of land and the remaining was distributed to the peasants who were given 5 acres each. Like other peasants, Baluch migrants who worked in agricultural activities prior to the revolution were often given the land. Those who migrated after the 1980s bought agricultural lands from local peasants. They now own their agricultural lands and work on their lands but are still stigmatized by both Persians and Turkmen as drug dealers. They are accused of buying land as a means to launder money. Negative perceptions about the Baluch community in Golestan province have led to their marginalization and their exclusion. For example, the Baluch are repeatedly accused of being fanatic, rootless, pitiless. A Persian/Mazandarani girl repeated the same accusations and insisted that a while before my visit a Baluch girl had befriended a Mazandarani/Persian boy. "The Baluch found out and brought the girls to the street and hit her head with cement blocks." My investigations, however, proved that the information was false and that no so such incident had happened. But the rumors participate actively in making negative perceptions about Baluch in Golestan.

According to my observations, Minoodasht area and the adjacent villages have a population of Turkmen, Persian/Mazadarani, Zaboli, Baluch, and Azari communities. When Baluch become the majority in a village, Persians and Turkmen (who in some cases tend to identify with Persian majority as a strategy of empowering their community) sell their lands and houses to the Baluch, and leave their village for a Persian- or Turkmen-dominated place.

Weber defined ethnic groups as having a subjective belief in a community of origin based on similarities in external habitus or morals, or both, or on memories of colonization or migration, so that this belief becomes important for the spread of communalization—regardless of whether or not a blood community exists objectively.[43] Along with language, history, and memory, religion (Sunnism) is one of the elements that allows the construction of a common sense of belonging. An awareness of cultural differences has thus developed.

In Golestan, many Persians declared that Baluch had their own traditions, behavior, and attitude that were very different from theirs, and not accepted by the locals. But these assertions are rooted in misperceptions rather than in reality.

Although stigmatized, the Baluch community, especially Baluch women, attempt to integrate within Persian-dominated environments. They are greatly influenced by the values of the majority and as a consequence of this hybridity they have abandoned aspects of their traditions. The role of certain cultural-symbolic practices that some defend in order to preserve the culture of their community has faded away. For example, polygamy is virtually non-existent among married Baluch men in Golestan; the Baluch allow and even encourage their girls to continue their studies; the minimum age of marriage for Baluch women in Golestan is around eighteen to nineteen; Baluch parents do ask the opinion of their daughters before responding positively to their suitors.

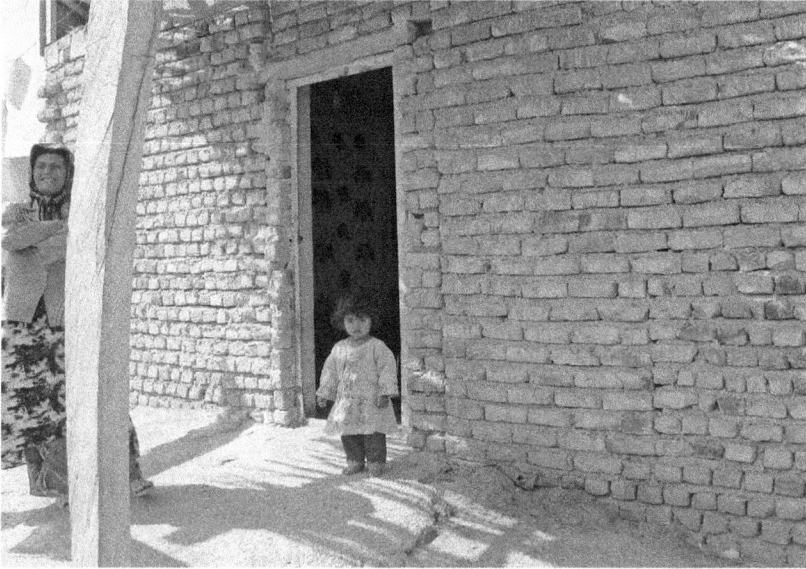

Figure 3.2 A Baluch women and her daughter in Kamâl Abâd. Picture taken in 2008 by Azadeh Kian.

Although Baluch, like Turkmen, and local Persians do marry within their own community and their own tribes (most Baluch in our Golestan survey are from Barahuyi, Naruyi, and Galeh Bacheh tribes), women are much more emancipated, they go shopping alone, and married women work as shopkeepers or peasants. Dress codes are also very different from Baluchistan. In Golestan, Baluch, both women and men, have adopted the local Persian clothes for themselves and their children. Baluch women in Golestan wear pants and a colored or flowery dress like local Persians. This adoption is both likely to ease their integration in the larger community and is a sign of their integration. As Vayda argued: "People do not mechanically act out a basic cultural pattern, but rather pragmatically vary [...] their behavior and respond to the different conditions in which they find themselves."[44]

Changing Gender Relations

Their marriage ceremonies too are very much influenced by the Persian model. They celebrate a one-day marriage ceremony, the bride wears a white gown, and the day after ceremony they organize a party called *pâtakhti* in Persian (a kind of bridal shower) when the gifts offered to the bride and groom are opened and announced in front of the guests. Pâtakhti is considered unlawful according to Sunnite religion in Baluchistan. More importantly, the tradition of zan talâq (divorcing the wife) does not exist. My interviewees all believed that among Baluch traditions which are still practiced in Baluchistan, *zan talâq* is the most humiliating for women. If a man makes a bet on accomplishing something (for example, to quit smoking opium) and swears in front of four male witnesses to divorce his wife if he does not succeed, or simply if he gets angry with his wife and declares he will divorce her, then the wife will be considered as a divorcee if the husband fails although she will not be legally divorced. She thus must quit her husband's home leaving her children behind. But she cannot remarry while the husband will not hesitate to remarry. According to some of my interviewees, this tradition has recently been questioned by educated Baluch people, and some Molavis (Sunnite clergy) are trying to provide a more nuanced reading of it in order to prevent unjustified divorces. It should be mentioned that among some traditional Kurdish Sunnites a more or less similar practice still persists—the practice of triple divorce (seh talâq). The husband repeats three times "I divorce you. You have become harâm (illicit) to me."[45] The divorcee women must return to their parents. However, this type of divorce is not authorized by law according to which all couples must file for divorce in a court and a judge pronounces the divorce.

Although most of my interviewees were literate, they were not very aware of women's rights and/or did not want to break with their traditions. For example, they did not know about the conditions they can set in the marriage contract, including the right to divorce. In matters of women's rights, they remain closer to their own customs and traditions than those of Persian/Mazandaranis in Golestan province. Like in Baluchistan, there is virtually no divorce. In case there is a conjugal problem, they do not go to the court, but rather solve problems amongst themselves, usually through the involvement of the elderly or the Molavis. Baluch migrants have combined Persian traditions with their own. Unlike Persians, however, it is the groom who offers the dowry (*jahiziyyeh*). The groom also offers the bride a dower (*mahr*) the amount of which depends on the social status of the bride. They argue that their religion forbids high amounts of dowry. The cost of marriage is entirely paid for by the groom himself. He thus must work to collect the money he needs to marry. For this very reason, many Baluch young men work in Mashhad or Tehran. The Imam Relief Committee also helps to provide the dower for poor families if the groom has done his military service. However, in Golestan as in Baluchistan, Baluch people said they are discriminated against by the Imam Relief Committee or the Organization of the Well-being (Behzisti). "My father had no insurance and a cancer. The Behzisti did not help us. I had to take care of all his health expenses," said one interviewee in Kamâl Abâd.

In summary, and despite some differences, the Baluch way of life in Golestan is much closer to Persian's than to their own relatives' in Baluchistan. As the people in my sample said, the influence of Persians is very important in matters of habits, customs, ceremonies, and dress code. When they visit their families in Baluchistan, they are no longer considered as Baluch. Yet the process of othering has made them total strangers in the eyes of both Persian and Turkmen sending them back to a position of vulnerability.

In the village of Kamâl Abâd near Minoodasht, all inhabitants are Baluch and they are all from Nâruyi tribe. They are originally from Sarakhs and are all relatives. They have constructed themselves a Sunnite mosque in their village. Young men work in a nearby cement factory; others are involved in agricultural activities. Women have abandoned the Baluch traditional dress and have adopted the local Persian dress and pants. They all watch Iranian national TV and tend to appreciate the educated active women and the cultural models they see in different soap operas. Contrary to their counterparts in Baluchistan who usually do not have the right or do not leave the home without being accompanied by their husband or a male relative, Baluch women I encountered in Golestan take the bus and go shopping in Gâlikash or Minoodasht without having to obtain their husband's authorization. One of the shopkeepers in Kamâl Abâd was a woman. In this village like elsewhere, Baluch marry their relatives. Men too are very different from their counterparts in Baluchistan. In Baluchistan, as Kheyr Bibi, an interviewee in a poor neighborhood of Zâhedân and a second wife of a bigamous declared, "Housework is the exclusive responsibility of women. If a man helps his wife, everyone will laugh at him. The Baluch don't appreciate it at all if the husband helps his wife or looks after the children. Whoever does so will be laughed at." In Golestan, however, Baluch men do not mind looking after their children while their wives are absent. They agree that their daughters go to high school in a different village or town, that parents should not impose unwanted marriages on their daughters. Among the younger generation, husbands always do ask the opinion of their wives and said they never make any decisions without their wives' agreement. Mr. Kamal's grandfather built this village in the 1930s. Then other members of the extended family came to visit and they decided to stay. Mr. Kamal was himself born here in this village. He studied up to the age of fifteen, and his wife who is his first cousin has finished primary school. As we can see in the Figure 3.3, he was building their new house himself. He is an example of the younger generation of Baluch men who have largely abandoned patriarchal traditions of male superiority. He looks after her two daughters while his wife is absent; he is not unhappy to have no sons, and said he did not want other children in order to better educate his two daughters.

Mânjârloo is a beautiful Baluch village of about 400 residents located atop a hill in front of Golestan forest. The village is, however, very hard to reach and villagers feel quite isolated especially in winter when the road is usually closed during periods of snow. The village has electricity, school, drinking water but has no gas and no bakery. People make their own bread which they do not find very comfortable. There is a school in the village, and like many other villages I visited there was no gender segregation at school, mostly due to a lack of teachers. The majority of inhabitants are from Barahuyi and Galebacheh tribes. Persians used to live in the village, but they left due to a lack of facilities, and were replaced by the Baluch most of whom cultivate wheat, cotton, and barley. Several of those Baluch who had better material conditions also left for Dâr Abad down the hill. The remaining inhabitants too now wanted to leave

Figure 3.3 A young father and his daughters in Kamâl Abâd. Picture taken by Azadeh Kian in 2008.

Figure 3.4 School children with their teacher in Mânjârloo. Picture taken by Azadeh Kian in 2008.

Figure 3.5 Safiâbâd. Picture taken by Azadeh Kian in 2008.

Mânjârloo and demanded to be resettled in one of the newly built small towns (shahrak) the public sector builds in the valley. "We don't have gas, nor a bakery. We have to make our bread ourselves. We are isolated during the Winter because it becomes impossible to reach our village," said an inhabitant. But Mânjârloo villagers say they cannot accept the preconditions that the central government and local authorities have set on them, i.e., that they disregard their tradition of hospitality and hand in to the authorities the wanted Baluch who every now and then hide in the mountains near the village. This is against Baluch tribal tradition of *mayar*, or giving refuge to the fugitives. The need to cohesion of minority groups determines life and moral style in helping other members of their ethnic group even when they are not right. Dignity and honor play a key role in these dynamics. But some Baluch who accept to overlook their traditions or collaborate with the state/local authorities on security issues, especially drug dealing, are given access to housing or other facilities.

The Relationship between Baluch and Turkmen

The relationship between Baluch and Turkmen in Golestan is very complex. Although Turkmen are Sunnite and share the same religion with Baluch, they often side with Persians against Baluch whom they too label as invaders. Persians/Mazandaranis do not openly stigmatize Turkmen in towns and villages where the population of Baluch migrants have become important. Conscious of their dominant position, however, Persians openly stigmatize the Baluch as drug dealers, violent, miserly, thieves, etc., but they declare having no problems with Turkmen whom they qualify as hardworking, honest, non-violent.

A Persian/Mazandarani farmer declared:

> Most of my agricultural workers are from Zabol (major town in Sistan the majority of whose population are Persian/Shi'ite). They work from 6 AM to sunset. But Baluch don't work hard. They are involved in smuggling activities and purchase land and well to irrigate the land. How can you possibly purchase land for millions of toman by picking cotton and gathering pumpkin seeds?

Likewise, a young man from Zabol declared: "My family lives here for a very long time. I was born here. We are not involved in illegal activities. Some Baluch, though not all of them, are involved in drug smuggling. They make their living illegally. Some are even famous bandits." His friend, who is also a migrant from Zabol and a local state employee, said: "Baluch are well known for their illegal activities. They have spent a fortune to build a mosque here … where does the money come from?" Zabolis, who are Shi'ite and Persian, consider themselves distinct from Baluch for both ethnic and religious reasons and feel superior to them. I met some mixed Zaboli, local Persian couples in villages near Minoodasht. However, some local Persian interviewees were reluctant to accept Zabolis because "they are close to Afghans both culturally and linguistically. They listen to afghan music." On the other hand, Baluch in Golestan dislike being qualified as Afghans. As mentioned earlier, solidarity among the subaltern in Iran is impeded by ethnic/religious boundaries that also function as social hierarchies.

The situation is quite different in Gonbad Kavoos or Gorgan where Turkmen are the second largest population after Persians and have a strong feeling of being discriminated against by Persians. Indeed, despite the population mixing in this province, ethnic and religious boundaries are quite tight. For example, we did not see or hear of any intermarriages between Turkmen, Baluch, and Persian/Mazandaranis. The three communities live side by side but show no willingness to remove ethnic boundaries or let their ethnic and religious identity be influenced by matrimonial alliances with other communities. "We do not marry our daughters to Persians" is both a Baluch and Turkmen motto. Although the Iranian civil code authorizes marriage between a Shi'ite woman and a Sunnite man (Article 1059), traditionalist clerics advise against such marital unions. "It is preferable that a Shi'ite woman does not marry a Sunnite because man's control over his woman might deviate her from her religious path."[46] In our survey, Persian/Shi'ites use religious and cultural differences as a pretext. While sipping tea with a Persian peasant family of tobacco cultivators in Dowlat Âbad, an exclusively Persian village, and discussing their daughter's upcoming marriage with a Zaboli, I asked whether they also accepted to have a Sunnite son-in-law. The father who worked for the tobacco factory became very angry and said that my question had "made his tea poisonous." Turkmen of Gonbad Kavoos and also those in the villages near Minoodasht had themselves built several mosques. For example, in Gonbad Kavoos, in the neighborhood where several of my interviewees lived (Oghoul, Zeynab, and Sahar), there was a Sunnite mosque belonging to Sahar's uncle (and Zeynab's grandfather). Zeynab and Sahar both mentioned: "On the night of Qadr (toward the end of the month of Ramadan, when according to the traditional Muslim belief, the God sent the Quran), all the Turkmen girls in the neighborhood get together and pray." She said: "We know how to read the Quran. The Quran has 30 parts. We ask each of them to read two or three parts and then we read the whole Quran. This can last until three in the morning. We also do it during the month of Ramadan or when someone dies. During Ramadan, some people offer to break the fast. Others give offerings (sadaqeh) to their neighbors. The day before yesterday, Turkmen bread was given as an offering. From time to time they give pastry as an offering (sadaqeh) but it is very expensive." In the areas near Minoodasht too, Turkmen were in the process of building their own Sunnite mosque, and two other mosques were under construction in two nearby villages. They chose their Imam themselves and paid his salary. There was also a women's Sunnite religious seminary in Gâlikash, and women had enrolled in the seminary to study the Sunnite religion. The Molavis, however, usually brought in from Baluchistan, turned out to be conservative.

In Shi'ite majority villages, men and women go to the mosque together. People go to the mosque not necessarily to pray but to socialize. In the absence of cafés or other gathering places, the mosque that exists in each Persian/Shi'ite majority village also fulfills this role. People gather there to organize pilgrimages to Karbala or Mashhad, to file for financial assistance, even to find a good match for their children to marry. A local Persian villager from Esboo Mahaleh

Figure 3.6 A Sunnite mosque situated between Kamâl Abâd and Dâr Abâd. Picture taken in 2008 by Azadeh Kian.

Figure 3.7 A Peasant family in Dowlat Âbad. Picture taken in 2008 by Azadeh Kian.

Figure 3.8 A Mazandarani family in Esboo Mahaleh near Gorgan. Picture taken in 2004 by Azadeh Kian.

Figure 3.9 A Mazandarani family in Esboo Mahaleh near Gorgan. Picture taken in 2004 by Azadeh Kian.

(15 kilometers away from Gorgan) declared: "On the occasion of the New Year (Nawrooz) we go on pilgrimage to Imam Reza's shrine in Mashhad with the village religious association (hey'at). Usually, we are around 150 to 200 people. They book houses in Mashhad and four or five buses. All men 15 years old and over can come." It is interesting to note that some Persian/Shi'ites combine a pagan celebration (Nawrooz) with religious ceremonies (pilgrimage). His wife continued: "There are also women who organize trips to Mashhad or Amol for example. Women have their own hey'at. We go separately. The ones who want to can become the tour leaders and then they go to Mashhad to book the houses and organize the buses and the trip. We went three times and it went very well. Little girls, young people, brides, everyone comes."

It is interesting to note that although Baluch are Sunnite, they too undertake pilgrimages to Imam Reza's shrine in Mashhad.

Non-Persian Women in Golestan: Building the Bridge between Ethnicities

In Golestan, several women from all religions and ethnicities cultivated the land. Gender division of labor, however, was paramount in agriculture as in other activities. Women who cultivated land worked with their hands and rudimentary tools, while men usually used machinery including combines, tractors, etc. As Paola Tabet argued, there is a gender-based differentiation of tools usage. While difficult tasks are accomplished by women, they are considered as degrading for men.

> In every activity, the most archaic operations are left to women, as far as the technical evolution is concerned, especially the operations of manipulation and direct motricity. In general, women use the tools where only human energy is used. [...] The relationship between tasks and tools must be reversed. Women perform certain tasks to the exclusion of others, depending on the tools to be used. It is in the forms of male control of the instruments of production that we must look for the objective factors, the constants of the gender division of labor.[47]

In Ismail Abad, a village in the plain, with Turkmen, Zaboli, and Baluch populations, women worked outside the home and were also involved in local politics. Some were shopkeepers and shepherds, others were farmers. Most Turkmen women weave carpets and sew for themselves but they usually do not sell them. Some work on their lands with their husbands or other family members. Likewise, in several Baluch villages, young men worked in Tehran or Mashhad, and the land was cultivated by the women who had remained in the villages with the children and the elderly.

Figure 3.10 Woman working the land with rudimentary tools. Copyright Sohrab Sardashti.[48]

Figure 3.11 Man using machinery. Copyright Sohrab Sardashti.

The Ismail Abad, the village council, was composed of five members: two Turkmen, two Zaboli, and one Baluch. All were men. Mr. Moghadam, who represented the Turkmen population in the village council, was a farmer and cultivated wheat and soybeans, but also had a shoe shop. On the issue of polygamy, he said that the number of polygamous Turkmen was very low, and mainly belonged to the older generation.

The village of Ghasem Abâd is composed of Baluch and Zaboli. Two women were elected to the village council. Mrs. Barahouyi was one of the two. A young newlywed woman whose husband worked in Tehran had opened with her counterpart, sewing, hairdressing, first aid, Quran classes. Additionally, they also taught to the predominantly Baluch women who attended, how to keep livestock and bird breeding. Quran recitation and prayer classes were attended by both Baluch and Zaboli women. The state does not help the Sunnite build their mosques. They had a mosque in the village which they had built themselves. Friday prayer is said by a Hanafi Sunnite cleric.

Religion remained a determining factor for marriage. Baluch all agree to marry their daughters to Turkmen but refuse to marry them to Persian/Mazandarani or to Zaboli. Also young Baluch married men in Golestan are not polygamous, contrary to Baluchistan, but some elderly Baluch are. Young Baluch disapprove of polygamy. Mrs. Barahouyi continued her studies, encouraged by her father.

Her husband is a distant cousin (her father's nephew). Similarly to Baluchistan, in Golestan they tend to marry within their own tribes. They speak the Baluch language together. Their relatives come to Golestan to visit, and continue wearing their own traditional Baluch clothes, the older ones disliking Persian clothing, contrary to the younger generation. As mentioned earlier, in Golestan, a process of Persian cultural hegemony is at work among Baluch migrants but they do not merely imitate Persian traditions and cultural values. The identity of the Baluch women in Golestan (and therefore their families) is undergoing change not through mere "imitation" of an idealized other,[49] but through hybridization.

As symbolic expression of the community,[50] the transformation of women's identity also implies identity reconstruction of the whole ethnic community. If we understand the family institution as a site of power and a space in which politics occur, change in gender relations within the family also changes relations of power within tribal structures of the ethnic community.

As mentioned earlier, Baluch girls usually continue their studies up to the age of seventeen or eighteen before getting married. In addition to schooling, several Baluch young girls said they absolutely wanted to have a computer and access to internet. They believe that "today, if you don't have a computer and access to internet it is as if you were illiterate." Young women I met also wanted to learn a foreign language (mainly English) but in their villages or nearby towns there were no English language classes. In this province, Baluch parents, like Persian and Turkmen, value education and continue sending their daughters to school after the end of the primary level. For these non-Persian-speaking migrant parents who belong to lower social categories and are themselves often illiterate or barely literate, education that was expanded in post-revolutionary Iran has become a cherished new value. The norms of these migrants are no longer shaped by reference to their primary ties but rather through identification with the urban middle class or the educated and active women they saw in their new environment.

Nâz Bibi, a twenty-four-year-old Baluch in Qasim Abâd village, finished primary school in her village. She wanted to pursue education and her father encouraged her. As there was no high school in her village, her parents allowed her to go to high school in Gâlikash. Every morning she took the school bus until she obtained her high school diploma. She was married at the age of twenty-three. Her husband, who is her first cousin, works in Tehran. Nâz Bibi is very involved in social activities and organizes different classes for women, most of them are peasants. She teaches illiterate grown-up women to read and write, organizes sewing classes for several widows so that they can one day earn their living by sewing. Although the majority of the village population is Baluch (here mostly from Nâruyi and Rakhshâni tribes), Persian and Turkmen women also attend her classes.

Mahnâz, another Baluch young woman in Qâsim Âbâd, married at nineteen with a distant relative who was her neighbor. Her parents asked her opinion. "We are much more free than Baluch girls in Baluchistan. When our female relatives from Zâhedân come here for their vacation and stay with us, they take us as their role models. For example, they dress like us or say they want to continue their studies. But their parents, especially fathers disagree. They are not happy that their daughters imitate us." Shâhin is twenty-two and was eighteen when she married her first cousin to whom she had been promised upon her birth (nâf bori), but says she wanted to marry him. She says that here Baluch men have only one wife and that young couples have much less children than in Baluchistan. "Younger couples have only one to two children. We don't want to have more because it is financially very difficult to have several children. Furthermore, if we have less children, we can give them a better education." When I was doing my field work, contraceptive devices were still distributed in dispensaries (called Health Houses) for free. As we shall see later, the free distribution stopped in 2015 when the Leader Khamenei, aiming to double the population, decided to end the Family Planning.

Although these young women belong to various religions and ethnicities, they have all constructed multiple identities and exist in a pluralistic way. They try to realize the reinvention of the self in the context of concrete constraints from which they contest power relations through bargaining with patriarchy[51] which also embodies the power of the state. Although their aim is not to upset the established social order, they are likely to weaken it.

A profound change requires the interaction of women and their lived experiences with such changes. It relies on their aspirations and their commitment to take control of their destinies, and a determined direction of change. If laws and changes are placed on or in juxtaposition to the reality of situations without penetrating it in depth, they will be unable solely to change the values of a society. As we shall see later, having a very limited number of children has become a value for the majority of women (fertility rate is only 1.6) and the Leader's will to force women to have many children does not correspond with the realities of their life (economic crises, women's better education, increase in the age at first marriage, cultural aspirations, etc.). Individual identities are redefined and reconstructed through a combined impacts of laws and changes from above, from the margins and sometimes from outside the society.

Hybridization as an active moment of challenge and political and cultural resistance[52] can remove the divisions between different categories of women, and even make it possible to wage common struggles against patriarchal powers within the both family and society. Women's strategies vary according to specific social, economic religious, or ethnic contexts. In some instances, they bargain with the patriarchy, while in other instances they confront it.

4

Structural Transformations: Impacts on Islamic Gender Regime and Social Relations of Gender, Ethnicity, and Religion

As Valentine Moghadam argued, and given the distinctive political-economy features of Islamic regime in Iran (e.g., authoritarian state, rentier economy, and corporatism in both polity and economy), Iran's public gender regime can be classified as neo/patriarchal.[1] "In the neopatriarchal form," she argued, "aspects of private/domestic patriarchy prevail, in terms of the retention of conservative family law, a rentier form of capitalism that limits female economic participation, restraints on civil society that impede sustained feminist organizing, and inadequate or non-existent legislation on violence against women. The importance of the family in societal and legal debates, constitutions and policies, family laws, childcare and elder care, kinship-based welfare outside formal employment arrangements, and contestations between feminists and Islamists—confirms that it remains the locus of female control (including the control of women's sexuality) and of social reproduction in neopatriarchal public gender regime."[2]

In addition, the Iranian-Islamic Civil code that maintains private patriarchy is often considered as a marker of national-Islamic identity and culture by Islamist authorities for who gender inequality is a stronghold against Westernization. Reinforcing private patriarchy thus consolidates the neo/patriarchal public gender regime.

However, as this chapter shows, the Islamic public gender regime, along with its legislation and institutions, has been increasingly questioned by women, especially the younger generation, belonging to both the majority and the minorities who, through subtle arrangements, alter gender social order.

The structural transformations (urbanization, modernization, expansion of education, etc.) that have taken place, especially since the 1970s, have led to better access for both Persian/Shi'ite and non-Persian girls to schools, university education, and the professionalization of a number of women. One of the outcomes of these transformations is that patriarchal family founded on male power and domination is questioned and is undergoing change. Despite class, religion, ethnicity, or rural-urban divide, many women share experiences and are likely to build a collective body of wisdom in matters of marriage, family, child bearing and child rearing, and education. These are themes that I will discuss and analyze in the upcoming pages.

The post-revolutionary Iranian society has become increasingly urbanized with over 75 percent of its population now living in urban areas,[3] fertility rates having dropped to 1.6 per woman as opposed to over 7 prior to or at the beginning of the revolution. Women are also increasingly pursuing higher education. The number of female university students increased from 57,000 in 1976 to over 2 million in 2016. The average age at the first marriage for women increased from 19 in 1976 to 24 today, with over 70 percent of Iranian women utilizing contraceptive devices until 2015, when its free distribution in dispensaries was halted following the Leader orders.

In the aftermath of the revolution, and to contain rural exodus, rural areas have been modernized. Over 90 percent of villages now have electricity, over 80 percent have tap water, almost all have roads, schools, and dispensaries. In some villages I visited, tap water was outside the homes usually on a square around which homes were built. Yet people were unhappy and wanted tap water inside their kitchens. Although the Islamic regime did not succeed in curbing rural-to-urban migration, the gap between town and country has narrowed, as illustrated in literacy rates among the younger generation in both urban and rural areas.

Women's better education has had critical impacts on their demographic behavior, as illustrated in the results of our quantitative survey showing that literate mothers fifteen years and older had given birth to 2.5 children against the figure of 6.4 for illiterate mothers. Amongst the literate mothers, a correlation can be established between the level of education and the number of children: 3.1 for primary level education against 1.4 for university level education.

Table 4.1 Number and percent of population of our sample by main age group and sex: (2002).

Main age group	Both genders	Both genders	Male	Male	Female	Female
Total	Number	Percent	Number	Percent	Number	Percent
	30,715	100.0	15,399	100.0	15,316	100
Under 15 years	9,394	30.6	4,803	31.2	4,591	30.0
15–64 years	19,551	63.6	9,637	62.6	9,914	64.7
65 years and over	1,770	5.8	959	6.2	811	5.3

Table 4.2 Percentage distribution of our sample population of 30,715 by local and ethnic language (2002).

No familiarity	Familiar with local and ethnic languages								Lacking the ability to speak
	Baluch	Turkman	Turkish	Arabic	Kurdish	Gilaki	Lori	Mazandarani	
45.5	2.4	0.7	23.3	3.4	6.7	3.5	9.8	4.6	0.05

Statistical Center of Iran, Tehran, 2003, P. 14.

Many poor and illiterate women respondents in our qualitative survey attributed their inferior status in the family and society to their lack of educational credentials, which, they believed, also prevented them to become autonomous from their fathers or husbands. Therefore, they advocated their daughters' education as a crucial means to their empowerment.

According to Iran's census of 1986, 7 percent of urban residents and 23 percent of rural residents out of a population of 49 million did not understand Persian at a spoken level.[4]

According to our quantitative survey conducted in 2002, 90 percent of sampled households could speak Persian, 5 percent could only understand Persian, and 5 percent could neither speak nor understand Persian, and 54.5 percent were familiar with at least one other language. This change illustrates the impact of schooling of non-Persian children, especially in rural areas.

A nationally representative survey on identity was fielded in late 2016 by phone across the country via landline to 5005 randomly selected respondents. Interviews were conducted in Persian (95 percent), Azari-Turkish (4 percent), Kurdish (1 percent), and the survey response rate was 64 percent. As many as 23 percent or 1,129 respondents answered "I don't know" to the question "to which Iranian ethnicity do you belong?" while 77 percent of the sample stated an ethnic category.[5]

The Crucial Importance of Education on Women's Demographic, Social, and Cultural Behavior

In our survey, the lowest literacy rate for women six years and older belonged to Baluch women (46 percent) and the highest rate belonged to Persian women whose mother tongue is taught at school (83 percent). Among literate Baluch women, 70 percent had only a primary-level education, as opposed to 33 percent

Table 4.3 Literacy rate of women aged six and over of our sample (2002).

Ethnic or local language	Literacy rate	Primary level education
Baluch	46%	70%
Azari	72%	40%
Lori	71%	46%
Arab	66%	47 %
Persian	83%	33%
Kurdish	68%	46%
Turkmen	71%	37%
Mazanderani	78%	34%
Guilaki	74%	29%

Table 4.4 Percentage of literate population aged six and over of our sample (2002).

Level of education	Both genders	Male	Female
Total	100.0	100.0	100.0
Primary	35.7	34.2	37.4
Lower secondary	25.5	27.5	23.3
Upper secondary	25.3	25.7	24.9
Last year of high school also called pish-daneshgahi	2.5	1.8	3.3
First and second year university	2.2	2.6	1.7
Other higher education levels (BA, Master, PhD)	5.4	5.8	4.9
Theology	0.3	0.4	0.1
Other*	3.1	2.0	4.4

for Persian women. The gap in male-female literacy rate was 7 percent for Persians and 18 percent for Baluch. It is interesting to note that Turkmen men had the highest literacy rate in our sample (95 percent) and the gap in male-female literacy rate was also the highest among Turkmen (24 percent). As the following table shows, a correlation can be established between the level of education and the number of children given birth by mothers regardless of their ethnicity and religion.

Moreover, the majority of mothers either Shi'ite or Sunnite said they did not want more than two or three children. Fatemeh declared: "I take pills and only

Table 4.5 Women six years and over by level of education, by regional and ethnic language (2002).

Total		Literate	First grade	Second grade Primary level	Second grade Secondary level	Last year of high school	Two years university diploma	Other university levels	other
13912	Total	10557	3953	2462	2624	346	179	514	465
Baluch	308	143: 46%	100	24	12	1	0	2	4
Turkmen	96	68: 71%	25	22	14	3	1	0	3
Azari	3346	2396: 72%	948	590	522	73	30	95	136
Arabic	447	293: 66%	137	79	51	3	4	10	8
Kurdish	926	632: 68%	290	149	110	13	1	9	60
Gilaki	524	388: 74%	114	102	100	13	9	18	30
Lori	1309	925: 71%	426	216	156	37	16	22	51
Mazandarani	632	490: 78%	169	124	131	13	12	25	15
Persian	6313	5216: 83%	1742	1153	1527	190	106	333	158

Source: *Socio-economic Characteristics Survey of Iranian Households (2002)*, Statistical Center of Iran, National Center for Scientific Research (France), French Research Institute in Iran. Tehran, Statistical Center of Iran, 2003.

wanted three children but I got sick (back pain) and it turned out that there was an incompatibility between the medicine and the pills. I got pregnant by accident."

Kaniz declared that she only wanted two children in order to better educate them and was taking pills. Her last two pregnancies were unintended. "Having children requires financial means," she said. "My son who is 15 years old argues with us because he wants to have such and such things and we don't have the means ... I tell my daughter-in-law that one child is enough and that if she wants other children she has to leave our home and go and live with her father."

The daughter-in-law replied: "She's joking of course."

Kaniz said "No. Not at all. I am very serious. If you are pregnant again, I don't want anything to do with you. The child has expenses. My elder son is unemployed so its us or my daughter-in-law's parents who provide for their needs."

Traditions still have a stronghold on some less-educated women in some parts of the country where men cherish a high number of children as important

Table 4.6 Average number of children born alive to married women aged fifteen and over by ethnic and local language and education level, 2002.

Language	Total	Literate	Primary	Secondary/1st	Secondary/2	Last year of high school	University 1&2 level	Other univ level	theological	Other	Illiterate
Total	4.08	2.53	3.12	2.18	1.79	0.26	1.88	1.41	2.60	4.42	6.46
Lori	4.90	3.01	3.23	2.34	1.76	0.33	1.67	1.67	0.00	5.53	6.64
Baluchi	4.81	2.26	2.26	3.33	1.40	0.00	0.00	2.00	0.00	3.75	5.83
Arabic	4.44	2.72	3.29	2.31	2.10	0.00	2.00	1.00	3.00	2.5	5.84
Kurdish	4.39	2.28	2.54	1.53	1.26	0.00	2.00	1.00	0.00	3.33	6.21
Azari	4.10	2.24	2.78	1.80	1.56	0.43	2.00	1.35	1.50	3.63	6.48
Turkmen	4.10	1.67	2.29	0.75	1.60	0.00	1.00	0.00	0.00	3.00	6.54
Gilaki	3.90	2.48	2.72	2.26	1.80	0.00	2.14	1.73	0.00	4.26	6.34
Persian	3.86	2.66	3.47	2.43	1.91	0.14	1.90	1.45	2.86	5.01	6.66

assets. Kheyr Bibi, a Baluch and a second wife, does not use contraceptives. "If I have only two children, it is because I could not have more. Two children are not enough. My husband would like to have more. He says that if I can't have more soon, he will take a third wife."

Maryam D, although Baluch in Zâhedân, declared that four children are more than enough, it is even too much. Besides, she used to take birth control pills, but the antibiotics she took for her sinusitis had obviously neutralized the effects of the pills, she said.

She is a housewife and has been to literacy classes for adults. Contrary to Kheyr Bibi whose husband is young, Maryam's husband was eighty and she could not imagine having more children with such an old man.

Marziyeh, a Persian/Shi'ite and the mother of six in Zâhedân, said "I promised myself that I would use contraception. I don't want to have any more children. My brothers and sisters only have one or two children each. They work and don't have time to have more. But I love children very much and when they are not around, I feel like I am suffocating."

Roqiyyeh, an illiterate Persian/Shi'ite villager in Sistan, had been pregnant thirteen times, but she had three miscarriages and had also lost three of her children at an early age. She did not use contraception. In 1991, the village was flooded and their house destroyed. They rebuilt it with a government loan that they have not yet paid back. Her husband was a farmer but more than six years of drought turned the farmland into a desert. Their livestock died for lack of food.

Sadigheh, a mother of three children, said she didn't want any more children, nor did her husband. "I took pills but I became pregnant twelve years after my previous pregnancy."

Hâjar, a Mazadarani/Shi'ite who lives in the village of Esboo Mahaleh, said: "I did not want more than two children and after the birth of the second son, I took pills. But my husband wanted a daughter and insisted on having a third in the hope that it would be a girl. I resisted a lot but after eight years I gave in reluctantly."

When questioned about the number of her children, Mrs. Peymani, a fifty-five-year-old retired Baluch school teacher in Zâhedân, said: "My husband and I wanted two sons and two daughters. But my first four children were all girls and in Baluchistan having sons is very important. I therefore continued to become pregnant in order to have two sons. Well we ended up having only one."

Contrary to many Iranian women, including Baluch and Turkmen, who give birth on average a year after marriage (which is a sign of the wife's fertility and the husband's virility and reproductive force), Soraya, a young, educated Baluch woman from Iranshahr, still didn't have a child two years into her marriage. "I decided not to have a child right away and my mother who encouraged me to study tells me to wait for a while. She says I should continue my studies and earn an M.A. My mother-in law who wants a grandchild now, however, keeps her pressure on us."

Fatemeh, from Esboo Mahaleh, is twenty years old, the wife of the fourth son of the family. The husband is twenty-two years old. They got married two weeks before the interview but had been engaged for two years. She would like to have one child, she said. "In these difficult times, if you have one child you can give him/her a good education, buy him/her things, take good care of him/her. But if you have more than one but you can't provide for them, what's the point?"

Maliheh, a young Turkmen from Gonbad Kavoos, said: "I only want two children because life has become so difficult. My husband is of the same opinion. I take pills." She also stated that "I would like my children to study. There is no difference between boys and girls. If we have the means, we will make them available to your children without [gender] distinction." As mentioned earlier, the interviews were conducted before the Leader's order to end the family planning.

Maryam C from Esboo Mahaleh took pills too. She wanted to have a tubectomy but her husband did not agree. So she started taking pills after the birth of her third child. "I don't want any more children. They are often sick. I'm really tired of children. Even three is already too much. I work, I also work on the land and my children are always sick."

Maryam, a Persian/Mazandarani villager in Golestan, said: "After school, my two older children come home to eat, do their homework, then play or watch TV. There are no extracurricular activities in the village. During the summer, the Basidj organizes Quran or sewing or ornamental flowers classes. The courses are not free of charge. My children have never gone to these classes because they don't like them. They don't need to go to Basidj classes to learn the Quran. We teach them ourselves." Her sister Zeynab declared: "We are a group of 30 to 40 women of different age groups who gather to recite the Quran." Maryam added: "When I don't have work to do, I watch TV, mostly movies and soap operas with family and social themes, and also watch the news. Here the main leisure activity is socializing with family, neighbors and friends."

With a strong emotional investment in their daughters, women in our survey from humble origins often attempted to compete with their husbands for authority over the family by taking over the management of the household. As they all believe that for a girl from a modest family and social background, education and cultural learning are the main vectors of social mobility and a better life, they mobilize all the means at their disposal to set up the necessary framework for this goal, as well as the factors likely to stimulate their daughter's ambitions.

Indeed, contrary to the past when the women dramatized their fates, or exorcised it, but never exposed it directly, younger women do expose their grievances directly. Although discrimination against lower classes, rural populations, and ethnic/religious minorities still persists, they are nonetheless valued by their own communities and are even likely to become role models for other women.

Children's Education

In the villages I visited, there was an elementary school for boys and girls and at times a secondary school for girls. Otherwise, students had to go to another village on foot or by car when it snowed or when the weather was too cold. All parents (with the exception of some Baluch fathers) wanted their children to continue their education as far as possible and agreed to mobilize their means to this end. The general understanding was that if they do not continue their studies, they will be unemployed. But in contrast, no extracurricular activities were offered to children in the villages.

However, according to a report published by the Research Center of the Islamic Parliament, 696,377 pupils stopped going to school in 2019 and more than 237,000 definitely abandoned school. The report mentions poverty to be the most important reason.[6] In 2020, under the coronavirus epidemic when schools shifted to online teaching, even more pupils quit school due to lack of digital devices such as tablets and smart phones. Several deprived pupils even committed suicide in remote areas for this very reason. According to the Ministry of Education, in 2021, over 1 million students withdrew from school for lack of digital devices: 210,000 school and 760,000 high school students.[7]

Fatemeh K is from Keykha village in Sistan-Baluchistan province, northeast of Zâhedân (in Sistan). The village of Keykha had about ninety households. There were schools for girls and boys and even a high school for girls. Fatemeh K is a thirty-six-year-old Shi'ite/Persian and a housewife. Their house, like others in the village, was destroyed by the floods of 1994. They obtained a loan from the government to rebuild it. They have a three-room house. She was married at the age of sixteen. Her husband is her first cousin and was twenty-one years old at the time of marriage. Fatemeh K has a very low level of literacy. Her husband is a teacher. They have one daughter and four sons. The children all go to school except the last one who is 3.5 years old. On children's education, she declared: "I will be proud if my children continue their studies and they want to do so too. I don't want my daughter to become a housewife like me. She must be able to work outside the home, for example in the administration. If she doesn't succeed, let her work in the crafts. My daughter is in the technical-vocational field. She is studying in the city (Zabol). She is staying with my sister there. She wants to study medicine at the university. She likes medicine. My son is in the first year of high school. My second son is in high school, first year." Fatemeh M, forty-seven, is a practicing Shi'ite. She lives in Zâhedân, but grew up in Gonbad Kavoos where her parents were farmers. Her father died there, and she came back to Zâhedân where she was married at the age of seventeen to her first cousin who died three years after the marriage. She has a twenty-four-year-old daughter from her first marriage who is married. Five years later, she remarried her second husband who was seventeen years older than her. They are not relatives but Fatemeh's brother was a butcher and worked with him. They have six children together. Their oldest daughter is twenty-two years old. She married at the age of nineteen after finishing high school and is the mother of a two-year-old child. Fatemeh and her husband also have a twenty-year-old boy who is in the military and married, a seventeen-year-old girl, a sixteen-year-old girl, a fifteen-year-old boy, and a ten-year-old girl. Like many illiterate persons, Fatemeh has been to the literacy program for adults (nehzat-e savad amouzi) but cannot read. The husband is illiterate and claims that the Prophet appeared to him in his dream and since then he can read the Quran!

Fatemeh M's husband, who was present during the interview, did not let his wife express herself. He answered on her behalf. Every time I posed a question, I had to ask him to let his wife speak. He was very cunning. They were very poor. Their house had fallen into ruin but they couldn't get any help to rebuild it. Although they were very religious, they were also very unhappy with the situation, their poverty and the lack of assistance from public or semi-public organizations. They had received help from the Imam's Relief Committee once every six months (about 20,000 tomans per month). But they had not received anything for the past six months prior to our interview. Despite their extreme poverty, all the children go to school except for one of their daughters who did not like to study. Both parents encouraged the children to continue their studies.

Kaniz, a Shi'ite, is forty-four years old and she has two grown-up children (a boy and a girl) from her first marriage and four children, two girls and two boys, from her second marriage. The oldest son is fifteen, the youngest son is twelve, the oldest daughter is sixteen, and the youngest daughter is five.

Kaniz was fifteen years old at her first marriage. Her daughter from the first marriage is married and her son lives with his father. All children go to school. She declared: "I told my children to study well. Try to get a higher [social] status. God is my witness that I am ready to clean other people's houses so that my children can continue their studies. Our parents did not allow us to study. Look at the result. We are illiterate. My husband and I have only done two years of Nehzat. Look at our miserable life."

Kaniz and her husband Avaz agree that their daughters should go to college. Avaz said jokingly: "At least in our time, God bless it, you didn't have to have a bachelor's degree or a master's degree to work. They asked us to work. That was all!"

Sadigheh, a young Shi'ite/Persian from Zâhedân, was married at nineteen after finishing high school. She declared: "I would like to have only two children. Life is too expensive and in this society having more than two children is really difficult. I take contraceptives. My husband doesn't want many children either. He says one is enough." Sadigheh's husband is a revolutionary Guard (Pasdârans) officer in Zâhedân and has a high school diploma. It is interesting to note the crucial gap between the Leader's discourse and official policy since 2015 aiming to double the population through both coercive means and financial incentives, on the one hand, and, on the other hand, the modern and rational demographic behavior of some revolutionary Guards or other proponents of the regime who are supposed to obey his orders and have them implemented. Sadigheh kept arguing for a low number of children: "I come from a large family myself and know the difficulties of such families." Sadigheh, her husband, and their son live with her parents-in-law on the same street as her parents. Her father-in-law is a low-ranking retired civil servant. Her brother-in-law lives in the same house with his wife and two children. Sadigheh and her husband had saved up to build the upper floor and now live in their own apartment. Their expenses are separate from the extended family.

"I want my child to study, to find a good job later, so that he doesn't need others. I wish he could have extracurricular activities. When I was single, I wanted to participate in these activities, especially sports, but my father did not agree."

Dornâz, an illiterate thirty-five-year-old Baluch/Sunnite mother in Zâhedân, is the first of the two wives of her illiterate husband Malang who is thirty-eight years old. The two wives, their children, and the husband all live in a house in a poor neighborhood of Zâhedân. Each wife has two rooms located in two separate parts of a small court yard. They share the kitchen. Dornâz is originally from Zâhedân and married at the age of fifteen. She is illiterate. Her husband is a relative and she does not know her husband's age. Dornâz has five children. "I couldn't have children and my husband took a second wife but once he remarried I started to become pregnant!" Zobeideh, a Baluch/Sunnite neighbor who participated in our conversation, says: "Her eyes were burnt by the lack of children." Kheyr Bibi, a twenty-six-year-old Baluch/Sunnite and Malang's second wife, laughed: "After my marriage, she (Dornâz) became pregnant first. I cried a lot. I said to my God why haven't I had a child yet. The God said to me: "Be patient, you will have children too."

Dornâz has three boys and two girls. The oldest was twelve years old. The last two had not yet reached school age, but the first three went to school. After the marriage, they were tenants for several years before her husband bought their house three years ago. Dornâz wanted her children to study as much as possible.

Her daughter Mahnâz, twelve years old, who was in the last year of primary school and very studious, said: "I want to continue studying. I would like to be a medical doctor."

But Zobeideh replied: "A doctor! She is dreaming. She will be married long before she reaches university age. You know, for us, it is a shame if the girl does not marry young and a pride when she marries very young." When I asked Zobeideh whether she agreed with this tradition, her answer was negative.

Kheyr Bibi has two children, an eleven-year-old boy and a seven-year-old girl. They both go to school. Kheyr Bibi, originally from Khâsh, 180 kilometers south of Zâhedân, was 17 years old when she married Malang. Her parents still live in Khâsh. She has six sisters and three brothers. She came to Zâhedân after her marriage. She finished elementary school and could hardly read but liked to read. When she had time, she picked up her children's school books and read. Her father prevented her from continuing her education. "He said that school changes the attitude and behavior of girls. Moreover, he said that there are boys in school. My brothers continued to study but all my sisters stopped at the end of primary school. We all stayed at home before we got married." She spoke Baluch with her children but they spoke Persian perfectly because they went to school. Her husband was illiterate and was currently unemployed.

I asked how he managed to pay the expenses of two households while unemployed. Kheyr Bibi replied: "God gives"!

Kheyr Bibi wanted her children to continue their education. Even for her daughter, she was not against her getting higher education, but for her the gender mix in universities is a main obstacle. "I would like my daughter to go to college but the problem is that the universities are not Islamic. There is gender mixing and we can't let our daughter go to that environment. People will say bad things about her. She will be annoyed, insulted [by the other Baluch]. Here, there is not the atmosphere of Tehran." She also stated: "Their father also wants them to study. He buys them what they need for school. Since he is illiterate, he has a lot of problems and wants his children to be well-educated." Kheyr Bibi said that her daughter wants to study and that she will not get married. "Nowadays, young girls don't like to get married early," she concluded. Kheyr Bibi thinks that one of Malang's boys would like to become a teacher. "The other two who are not strong in school cannot continue. Their father will force them to work."

Maryam D, a Baluch/Sunnite, is twenty-eight years old. She is originally from Zâbol but grew up in Zâhedân. She has two brothers and six sisters. The brothers dropped out of school to work, the sisters finished primary school before getting married. Her husband is eighty years old and illiterate. She was married at the age of fourteen to this polygamous man fifty-two years older than her. They have four children together: one boy and three girls. Her son is thirteen years old, her daughters are twelve, ten, and five years old. With the exception of the last one who is not yet old enough, the others go to school. Concerning her daughters' education, Maryam D said: "We are very poor but I wish my children to continue their studies as far as possible. We did not succeed our lives and I strongly hope my children can come up with a better life thanks to their education."

Marziyeh, a thirty-two-year-old Persian/Shi'ite, lives in Zâhedân and comes from a family of ten children. She got married at the age of thirteen after only three years of schooling. "My parents were not against my education. On the contrary. They asked me to continue. But because of my thyroid, I didn't feel well and couldn't concentrate. My brothers and sisters all went to school. My sisters even graduated from high-school before they got married. One of them is a teacher." Her husband, who is a distant relative, was twenty-six when he came to propose to her parents. Marziyeh had six daughters and was pregnant at the time of the interview. Her oldest child was seventeen years old and the youngest was three. Except for the last one who had not yet reached school age, the others were all enrolled in school. She had not used contraception because of her thyroid condition.

"I want my girls to continue their education, to get a higher education. I think they should even get a job before they get married because after marriage they won't have the opportunity. If I were educated like my husband, I could have a job and earn a better living. But since I am not educated, I became a shopkeeper."

Effat, Marziyeh's eldest daughter, studied building design and wanted to continue her studies in the same field and then work. Fatemeh, Effat's friend who I interviewed, was eighteen years old and was studying. She was the eldest and had five sisters and one brother. She is Shi'ite. Her father worked at the university and her mother was a housewife. All the siblings went to school and wanted to continue their studies. Their father encouraged them to pursue their studies. Their mother had very low literacy skills. Concerning the Baluch girls who do not study after the age of twelve, Fatemeh said: "Among the Baluch, it is mostly their families who do not let them continue. Persians, in their great majority, do not have this kind of problem. Even among the Baluch, those who have a high cultural level let their daughters continue their studies. Among the others, the mothers often agree that the girls should continue, but it is the fathers, and the brothers who prevent them from doing so."

Roqiyyeh, a sixty-year-old Persian/Shi'ite, lives in Keykha village. She was twenty when she was married to her first cousin who was twenty-six. They have seven children together (five boys, two girls). Roqiyyeh and her husband are religious and illiterate. "My parents did not let me go to school," she regretted. Roqiyyeh and her husband shared liberal views on their daughters' education, employment, and marriage. All their children were educated but several were unemployed except their eldest son who was a law enforcement officer, and one of the daughters who was a single thirty-six years old and worked as a cook. Roqiyyeh's husband thought that given the high number of unemployed men, it is better to give priority to men's work.

The family received aid from the Imam's Relief Committee, the Rajayi Plan (a small financial aid destined to poor and unemployed men aged sixty and over) and also received flour to make their bread.

Zahra, their youngest daughter, was eighteen years old and a high school student. If she had the financial means, she wished to continue her higher education in Zabol. Her parents had no objection. "I would like to become a teacher," Zahra says. "For the AP courses, we have to go to the city and we don't have the financial means. In this village, most of the young people have finished high school but are unemployed. They could not continue their studies because of lack of financial resources. Most of the girls here get married at the age of 20 or 21. They finish high school before getting married. They are often engaged but do not get married until they finish school."

Roqiyyeh, like many other illiterate mothers in our survey, encouraged her daughters to study and to work: "Zahra should study and work. I am illiterate and I really wish that Zahra could study and find a job. I will be honored for both my daughters and my sons." Through insisting on their daughters' education and financial autonomy, they differentiated themselves from the Baluch and asserted their cultural superiority. "We are not like the Baluch. We have no problem with the education and employment of our girls." Her husband agreed: "All jobs are suitable for women. Teaching or computer science or everything else. Anything that allows them to earn a living."

Sadigheh H also lives in Keykha village. She is forty years old and was married at the age of twenty. Her husband was twenty-six and they are not relatives. They have four daughters. Her oldest daughter is nineteen years old and was married at the age of eighteen after finishing high school. Sadigheh said: "She had even finished the preparatory courses for university but her husband (who is her cousin) does not allow her to continue. He says he doesn't like his wife to study even though before marriage he said he did. So she is a housewife in Zâhedân."

The second daughter is in pre-school, the third is in high school, and the last one is too young to go to school. "My daughters go to high school in Mohamad Abâd (another village a few kilometers from Keykha). Someone with a car takes them there and back. They have no extracurricular activities because there is nothing to do in the village. During the summer, the Islamic propaganda organization or the Basidj organize courses and my children participate in them. Quranic classes, sports. From time to time they organize outings."

Oghoul, a Turkmen from Gonbad Kavoos, regretted not having had the opportunity to go to school. "At that time there was a lot of work to do and the children had to participate in this work. Parents did not send their children to school." Zeynab, her niece, emphasized: "But today, it is mostly the parents who insist that the children study and continue their studies at the university."

Shahnâz, forty years old, illiterate, is married and mother of three children aged twenty-five, twenty-three, and twenty. She is Baluch and lives in Zâhedân. She was married at the age of twelve to a distant relative, a man who was eighteen years older than her. Five years after their marriage when her youngest daughter was only six months old, her husband left her. He did not agree to divorce her. Shahnâz had a small two-room house in a modest neighborhood in Zâhedân. Abandoned by her husband and devoid of financial means, she took up sewing to earn a living and provide for her children. "I work at home. My customers are neighbors. But my eyesight has become very poor as a result of sewing. I don't know how much longer I can do this." Unlike other Baluch from poor and traditional backgrounds, who do not allow their daughters to continue their education after the end of primary school, her daughter graduated from high school and tried to take the university entrance exam in Tehran but did not succeed. "She liked to continue her studies. I also wanted her to study at the university. But she was not admitted. As a result, she had to get married to her first cousin."

Parvaneh, sixty years old, is one of twenty-two children, born to a very well-known polygamous Baluch chieftain who had four wives. She lives in Iranshahr (south of Zâhedân) and considers herself a feminist. She presented her candidacy in the 2008 legislative elections but was not approved by Molavis (Sunnite clerics) and traditional people. Parvaneh was thirteen and had just finished primary school in Khâsh when her father forced her to marry a thirty-year-old man who had already three wives. Parvaneh is the mother of two daughters and four sons. "I did not want six children but had no choice. Today, women can decide how many children they want to have. One of my daughters is married for ten years but has only one child." Like several of her counterparts, Parvaneh, who could not continue her studies, encouraged her daughters to get education despite her husband's disapproval. "My dream was that my daughters be highly educated and financially independent. But when my older daughter finished high-school in 1975, there was no university in Iranshahr and thus could not pursue her higher education. My younger daughter is studying English literature in India where she lives with her husband who is a medical doctor. I agreed to marry her only if her husband authorized her to pursue higher education." Both of Parvaneh's daughters were married after graduating from high school. But their marriage was arranged by their parents.

Soraya is a twenty-four-year-old woman who was born and raised in Iranshahr, studied at the University in Châhbahâr, and moved to Zâhedân with her husband a year ago. She does not have a child yet. She has an MA in English literature and teaches English. Her father was a school teacher; her mother is illiterate. Two of her sisters have primary-level education and are housewives. The third is a school teacher. Her five brothers are all educated and work. "I am the youngest child and much more educated than my sisters. My brothers and sisters thus allowed me to decide for myself. Education now plays a crucial role in changing mentalities."

Saideh, a thirty-three-year-old Baluch woman, was born in Bampur south of Iranshahr, where his barely literate father was a chieftain. He was twenty-three when he married Saideh's mother who was only seven. "She still had her milk teeth when she was forced to marry my father who was a widow. They had nine children together." Saideh's family is very traditional and her father and brothers were against girl's education.

I was twelve when they forced me to marry a man twenty years older than me. I had my menstruation at his house. My first child was born when I was only thirteen. My husband was a good man and taught me to read and write and bought me books about marital relationship. He respected me and we gradually became friends, but he was killed in a car accident when I was 18. I had just given birth to my son. A year after his death, I started to study, obtained my high-school diploma, then went to university and earned a B.A. in accounting in 2005. My father completely changed when my older brother and my husband died. He gradually abandoned his traditional views and accepted that me and my sister go to university, to drive cars, etc.

Mrs. Peymani, a fifty-five-year-old retired Baluch school teacher in Zâhedân, is an exception to the rule. She was twenty-two at the time of her marriage, the highest age at marriage among women of her generation whom we interviewed, and her husband was not a close relative. Even more, his origins were much lower than hers' which led her extended family to disapprove of their marriage. But her father, although a landowner, and a polygamous man, cherished education and agreed because her suitor was an educated man.

"Today, everyone sends their daughters to school. But when I was a child, only my sister and I were going to school. Our schoolmates were all boys. My father wanted us to study but our extended family were against the idea. In order to let us pursue our studies, my father sent us to Bandar Abbas [in Hormozgan province]." Mrs. Peymani values education and has encouraged her six children to study. "My daughters are dentist, chemical engineer, architect, and biologist. The youngest is a high-school student. My son is studying engineering. My sons in law are also all well-educated. They're all Baluch. Two are relatives, two are from another tribe. My daughters were almost free to choose their husbands and continued their studies after marriage."

Despite unequal access of women to education, our respondents overwhelmingly valued education. In her work on Bedouin women in Egypt, Lila Abu-Lughod revealed the tactics of resistance and the subversive practices of women. Her analysis shows how power and gender work through the self and the social, but also through emotions and cultural narratives.[8]

Women's access to education and knowledge is likely to lead them to challenge male authority both within the family and in society. As Mary Wollstonecraft argued in *A Vindication of the Rights of Woman* published in 1792, education is a tool of emancipation that allows women to escape from the automatism of tradition. Its purpose is to expose the ideological function of authority and obedience in the reproduction of established hierarchies.

The tremendous increase in literacy rates and the level of education attained by children and the youth from lower-class origins after the revolution have strengthened the authority and prestige of the youth within their families. Additionally, it has contributed to the weakening of parental authority over their children.

Marriage, Kinship, Family

I examine the family institution as a site of power and argue that, by analyzing family dynamics and women's everyday life, we can better understand the politics of ordinary Iranians and the relationship between state and society. The underlying assumption is that the private and public spheres are not separable worlds, but rather they are interconnected and are aspects of the same socio-economic system. I also consider the family and the laws that govern the relationship between its members as an institutional domain in Iran's gender regime.

The control of women, their bodies, and sexuality, which is the foundation of neo/patriarchal power, is exercised through the family institution based on patrilineal marriage or the exchange of women among men. It is therefore men who are the beneficiaries of the product of these exchanges—social organization. As Lévi-Strauss pointed out:

> The global relation of exchange that constitutes [patrilineal] marriage is not established between a man and a woman who each owes, and each receives something: it is established between two groups of men, and the woman appears in it as one of the objects of the exchange, and not as one of the partners between whom it takes place. This remains true even when the girl's feelings are taken into consideration, as is usually the case. By agreeing to the proposed union, she precipitates or allows the exchange operation; she cannot modify its nature.[9]

In Iran, the religious and political elite attempted to Islamize the family through the Islamic laws in order to make this institution a place of rapprochement between society and the Islamic state. Moreover, in the absence or because of the dysfunction of social institutions, the family also fulfills certain social functions. It is thus considered by the authorities as the main resource for regulating social problems. This is one of the reasons why the value of the patriarchal family is reinforced by means of a public policy that encourages marriage, especially among young people, as the foundation of the "sacred institution of the family." To this end, in addition to lowering the minimum age of marriage, financial provisions are made for young married people with low incomes. This includes the granting of advantageous bank loans and/or credits, a family allowance which is granted to them, the benefit of priority access to housing, employment, etc.

In addition to financial incentives, Iranian clerics widely echo the following statement attributed to the Prophet to encourage marriage in general, and youth marriage in particular: "Youth, get married! Those who have the opportunity to marry but refuse to do so do not belong to us. Marriage is my tradition and he who refuses it is not of mine. Hell is composed in its majority of single people. The one who refuses to marry because of poverty does not really believe in God. Marry you, otherwise you are considered as someone who has committed a sin." Many hadiths (acts and words attributed to the Prophet and his successors) and Islamic texts are used to legitimize the marriage of young people. For the supporters of this vision, young girls are the main beneficiaries of early marriage. Ayatollah Khomeini, the leader of the 1979 revolution, was among the clerics who favored early marriage, especially for girls. In his religious treatise he stated: "It is better for girls to marry as soon as they reach puberty."[10] To reinforce his argument, he quotes Imam Sadeq, the sixth Imam of the Shi'ites, who is said to have said, "Blessed is he whose daughter has not menstruated in his house."

Iranian traditionalists, for whom "no religion has discussed marriage as much as Islam," use every argument to encourage young people to marry: "If the majority of young people married at the age of puberty, an important part of the social ills and problems would be solved." Or, "According to Islam, marriage during youth produces a strong generation." They summarize the main purposes of marriage according to Islam as follows:

- "To ensure procreation and renewal of generations,
- to prevent births outside marriage,
- To satisfy the sexual instinct,
- to achieve stability and calmness, ..." [11]

Ali Qaemi, a best-selling religious author on marriage and married life, who, in the early years of the revolution, hosted a radio program on the family, and before the revolution contributed to some magazines including Nasl-e Naw (new Generation in 1976), stated: "Contrary to the analyses of sociologists claiming that marriage is a cultural trait, what motivates marriage is nothing but human nature and the existence of sexual instinct. Thus, procreation and sexual intercourse that is not permitted outside of marriage are the primary reasons for marriage."[12]

As the results of some recent research on white marriage show, a new type of marriage has emerged among the educated urban middle-class youth, who reject the compulsory traditional marriage structure, to the benefit of a common life with no formal religious or civil wedding.[13] However, white marriage is unlawful and its aim is not procreation and its scope remains small in comparison to classical marriage.

Table 4.7 shows the ages of women at their first marriage from our nationwide survey.

The increase in the average age of the first marriage and the decrease in arranged marriages are among the consequences of the youths', especially girls', better education. Marriage by free choice is much more common among the younger generations. The rate is 53 percent for women in the age group fifteen to nineteen, and 55 percent for women in the age group twenty to twenty-four, and 46 percent for women in the age group twenty-five to twenty-nine, against 33 percent for women in the age group forty to forty-four, and 23 percent for women in the age group forty-five to forty-nine years. This rate is even much lower for the generation of grandmothers: 17 percent for women in the age group sixty to sixty-four and 11 percent for women in the age group sixty-five years and more.

Table 4.7 Age at the first marriage among ever-married women fifteen years and older, by local and ethnic language (2002), by number.

Local and ethnic language	Total	<15	15–19	20–24	25–29	30–34	35 +
	7746	1235	4162	1808	421	82	38
Baluch	161	52	86	18	2	2	1
Turkmen	48	4	25	12	6	1	0
Azari	2029	345	1117	473	75	13	6
Arabic	237	43	118	59	13	1	3
Kurdish	506	74	273	113	37	6	1
Gilaki	353	20	156	127	40	6	4
Lori	650	151	370	104	19	3	3
Mazandarani	402	30	217	118	28	6	3
Persian	3357	516	1798	781	201	44	17
ND	3	0	2	1	0	0	0

Source: *Socio-economic Characteristics Survey of Iranian Households (2002)*, Statistical Center of Iran, National Center for Scientific Research (France), French Research Institute in Iran. Tehran, Statistical Center of Iran, 2003.

Table 4.8 Rate of early marriage (under fifteen years) among ever-married women fifteen years and older by local and ethnic language, 2002 by percentage.

Local and ethnic language	Rate
Baluch	32
Azari	28
Lori	23
Arabic	18
Persian	15
Kurdish	15
Turkmen	8
Mazandarani	7
Gilaki	0.56
Average	16

Source: *Socio-economic Characteristics Survey of Iranian Households (2002)*, Statistical Center of Iran, National Center for Scientific Research (France), French Research Institute in Iran. Tehran, Statistical Center of Iran, 2003, P. 80.

Table 4.9 Rate of consanguineous marriage at the first marriage among ever-married women fifteen years and older, by local and ethnic language (2002).

Local and ethnic language	Rate
Baluch	45
Arabic	38
Turkmen	33
Lori	26
Persian	22
Mazandarani	18
Azari	16
Kurdish	17
Gilaki	13
Average	21

Source: *Socio-economic Characteristics Survey of Iranian Households (2002)*, Statistical Center of Iran, National Center for Scientific Research (France), French Research Institute in Iran. Tehran, Statistical Center of Iran, 2003, P. 82.

In our survey, the rate of arranged marriage is 55.6 percent for women. It is supposed both to promote the wife's upward social mobility and to secure and strengthen patriarchal authority and male domination. According to traditional cultural precepts, the groom had to be better educated, much older, with a higher social and economic status than the bride.

As we can see, the highest rate of both early and consanguineous marriage, which is twice as much as the national average, belongs to Baluch women in Baluchistan. Likewise, the age difference between husbands and wives can be huge, especially in polygamous marriages where the bride is the second, third, or fourth wife. Through the tradition of "bride price," old men with a higher status and a better financial situation than the bride's family can pay and purchase her from her parents. Likewise, our poll among 2,717 single unmarried women aged fifteen to twenty-nine who lived with their parents showed that 73 percent of Baluch youth in our sample agreed with consanguineous marriage. This was the highest rate in our sample, followed by those who spoke Arabic (42 percent), Turkmen (37 percent), Lori (36 percent), Persian (27 percent), Azari (18 percent), Kurdish (18 percent), Mazandarani (16 percent), and Gilaki (7 percent). The agreement rate with consanguineous marriage for unmarried boys aged fifteen to twenty-nine who still lived with their parents was Baluch (69 percent), Turkmen (69 percent), Arabic (62 percent), Lori (43 percent), Kurdish (34 percent), Persian (29 percent), Azari (21 percent), Mazandarani (18 percent), and Gilaki (9 percent) speakers.

Change in Continuity

In Baluchistan, divorce, the rate of which was 11 percent in our sample, continues to be very stigmatized. Even-married educated and financially independent women who, thanks to their educational credentials and jobs, are able to support themselves, usually do not initiate divorce even when their husbands remarry or even when they are mistreated or are unhappy with their lives, or if their husbands are sterile. They do not seek divorce in order to preserve the "honor" of their family. Under these circumstances, it is understandable why women, including young women, still prefer marriage with relatives (now increasingly distant relatives) so that in case of conjugal problems, the extended family intervene and the problem is solved.

Tribal structures of the Baluch community emphasized on kinship and descent as organizing principles in the absence of significant resources or other capital on which to base economic and political relationships. In the aftermath of the revolution and with the expansion of modernization policies to more remote provinces and areas, an educated middle-class with lower-class origin has emerged in Baluchistan (as elsewhere in the country). According to our qualitative survey, they tend to define themselves overwhelmingly by referring

Table 4.10 Registered marriages and divorces in urban and rural areas, 1398/2020.

Total country	Total marriage/divorce	Urban areas marriage/divorce	Rural areas marriage/divorce
Year 2020	530,225/ 174,831 33%	468,304/ 162,907 35%	61,921/ 11,924 19%
Sistan & Baluchistan	23,883 1,945 8%	20,031 1,782 9%	3,852 163 4%
Golestan	14,335 3,865 27%	9,290 3,201 34%	5,045 664 13%

Source: Iran Statistical Yearbook, 1398/2020, P. 168.

Table 4.11 Divorces registered by duration of marriage, the year 1398/2020.

	Total	Under One year	One year	Two years	Three years	Four years	Five to nine Years	Ten to fourteen Years	Fifteen years and over
Total country	174,831	12,573	15,065	13,726	12,225	10,793	41,876	28,797	39,776
Sistan & Baluchistan	1,945	202	218	202	134	133	514	274	268
Golestan	3,865	248	352	327	258	266	967	687	760

Source: Iran Statistical Yearbook, 1398/2020, P. 170.

to their occupational or educational credentials. However, those who belong to upper and upper middle classes emphasize a belonging to their tribes. In general, for Baluch upper classes, social status is still largely determined by tribal affiliations, while levels of education and types of occupation are variables through which the Baluch from lower-class origins attempt to re-construct their identities.

The Baluch tribally organized family institution has been concerned with genealogies, group boundaries, and networks of kin.[14] Women as biological and cultural reproducers of the ethnic community, responsible for transmitting cultural values to their children, are considered as the guardians of culture. For the time being, Baluch women's social, cultural, and demographic behavior remains more traditional than their Persian counterparts. Women's subordination to men and to the family is believed to be vital to the community's unity and survival. Women, especially the less-educated, largely endorse such a belief. In Baluchistan, the rates of early marriage, fertility rate, and polygamy are much higher than other ethnicities; the age difference between husband and wife is significant, the rate of women's employment is very low. Although the younger generation is overwhelmingly literate, the level of educated lower-class Baluch girls remains low in comparison to other ethnic minorities mainly due to tribal customs and traditions. They usually stop going to school after puberty, and remain at home to preserve their chastity and wait for suitors who do not approve of educated women. Even some working women are not financially independent from their husbands. Several of our interviewees who are school teachers said they never go to the bank to deposit their pay checks or to withdraw money. Their husbands do on their behalf.

Although Baluch women continue to surrender, they have started to disagree. Indeed, relations of authority are undergoing change as a result of young women's access to better education, lower fertility rates, and an increase in the age of the first marriage. As a result, Baluch women increasingly take educated active women as their role models and raise questions around gendered relations within the family, and women's submission to men's control.

Despite crucial social change, mixed marriage between the Baluch and Persians is still unimaginable. Even the most active and educated Baluch women in Baluchistan as well as Baluch migrant women in Golestan do not wish to have Shi'ite/Persian sons-in-law or if they are young, they prefer to marry Baluch men. As Zeynab, a retired school teacher and a social activist in Iranshahr, mentioned: "We prefer that our daughters marry Baluch men. Marrying a Persian will create problems at the religious level. Some mixed couples exist but we have all seen that their children have problems because each parent wants to attract children to their own religion."

A recent qualitative survey of interfaith (Sunnite-Shi'ite) couples in Sistan-Baluchistan was conducted with a sample of twenty-three people, ten Sunnites (four women, six men), and thirteen Shi'ites (eight women, five men).[15] However, the study does not specify the place where the interviews were conducted. There are important cultural differences between various Baluch towns, between the North (Zâhedân) and the South (Châh Bahâr a port at the Oman Sea), or between the border towns and the ones that are far from the borders. Likewise, when the authors quote the interviewees, only their age and religion are mentioned. A general table of interviewees is presented elsewhere in the article which also hold the educational and professional information. The oldest interviewee is a man aged forty-nine and the youngest is a women aged twenty-two. The duration of their marriage varied between two and twenty-four years. The average number of their children is 1.4. Among the women, one is a teacher, two are state employees (all three are Shi'ites), and the others are all housewives. The men both Shi'ites and Sunnites are all self-employed with the exception of one Shi'ite teacher.

The results of this research show that the majority of mixed marriages between Shi'ites and Sunnites have occurred between Sunnite men and Shi'ite women. Shi'ite women are more easily accepted in Sunnite families than Sunnite women in Shi'ite families. This finding corroborates the results of my survey in Baluchistan and Golestan both among Turkmen and Baluch communities where the motto with regard to intermarriage with Persian/Shi'ites was "We don't give them our daughters but agree to take theirs."[16] The authors argue: "Ever since the ethnic/religious identities in Sistan-Baluchistan province have become politicized, interfaith marriages have decreased and are facing problems and challenges."[17]

The authors emphasize cultural/religious tolerance as the major reason behind successful interfaith marriage. However, tolerance does not imply equality. As can be seen in the following quotation, some men allow their wives to practice their religion without considering it as a fundamental right of their wives. A forty-seven-year-old Sunnite man who has a high school diploma and is a teacher argued: "During the past 22 years of conjugal life I have never forbidden my wife to participate in Shi'ite religious ceremonies. Contrary to many men who even force their wives to change their religion, I always preferred to leave my wife to deal with her religion as she pleases." Some married couples tolerate each other to preserve their conjugal families. A thirty-five-year-old Shi'ite woman, who has an MA and is a teacher, declared: "Until now, whenever there has been a quarrel, I have always given in so as not to make our problems worse. I have always been patient because I love my children and my family life."[18]

In addition to religious tolerance, marriage based on love, the approval within the family, of religious diversity and difference, and a democratic family are said to be other major reasons to a successful interfaith marriage. A thirty-seven-year-old Sunnite man, who has university education and is self-employed, declared: "I was in love with her and did not mind at all her religion. I believed that the major pillar of our relationship was love and that religious and cultural differences could not keep us apart." A forty-year-old Shi'ite woman who holds an MA and is a state employee said: "We met at university and later fell in love with each other and decided to marry despite all problems and our families' disapproval."[19] A twenty-nine-year-old Sunnite woman, who is a graduate

156   *Rethinking Gender, Ethnicity, and Religion in Iran*

student, declared: "At the beginning of our marriage, we had a very hard time because we had married despite the disagreements of our families. My family-in-law treated me very badly and my own family was not kind with my husband. They each thought their religion to be the best. However, after some years the relationship has improved."[20]

As our quantitative and qualitative surveys showed (see the discussion on permissive upbringing below), permissive-type upbringing is becoming the dominant type of child education within families. One of the implications is to leave children choose either parents' religion. A forty-seven-year-old Sunnite man, who has a high school diploma and is a teacher, said: "From the beginning, we agreed on our children's education. We decided to present our religions to them and leave our children decide which one they prefer. We have two daughters. My elder one is Sunnite like me, the younger on is Shi'ite like her mother and they are in very good terms with each other."[21]

For Fatemeh, a practicing Shi'ite mother who lives in Zâhedân, the ideal age for marriage is after the age of eighteen for girls. She, however, added: "But if there is a suitor before this age, I agree that they get engaged." Sadigheh, her daughter, was engaged at the age of eighteen and married at nineteen after

Table 4.12 Kinship ties with first husband among ever-married women fifteen years and older (2002).

Age	Total	First cousins	Other relatives	No kinship ties	NA
	7,746	1,635 (21%)	1,548 (20%)	4,544 (59%)	19
10–14	8	1	4	3	0
15–19	395	124	85	185	1
20–24	840	220	165	454	1
25–29	930	181	195	553	1
30–34	972	193	213	565	1
35–39	955	125	537	209	62
40–44	818	153	166	498	1
45–49	729	164	131	433	1
50–54	546	113	99	334	0
55–59	412	85	72	254	1
60–64	334	60	61	212	1
65 et +	807	155	149	493	10

Source: *Socio-economic Characteristics Survey of Iranian Households (2002)*, Statistical Center of Iran, National Center for Scientific Research (France), French Research Institute in Iran. Tehran, Statistical Center of Iran, 2003.

Table 4.13 Ever-married women fifteen years and older by age-group and choice in the first marriage (2002).

Age	Total	Parents advice	Under relatives' advice	Under family friend's advice	Under friends' advice	Personal choice	NA
	7,746	4,309	408	326	93	2581	29
10–14	8	3	0	0	0	5	0
15–19	395	159	16	6	2	210	2
20–24	840	303	37	33	6	459	2
25–29	930	402	45	39	13	431	0
30–34	972	453	73	39	18	386	3
35–39	955	125	537	209	62	16	6
40–44	818	472	33	34	9	267	3
45–49	729	488	31	32	11	167	0
50–54	546	366	33	20	4	123	0
55–59	412	304	25	14	4	62	3
60–64	334	244	16	14	2	56	2
65 et +	807	629	34	34	8	89	13

Source: *Socio-economic Characteristics Survey of Iranian Households (2002)*, Statistical Center of Iran, National Center for Scientific Research (France), French Research Institute in Iran. Tehran, Statistical Center of Iran, 2003.

finishing high school. She had a two-year-old son. She is distantly related to her husband who has the same name. But they had never met before. "When I was participating in the technical-vocational courses organized by the Imam Relief Committee, we met in the street. Then he conducted his investigation about me and my whereabouts before asking my parents for my hand in marriage."

Kaniz's first husband was not related to her. "I was very young. My parents decided to marry me to someone I didn't know without even asking me. I didn't even know what marriage was. I didn't have a good life with him. He had no father or family. At first we stayed in Zabol, then we went to Gorgan. We had nothing. My brother who lived in Tehran took us there. We lived there for a few years, but our life together could not continue. So we got divorced. He kept the children and remarried." Kaniz was twenty-four when she remarried. Some of her second husband's family members lived in the same village as Kaniz's father and so they introduced her to Avaz and she accepted. Avaz was a widower and had seven children from his first marriage. Kaniz said: "When he married me, he still had four of his children from his first marriage, two girls and two boys. I took care of them and married them myself and they built their own lives." Avaz said: "My first wife was very sick and died. My youngest son was 2 years old, I used to take him with me to my work place. Then, when he was five years old, I got married again."

Dornâz was related to her husband but they had not seen each other before the marriage. No one asked Dornâz's opinion. I asked her what she would do if one day her husband does not pay her nafagheh[22]. She said: "Nothing. I sleep without anything."

And what if he beats you? "I'll stay at home and cry." I asked if he beats her often and she replied: "Yes, when we fight. But not every day." Her eldest son, who was doing his homework and was listening to our conversation, added: "He beats her when he gets angry."

Dornâz and Kheyr Bibi, her husband's second wife, both think that the family ties with the husband protect women from domestic violence because of family considerations.

For Dornâz, the age of twenty is an ideal age of marriage for both girls and boys. Kheyr Bibi said: "The Baluch do not hesitate to marry their daughters even if the suitor is already married with ten children. Polygamy is a tradition here. But I would have liked my husband to be monogamous." Kheyr Bibi, who came from Khâsh to Zâhedân after her marriage, did not choose her husband. Her parents decided for her. "At that time he was already married [to Dornâz] but had no children. He had come to Khâsh to attend a wedding ceremony and wanted to take a second wife himself. He was told that my parents had a marriageable daughter. Her father is my father's cousin. He came to my parents with his mother to ask for my hand. Nobody asked whether I agreed. It was my father who decided. I did not want to be the second wife of my husband."

Kheyr Bibi says:

Among the Baluch, it is not the girls who decide. It is the parents. Then you obtain the girl's agreement. So if someone we think is good asks for our daughter's hand in marriage, we may accept even if she is only 13 years old. Baluch, whether rural or urban, want girls to marry very young … That being said, from the bottom of my heart I don't agree that my daughter marry too young, but what do you expect. That's the tradition here. If a girl who has reached the age of 18 is not married yet, tongues will wag against her. Everyone will say that she is too old and that she will not have a suitor. Then they will say nasty things about her. The Baluch culture wants girls to get married early. I would like my future son-in-law to be well educated, to have done his military service and to have a job before getting married.

Both Dornâz and Kheyr Bibi agree that girls should get married first, then continue their education or work. But as long as a girl is single, she should not do so in order to avoid bad tongues. Kheyr Bibi like Dornâz has an ambivalent view of traditions. She respects these traditions but deep down she disapproves of them. When I asked her if she agrees that parents should choose their daughter's husband, she replied, "If I had the choice, I would have decided myself. Now I regret that I couldn't decide. I think that girls should choose their own husbands." Or, "These traditions are to the detriment of women, but we are forced to respect them and follow them. It is the men who force us to do so. Of course they take advantage of it." Zobeideh, a neighbor and a friend, who attended the interviews, believed that it is necessary to improve the laws. "Women must also have the right to live, to make decisions. Women should be able to divorce," she said. Kheyr Bibi replied bitterly: "Yes but after the divorce, she can return to her mother or her brother. But the husband will keep the children." Dornâz said she shared Kheyr Bibi's views. Although Kheyr Bibi, Dornâz, and Zobeideh feel unable to implement change in their lives, they say they would have liked to have a different life, a better life.

Maryam, a poor Baluch woman, shared the same faith as her counterparts: "My parents forced me to marry a 66 years old man when I was 14. Baluch parents do not ask the opinion of their daughters. They told me that his first wife was ill and for this reason he wanted to remarry. But after our marriage, I realized that he had lied. Although his first wife is much older than me, she is in good health." Maryam belongs to a poor family of nine children. Her two brothers abandoned school to work; her sisters married after they finished primary school.

Maryam and her husband have four children together. She thinks that "girls should get married in an age when they are able to understand what's going on around them. Not before the age of 17. But Baluch do not agree. Even when girls go to school, they force them to withdraw to marry. I think parents should not give their daughters to the first suitor and should also ask the opinion of their daughters." Maryam, however, does not think that her daughters will be given the opportunity to choose their husbands themselves.

Maryam is not related to her illiterate husband. He was a neighbor of a relative. Being old, he received financial assistance from the Shahid Rajayi Plan and also worked with his son (from another woman). They sold second-hand clothes brought in from Pakistan. His sons helped him financially. He was still married with his first wife who lived with his sons. But he lived with Maryam. She said her husband has not beaten her for a long time. "If a man is violent, the woman has no choice but to endure. I'm tired of this life, I ended up with a heart disease and I am also very nervous. If I didn't have a daughter, I would have left him. But I don't want my daughters to suffer from a stepmother. So I was forced to stay. I think that women should also have rights. There are some who leave, others who stay and endure a difficult life. Moreover, women do not know where to go. For example, I cannot go back to my parents."

Contrary to the Baluch women, many Persians declared that their parents did ask their opinion before agreeing to marry them. They, however, do not make a decision in a vacuum and are influenced by their environments. They also realize what their parents' expectations are.

Marziyeh said: "Despite my young age, my parents asked my opinion. I said I agreed."

Despite the legalization of polygamy in Iran (up to four permanent wives, and an undefined number of temporary marriages for Shi'ite men), many Shi'ite women in our survey expressed themselves against polygamy. For example, Marziyeh declared: "I am for monogamy. Polygamy poses many problems for both wives and children. They will be embarrassed. If my husband takes another wife, I will hate him and refuse to see him for the rest of my life. In my family, no one is a polygamous." On the issue of conjugal violence, she said: "My husband is not violent but I know that conjugal violence exists and even a lot here. If a woman is beaten or abused, she must file a complaint. I saw on a TV show that a man had hit his wife in the face. Just watching that made me angry. How do you expect a woman to live with such a violent man? She has to break up with him."

Effat, Marziyeh's daughter in Zâhedân, believed that "young people have to get married after they finish their studies and find a job. That is, not before the age of 25." And her friend Fatemeh argued that unemployment was the main obstacle to marriage. "Young people do not have the means to get married. They also sometimes cannot find the ideal girl or boy—the person who would fit their criteria."

In the absence of laws, regulations and measures to protect women from conjugal violence, many families, Sunnite and Shi'ite alike, prefer that their daughters marry relatives. Originating from shared bloodlines, at least the same neighborhood is thought of as a guarantee for the safeguard of their daughters.

Roqiyyeh, an illiterate Shi'ite villager, believed that "for marriage, girls should be grown up. After they finish their studies and find a job. It doesn't matter if my daughters are related to their husbands. But actually it is better to marry a family member because the woman will be better protected."

Sadigheh B's sister and her husband's sister are sisters-in-law. "We were neighbors. He asked my mother for my hand, my father had passed away. My mother and sister asked my opinion and I agreed." She admitted the role of parents in reinforcing patriarchal traditions. "To my oldest daughter who wished to continue her studies but is prevented by her husband, we say it's okay. Listen to your husband. You have to obey him. He doesn't want you to study, so you shouldn't study." But she joyfully added that her second daughter, on the other hand, is very assertive and vocal. "She refuses to obey."

Kaniz bitterly states:

> Given the failure we have experienced in our lives; I think girls should be at least 20 years old to get married. Look at my beautiful daughter. She is only sixteen years old. What does she understand about life? Women like me who were married by their fathers at the age of 13-14, what did we understand about life? My two children's lives were ruined too. I, in the end, remarried someone else and made a new life for myself but my two children from my first marriage, their lives were destroyed. My daughter, thank God, graduated from high school and got married, but my son is not educated and is subjected to his step mother.

Kaniz, like many others in her status, prefers consanguineous marriage: "I prefer my children to marry family members. If they tell me that they want to marry someone I don't know, I will say no. I have to know their family. Their father, their mother, their religion, their attitude and behavior, their social status. Does he or she have a higher or lower social status than us. Gone are the days when we married our children, especially our daughters, to people we didn't even know. I am not confortable with my daughters marrying strangers."

Shahnâz was abandoned by her husband only five years after their marriage. "I was not unhappy when he left. He was very violent. He quickly remarried and has seven children with his second wife who is a bit younger than me. But he refused to divorce me and I did not want to get divorced either. Baluch women don't initiate divorce." I was very touched by Shahnâz's story. She told me that she had applied for financial aid from the Imam's Relief Committee but she was told that as a married woman she was not entitled to financial help. I, therefore, encouraged her to file for a divorce since the husband had left her and the children many years ago, and never paid the alimony (nafaqeh). I thought that this way she could at least get some assistance as a divorced head of the household. She disagreed and told me that she could not file for divorce and explained why. "Here divorced women are rejected from their family and environment. Although he has not helped us financially, I still prefer that the shadow of his name stands above our head. After all, polygamy is very common in Baluchistan. It is very well accepted." Her argument was powerful and related to the cultural and social reality of her life, her gender, social class, and environment. I realized that instead of encouraging her to file for divorce and take the risk to be cut off from her family and friends, or exclude her from every aid under the pretext that she was married, it was the responsibility of the state and local Shi'ite authorities to take into account Baluch traditions and to adapt their administrative rules accordingly in order not to further weaken these women.

Shahnâz believed that girls should not marry before the age of eighteen. Arranged marriage still remains a norm in Baluchistan despite women's higher age upon first marriage, and the much higher literacy rates among the younger generation than the generation of their parents. Zoleikha, Shahnâz's younger daughter, was only six months old when her father left her mother and remarried. When speaking about her father, she does not use the word "my father" but says my "mother's husband." Zoleikha has a high school diploma and wished to continue her studies. Her mother shared her hopes, and contrary to more traditional families who do not agree to send their daughters to school after the end of the primary level, she even wanted her to have a university education. She, however, did not (or could not) oppose her arranged marriage with her first cousin. Zoleikha said she did not choose her husband and was forced to submit herself to the tradition of *nâf bori:* "Right after my birth, and according to the Baluch tribal traditions, I was promised to my first cousin. I was therefore forced to marry him nineteen years later." It is striking that her "father" who abandoned them years ago still decides for their life. Zoleikha wanted to pursue her studies but her husband disagreed. She had her first child less than a year after the marriage. She emphasized bitterly: "Even after marriage, I wanted to continue my studies, but my husband did not want me to. Among Baluch, it is men who decide. Women have no value. They are subject to a humiliating treatment by men."

It should be mentioned that women do have the possibility to initiate and obtain divorce under certain conditions. According to the law enacted in 1980 and provided that both spouses sign the corresponding articles in the marriage booklet, the wife can initiate divorce, even in the absence of her husband, if he has given her the power of attorney. A married woman can also initiate divorce based on the following conditions: if she is mistreated to the point that her life is made unbearable, if the husband is drug addict, impotent, or sterile, if he suffers from an incurable disease that would endanger the life of his wife, if he suffers from insanity, if he is sentenced to more than five years of imprisonment, if he refuses for at least six months consecutively to pay his wife's alimony, if he has been absent from the home for more than four years, and if his job endangers the honor of his wife and his family. However, at the time of their weddings many women either ignore the existence of such legal measures or refuse to require the right to divorce, or to study or to work, etc. Sadigheh, a Shi'ite/Persian married to a Pâsdâran, did not ask her husband to sign the clauses of the marriage certificate, to give her the right to divorce. "No. I didn't ask him because I wanted to live with him! Anyway, I have the right to divorce according to the laws. Besides, asking for a power of attorney for divorce does not exist in my family."

Some of our interviewees declared that some religious notaries encouraged the bride and groom to sign conditions in the marriage contract giving the bride the right to divorce, and other rights that are not against the Islamic laws. But with the increase in the divorce rate, they no longer inform the brides of these rights. They just register the marriage.

When I asked Sadigheh what would she do if her husband decided to take a second wife, her father replied: "She should let him do." But Sadigheh disagreed: "No. I won't agree. I won't let him remarry." I told her that she couldn't do anything. That it's his right. It's in the law. Her father said I was right and her mother declared: "If he can pay her child support, why not?" Sadigheh's father agreed. Her mother added that her husband must also pay her pension.

I asked them if married life was just about paying alimony? Sadigheh said: "No. It's also about loving each other. You have to cooperate in life. The wife has to make concessions even when her husband doesn't in order to avoid this kind of incident."

I asked "what if, in spite of this, he wants to take a second wife?" Her father stated again: "Let him do. That is his right." Sadigheh said: "I am against it. I will file a complaint." I said: "Well you can't file a complaint because he will be exercising his right. All you can do is ask for a divorce." Sadigheh replied: "Then I will file for divorce." I followed up by asking, "Then what would you do? Would you move back in with your parents? He can also get custody of your son." Sadigheh replied: "In that case, I would cash in to stay with my son. For sure these laws are not to the benefit of women." She finally realized that signing the marriage booklet was not a bad idea. Sadigheh believed that women should be given "some kind of freedom." "The authorities should talk about women's rights on TV, they should publish pamphlets and distribute them everywhere including in the dispensaries so that women know what they are entitled to and what they are not."

Concerning the role of the media and modern communication devices in the province of Sistan-Baluchistan, only 4.47 percent of women aged fifteen to fifty-four have access to the internet, the lowest figure in Iran. Only 10.01 percent of women in the province have access to a computer. Women in Sistan-Baluchistan are also at the lowest level of the national average in terms of access to the media, with more than 8.39 percent of them having no access to any type of media.[23] Nonetheless, all households I visited had a small TV set, often black and white, where families watched the national TV programs. Many young people also listened to Radio Farda, an American radio broadcasting in Persian from Prague. They told me that the Iranian pop music of the radio station captured their attention.

A decrease in the number of polygamous marriages correlates with the increase in the educational level of Baluch men and women. This has been made possible in post-revolutionary Iran, especially from the 1990s onward when schools started to expand in Baluch towns and villages. Sara, a thirty-seven-year-old faculty member (University of Payam-i Noor and Azad University) who was also in charge of the Family Counseling Center in Iranshahr, explained: "The more people are educated, the less they accept early and arranged marriages. Today, most of my female students neither accept to be the second wife of their husbands nor allow their husbands to marry a second wife." Sara, who is very proud of her upper-class background from Naruyi tribe, is known in Iranshahr as a socially active woman and is a role model for many women, especially the youth. Sara was forced by her polygamous father and uncle to marry at the age of fourteen. After four years of unsuccessful marriage, her husband finally agreed to divorce her and she could thus continue her studies. "Had I not been the generation of the Revolution, I could not have been to school. Although my father was educated and had spent several years in Tehran, my uncles persuaded him not to let me pursue my education after the end of the primary school. I was a very good pupil and insisted to continue for another three years. Then I had to stop when I was married." After her divorce, she went to high school and obtained her high school diploma. In 1996 she was admitted to Zâhedân University and studied educational sciences and obtained her BA degree in 2002. She then went to Tehran and obtained her masters in psychology at women's al-Zahra university in Tehran in 2004.

> My family prevented me from studying and doing social activities. Traditional and tribal perspectives were then dominant. Nobody encouraged me to study or to work. I did succeed thanks to my own capabilities. Later, when I was a student, one of female faculty members became my role model. I myself have now become a role model for other women, including my cousins, the daughters of the same uncle who did not want me to go to school. They are now university students." Sara believed that one of the major problems of Baluch women is their lack of knowledge of the law. "They ignore that no one can force them to marry a person they don't want to.

Golnessa, a social activist in Iranshahr, is thirty-two and has a high school diploma. Her father is a chieftain but is not polygamous. "Both of my grand fathers who were chieftains had four wives. But from their generation onward, no other man in my family has several wives." She was sixteen when she married her first cousin, like her seven brothers and sisters. Although Golnessa's parents did not seek her agreement, she liked her suitor who was not much older than her and did not oppose her pursuing education after marriage. "My husband who is a high-school principal is very open-minded. We decide everything together. For example, contrary to Baluch norms, we decided to have only two children."

Baluchistan, however, is still marked by tribal structures. A powerful tribe/clan/family is the one with substantial number of members, and early and polygamous marriage is not peculiar to lower-class Baluch. Men thus marry several wives to have as many children as possible. Fifteen to twenty children per older Baluch man is quite current. This also explains the important age gaps between husbands and third or fourth wives. In my sample, several men were fifty to sixty years older than their youngest wives. When asked how they felt marrying such young girls, some responded: "I have paid for her!"

Nasrin, a Baluch gynecologist in Iranshahr, declared:

> Many Baluch still marry their daughters at an age when instead of playing with dulls these girls are forced to play the role of a spouse. Well, this makes their souls and bodies sick. For example, one of my patients who is 15 and married kept telling me that she was in pain. I examined her and realized she did not have any physical problems. Then one day, she came to see me with an old, toothless, bald, fat man who complained about the money he was spending and my inefficiency to find a remedy to the young woman's pain. I asked him whether he was her father and he said he was her husband! I told him that he was the reason of her pain. That she has problems having sex with him. He turned very angry and said 'Our Prophet was 60 when he married a 9 years old woman'.

It should be mentioned that in their plea, some Shi'ite defenders of polygamy do not hesitate to accuse opponents of its legalisation as being against the Islamic system because, they say, this right is recognized for men in the Quran. According to its supporters, there are several reasons why polygamy is right:

1) Some women are infertile or have congenital diseases. What is the husband supposed to do in these circumstances? Divorce his wife? Have extramarital sex? Deny himself sexual pleasure?

2) The man is prohibited from having sex with his wife during her menstruation. What should he do if he wants to have sex during this

period? Can he be told to refrain from it, to be patient, and to neglect his natural urges? Can he be advised to commit adultery? Polygamy is an appropriate response to these crisis situations.

3)   External factors such as climate, economic, and social conditions influence the sexual instinct of men who cannot be satisfied with one wife. Preventing them from having several wives is likely to cause dangers.

4)   The male genital organ is constantly erect. The main reason for this is that unlike the female genital organ, the male genital organ is outside the body.

5)   Polygamy also serves women. Everyone has the right to marry. Imagine a widow or a young woman who feels the need to marry. If single men refuse to marry them, married men should be able to marry them.[24]

One Baluch man tried to justify polygamous marriage by accusing Baluch women of contributing to the continuity of this tradition. He said that gold and jewelry are of crucial importance for Baluch women and sometimes constitute as their only source of satisfaction in marriage. He said that Baluch men instrumentalized Baluch women's passion for jewelry to perpetuate polygamous marriage. Women accept their husband's polygamy against gold and jewelry!

Zoleikha, Shanâz's daughter, thought that "men take advantage of these traditions which are to the detriment of women. They only think about themselves. They are very selfish."

Her brother said: "Each region has its own traditions. And then, here most women are illiterate. It's only in the last years that most girls are going to school. We have just started to have educated women who are likely to challenge traditions in order to participate in activities outside the home. But this will not happen soon. It will take time."

Out of the various markings of social and power relations such as social class, religion, and ethnicity, religion seems to be a much more important differentiating factor among Shi'ites and Sunnites than ethnicity or class. Avaz, Kaniz's husband and a retired employee in Zâhedân who is against mixed marriage, declared:

We [Shi'ites/Persian] do not participate in Baluch ceremonies. The Persians do not invite the Baluch for religious ceremonies, especially during the month of Ramadan, because the Baluch break their fast before us. So everyone according to their own traditions. Moses according to his religion, Jesus according to his. For marriage, it's the same. The Baluch among themselves, the Persians among themselves. If I want to marry my son, I will find him a Persian girl, my daughter too will marry a Persian. What do I know about what my Baluch neighbors do at home? They don't know what is going on in our home either. Each according to his own traditions. We don't interfere in their affairs and neither do they.

Likewise, Marziyeh and her family who are practicing Shi'ites go to the mosque to participate in religious ceremonies. Twice a year, during Ramadan and Moharram (the month of mourning) they celebrate at home and invite Shi'ite families and neighbors. "We don't invite the Sunnites. They don't come anyways." On inter-religious marriage she said it depends on the families. "In my family, we don't marry Sunnites. I prefer my daughters to marry Shi'ites. Around me, there are very few mixed marriages. Besides, those who married Sunnites had problems and had to separate". Having said that, my father-in-law was Shi'ite and my mother-in-law was Sunnite, but they never had any problems and loved each other to the end!"

As mentioned earlier, religion was not such a major problem prior to the revolution when mixed marriage between Sunnites and Shi'ites was more common. It became an issue when Shi'ism was declared the official religion, and a Shi'ite jurisconsult was promulgated the leader of the Islamic regime. Religion as politics thus interfered with the private lives of Iranians.

In addition to religious and ethnic barriers to mixed marriages, in Baluchistan, in both the North and South, most marriages take place within the same tribe and social class. As other marriages, the husband is usually from a higher social status. However, in recent years some educated young men who had secured their social mobility have decided to marry outside their own tribe or class. Baluch women, however, are still devoid of this opportunity.

Esmat, a retired 55-year-old mother in Iranshahr, was a school teacher and a school principal. Her father was a school caretaker. She married at the age of seventeen to her cousin to whom she was promised right after her birth (nâf bori). After their marriage, her husband married three more wives. As a sign of protest, Esmat lived alone for eight years. She has two sons and two daughters all of whom are educated. One of her daughters is a high school principal and the other is a nurse. Esmat is unhappy because both of her daughters have refused to marry. Esmat says that the rate of polygamy is much lower in Iranshahr compared to Zâhedân and Khâsh because Iranshahr has a much more educated population. Nonetheless, she thinks that the rate of polygamy in Baluchistan is high because temporary marriage is illicit for Baluch who are Sunnite.[25]

Soraya was married at twenty-two with her cousin who is a school teacher. Concerning the type of marriage (arranged or free choice) she says: "I was not forced to marry my husband. The final decision was mine. This was not the case of my sisters whose husbands were chosen by my father. But he died before my marriage. Besides, people are becoming more open to the outside environment. My nieces for example have married distant relatives."

Although the number of Baluch female students in university is increasing and they meet men outside their family circles at the university, the tradition of marrying relatives who are from the same class still persists today but it now also includes distant relatives. Pointing to the question of social status, Soraya declared: "Class is not defined by financial means or level of education. Class is related to the family name one has."

Sima, thirty-five, is a mother of two daughters, both students in Zâhedân. She was born near Iranshahr but migrated to Pakistan with her family after the Revolution. They recently came back from Pakistan and now live in Châhbahâr. Sima went to school in Pakistan and obtained her high school diploma there. She was married in Pakistan at the age of twelve. "My mother forced me to marry. My husband was 25 years older than me. He was a Pakistani Baluch and a remote relative. He was a lawyer. I was his first wife but I lived with him only three years. I left his house and went back to my fathers'. My husband was a good man and did not oppose me going to school. He did not remarry. I finally obtained my divorce recently and returned my dowry." Sima has eight brothers and sisters. Her own father is not polygamous but her grandfather was, as are several of her family members.

In Baluchistan, I struggled to find monogamous men. Only highly educated young men resist this tradition. In our research, highly educated young men encouraged their wives to continue their education. When asked about polygamy in Baluchistan, a Baluch female high school student in Iranshahr declared: "I'm not an illiterate woman and will not authorize my future husband to remarry with two or three more wives. I will definitely oppose his polygamy."

Although Turkmen are Sunnite and my sample of Turkmen was not socially very different from the Baluch, important differences exist among them: they cherish education, according to their traditions, girls usually do not get married before the age of eighteen to twenty, parents ask their daughter's opinion on the marriage, men are usually monogamous, and the age gap between the bride and the groom is low.

Bibi Latifeh, a thirty-eight-year-old Turkmen mother in Gonbad Kavoos, was twenty when she married. Her husband, who is her distant relative, was twenty-three. They knew each other before the marriage because their families were acquaintances. Her parents asked her opinion and she agreed to the marriage. She finished elementary school; her husband has finished high school. Bibi Latifeh was born and raised in Gonbad, her husband was born in a village near

Gonbad but lost his father when he was four years old and came to live with his maternal grandfather in Gonbad. Her husband is monogamous, their parents too. But her maternal grandfather had two wives. However, among people of her generation, she did not know or had not heard of anyone in her family, friends, or neighbors who were polygamous.

Bibi Latifeh and her husband own their home which they built themselves. Their family is nuclear. They own a few cows that they keep in the barn located in the yard.

After their marriage, for two months they lived with her husband's family and then the family asked them to leave. Her husband declared: "The house was my father's inheritance. At that time, I had just gotten married. I had no means. Finally, they forced us to leave and I had a lot of problems and could not go to university." Her husband was wounded in war (janbâz) and is disabled (25 percent). Before the marriage, he completed his military service during the war and therefore went to the front. He was wounded on his back.

Bibi's father and her husband's father are both dead. Their mothers are alive and live in Gonbad not far from them. Despite the fact that his older brother and other family members were not kind to them, they continued seeing and inviting them. Bibi Latifeh has four sisters and two brothers who are all except her elder brother in the same province, in Gonbad or Bandar Turkmen. Her sisters are illiterate but her brothers are educated and are teachers or employees. They see each other several times a year. Her husband has three brothers and two sisters who live in Gonbad or Bandar Turkmen. Bibi Latifeh is a housewife but weaves rugs for herself. She had also woven some for her trousseau. Her husband is a construction worker. He has been doing this job since before the marriage. They have four children, two boys, two girls. The eldest is seventeen years old and in high school. All the children go to school and the mother agrees with the higher education of her daughters if they too are willing.

Bibi Latifeh believed that the right age for her daughters to get married is after the age of twenty, after finishing high school and eventually even after finishing college—for boys, after the age of twenty-eight, after finding a job. Her husband agreed and believed that girls should not marry before eighteen years and boys before twenty-five years and even older. Less than that is not good, they stated, because they will not be mature. Bibi Latifeh said that although they have relatives in Turkmenistan, they have never been there, but the family members come to Iran to visit. She said they do not marry with Turkmen of Turkmenistan. Bibi Latifeh prefers her children to marry the Iranian Turkmen. "Turkmen marry each other but from time to time they also take Persian women but not in our family." According to her husband, "It is a question of tradition and customs. It is not possible to marry someone who is not part of your tradition." What would you do if your daughter decides to marry a stranger to the community, I asked. He replied: "We have to investigate whether he is good or not, about his attitudes, because children are young and don't understand everything. We have to see if he is a Muslim or an infidel (kafar)." Bibi Latifeh argued: "He has to be a Muslim, but if he is Persian [Shi'ite] we will not be against it." Her husband disagreed: "Traditions and customs always win. Our traditions are different from theirs."

Hâjar a Mazadanrani/Persian in the village of Esboo Mahaleh, is thirty years old, her husband is forty years old and is a school teacher. They have three children aged fifteen, eleven, and one. She married at the age of sixteen and had to abandon her studies. She preferred to continue her studies and did not want to get married at such a young age, but gave in under pressure from her parents. Her husband is the brother-in-law of her sister. Hâjar has four sisters and two brothers. She is not against consanguineous marriage but said it will depend on what her children themselves decide. "My parents-in-law were so happy with my sister's marriage to their son that they wanted to take a second daughter from the same family. My parents first disagreed saying 'We gave you one. You have a family of your own. Find a girl within you own family'. But they insisted and my parents finally agreed." Hâjar and her husband own their small house. "When we first got married, we lived with my father-in-law for several years. It was him who gave us the land and we built it. We borrowed from the bank." Her mother-in-law died a long time ago before their marriage. Then the father-in-law remarried. "They don't interfere in our life. They just give us advice. Especially in the beginning when I had no experience. My parents don't interfere in our lives either. They have always helped us with childcare. My mother helped me to take care of my children when they were little."

On her willingness to study, Hâjar explained: "I was a high school student and wanted to continue my studies, but after I got married, the high school officials did not allow me to continue going to school because I was married. At that time, married women were not allowed to attend school [for fear that they would talk about sex to their high school mates]. My husband, who is a high school teacher, told me that he would help me to continue studying at home in order to prepare for the high school diploma exam. But one year after the marriage, I gave birth to my first child and it was very difficult for me to study under those conditions. I took care of the housework and the children and also worked from time to time on our farmland which we own. When my husband was busy with his work and it was necessary to supervise the farm workers who worked for us I would go there. I would make tea for them. I also helped to grow tomatoes, cotton. Now we mostly grow wheat which is much easier to do." Hâjar thinks that girls should not marry before the age of twenty and boys before the age of twenty-six. Referring to her own experience, she added bitterly: "However, in the villages, girls still get married quite early. Parents don't let them continue their studies. As soon as there is an acceptable suitor, they give their daughters away. They do not pay much attention to what the girl thinks or asks."

Jahan is a fifty-three-year-old Mazadarani/Persian who lives in Esboo Mahaleh (her husband specified her age); the husband is one year younger than her which is rare in the villages. They were married thirty-four years ago when she was nineteen and he was eighteen. "He came with his father to ask for my hand. I didn't really know him. It was my parents who decided for me. I said that I would accept what my father decided," Jahan said. Her husband added: "She was under the guardianship of her father." They have four boys and a girl, and have lost a child to illness. The elder is thirty-two years old; the younger Soudabeh is nineteen years old and got married four years ago. She has had two miscarriages and has not yet had any children.

Their marriage is not consanguineous, but in the village they are all related and Jahan and her husband too have a distant relationship. Her husband declared that "80% of the inhabitants of this neighborhood shared the same family name"!

Jahan is illiterate, and her husband has two years of schooling and can read and write.

Their children are not highly educated either. The daughter was in the first year of high school when she married, the boys did not manage to get their high school diploma, and the youngest son left high school to become a mechanic. He was successful and is currently working. Their other son (who lives with his young wife) works in building decoration. Another is a combine driver and works on his father's combine. The fourth boy is a cab driver in Gorgan.

Jahan's husband has seven brothers and one sister. He owns his house, which he inherited from his father. They live with the younger son and his wife. He is a farmer and owns his farmland. He grows wheat, cotton, soybeans, etc. He also works with his combine for others and goes quite far to Zanjan, Mashhad, Fereydoon Kenâr, and Mahmood Abâd (in Mazandaran). Jahan used to help her husband, especially in the sowing and harvesting of rice and cotton, considered to be a "woman's job." They both agree that the best age for girls' marriage is around twenty-five so that they know what life is like, how they should educate the children. Her husband thinks that "she will live better. At that age, she will be able to understand her husband better. If she is too young, the husband has to guide her, but if she is old enough, she can guide herself. I got married very early because my mother had six boys and one girl. The children were all small. It was very difficult for her because she had no help. My other brothers also got married early. But nowadays children get married at 30."

Fatemeh, her daughter-in-law, interrupted her mother in law and said: "Yes, but your children married early.". Jahan replied: "It was not early. They were 21 or 22 years old."

Jahan states: "Except for the girl who got married very young, the boys got married at the age of 25 or 26. They finished their military service and then they got married. They chose their own wives and then we went to ask for their hands. Two of our daughters-in-law are from our village, two others from two other villages."

Fatemeh said: "Three were related but I am a stranger to their family."

Jahan's husband said: "The fourth boy chose his wife himself, we went to ask for her hand in marriage and then we took them to Karbala and they got married there. I also took my mother with us. In fact, my wife, my mother and I wanted to go to Karbala. My son cancelled his trip to Mashhad and told me that he wanted to come with us. So we took him and his fiancée with us." Toward the end of our interview, the wife of their eldest son entered with her little school boy named Dânial. Children learn Persian at school, but at home they speak Gilaki in this part of Golestan.

When I asked whether Jahan would agree that one day her husband marry a second wife, she laughed and said: "I will not let that happen." How would you do that? It is his right. It is in the law, I said.

Jahân replied: "I have no knowledge of the law. And I don't care if it's in the law. But as long as I live, I will not let my husband take a second wife. He can't have other wives. One head one bed!" Her husband laughed and said: "But I don't need your permission."

Jahân and Fatemeh together proclaimed: "**God is one, wife must be one too.**"

Maryam C, a Mazandarani/Shi'ite, lives in the village de Esboo Mahaleh and is thirty-seven years old. She married at the age of twenty-two; her husband with whom she is distantly related is the same age as her. They were neighbors in the village. They have three children aged five, ten, and thirteen. Their house has two rooms: a bedroom for parents and children together, and a living room.

Maryam C and her husband are farmers. They rent a plot of land and grow tomatoes and cotton. Then they share the produce with the owners: 50 percent or 40 percent. Maryam C also is an agricultural worker. She is almost illiterate. She did not attend school but went to adult literacy courses several years ago. Her husband has finished primary school. She has two brothers and four sisters. One of the brothers has a high school diploma, the other has a bachelor's degree. One of her sisters (Zeynab) has a bachelor's degree, another one has finished school. Maryam C and her older sister did not go to school because their working parents needed them to look after the siblings or to work. Maryam's father is a shepherd. Her father-in-law is a gardener (in Gorgan) and farmer. Her mother-in-law works on the land. But they own their farmland.

Maryam's husband has four sisters and three brothers. They are much less educated than Maryam's siblings. The husband also works as a tractor driver for the others, and is also a carpenter. They own their house which they build gradually when they have some money. Our interview took place at Maryam's parents home, as that day the city gas was being installed in Maryam's home.

She said that domestic violence existed but much less in their village because "here people are Persian, belong more or less to the same social and even family environment. Couples are often related to each other. They have the same culture and therefore understand each other better and there is less tension between them." She considers the best age for marriage to be "at least 20 years old, because when they are younger they don't know what life is like.

In rural areas, they don't ask the same conditions for marriage as in the cities. They don't ask the boys to have a car or a stable job. The parents ask that the boy be healthy, that he not be on drugs. That he be religious and practicing. Boys who don't have a house of their own yet, take their wives to their parents." Likewise, Maryam C's mother thinks: "I ask my sons to marry. I agree that my son should bring his future wife to our house. Here, the mothers-in-law agree. It's more the daughters-in-laws who don't want to live with their parents-in-law. They prefer to be independent." Maryam had no opinion on consanguineous marriage and preferred to wait until the children grow up to make up her mind, but said that her two sisters married their cousins (on her mother's side). Her educated sister Zeynab who at thirty-three was single, and held a BA in biology, stated that this type of marriage was not desirable for genetic reasons. She also argued: "For a successful marriage, the age gap between the spouses must be small. They should be culturally close, and have more or less the same education level. It is also necessary to have the same religion, etc. Thus, the differences and tensions will be less." Zeynab also argued: "There is a lot of difference between young people and their parents' generation. I don't say that we have to reject our traditions but that we have to reject some of its aspects. We have to reform the traditions."

Maryam C said:

My mother helped me to look after the children, but not my mother-in-law. When children were small, I took them with me to the land or left them with my parents and my mother looked after them. My parents-in-law never looked after my children and did not help me. At the beginning, we stayed with my in-laws, but then they kicked us out. They told us to leave their house. To rent a place. They didn't want us to stay with them anymore. That's how we thought of buying a piece of land and building our house. We stayed at my father's house until the construction was finished. My parents-in-law didn't even let us stay with them during the construction work.

Similarly to Baluchistan, in Golestan the extended family often lives in the same neighborhood.

Maliheh is a nineteen-year-old Turkmen living in Gonbad Kavoos. She grew up in a family of seven children. Her father was a construction worker and no longer works due to illness. Her father-in-law had more or less the same status and no longer works. She is the youngest child and was married at the age of eighteen. Her husband, who is a distant relative (their grandparents were cousins), is nine years older than her. They have a six-month-old baby. They built a small one-bedroom house in the backyard of her in-law's house. Her husband also has six brothers and sisters. They all live in the same neighborhood. Her husband has a small store in the neighborhood and finished high school. Maliheh went to high school for two years but dropped out because she didn't like school. "I wasn't smart at school and dropped out. So I stayed home and helped my parents for about three years before I got married. My husband sent his parents to propose to me. We knew each other. We were neighbors and also distant relatives. My parents asked my opinion and I told them I agreed."

Oghoul is a forty-six-year-old Turkmen. Like everywhere else, my arrival attracted several curious neighbors, one of whom named Zeynab spoke good Persian and seemed to know the inhabitants of the house well. She turned out to be Oghoul's niece. I told her that I wanted to interview the lady of the household. Being illiterate, Oghoul did not speak Persian and her niece Zeynab and her sister-in-law Sahar agreed to be interpreters. Oghoul who was in her forties looked much older than her age. She was married at the age of twenty-one to her first cousin who was three years older than her. Their marriage had been decided since childhood, and she had been promised to her cousin. She did not attend school but attended adult literacy classes for a short time which she could not continue due to her responsibilities as a mother and wife. She has five children: four boys, one girl. The eldest is twenty-four years old, then an eighteen-year-old disabled girl, a boy (who is blind and is in a specialized boarding school in Gorgan to learn to read), and her youngest son is five years old. She looked after her five children alone without any help because her mother was ill.

Oghoul's husband bought his father's house which is composed of a courtyard around which rooms are located. Like other families I surveyed, they were nuclear.

Oghoul works at home as a tailor. She accepts orders to make traditional Turkmen clothes with needlework (suzanduzi). When she was younger, she also wove Turkmen rugs.

In their neighborhood, everyone is Turkmen. A number of consanguineous marriages have occurred among the Turkmen (33 percent according to our survey), especially among the previous generations, but also among the younger generation. Zeynab said: "Oghoul married her cousin, my parents are cousins, Sahar's parents too. Even my brother and my cousin married their cousins. But my two sisters are not related to their husbands. When my elder sister wanted to get married, as her would be husband was not from the family, my parents did a lot of investigation on him. But we knew my second sister's husband."

Like many Turkmen, Oghoul's husband is monogamous. Sahar, nineteen, is Oghoul's sister-in-law and Zeynab in her early twenties both think that polygamy is not very common because one has to be rich to be polygamous. Except when the wife is sterile and her husband remarries to have children. "It is accepted to give unmarried girls who are too old (e.g. 35-40 years) to men who are already married. But we do not accept to marry a man who is already married. Our parents always ask our opinion. If we have suitors, our parents say that they must first ask their daughter's opinion. Nowadays, many Turkmen ask their daughters' opinion." I asked how they explain this change. Oghoul's answer was: "Because it is necessary to advance with time." Zeynab explained: "The previous generations were often forced to marry the one chosen by their parents and were unhappy in their lives. That is why today they prefer not to impose a marriage on their children. For example, my parents married by force. But when I have children, I will let them marry whoever they want." Oghoul, however, thinks that marriage by free choice has its own problems: "Yes, but if a girl marries whoever she chooses and she is not happy in her life, she must suffer the consequences of her own choice. She cannot expect her parents to support her."

Like Zeynab, Sahar disapproved of consanguineous marriage. However, they did not agree to marry Persians either. "Generally speaking, our parents do not allow us to marry Persians. They are vehemently opposed to it. It happens that Turkmen boys marry Persian women, but the reverse is very rare. We don't give girls to the Persians but take their girls. If a Turkmen girl marries a Persian man in spite of her family's objection, she will have no other choice but to break with her own family." Sahar also emphasized that in her family, they have never married with Turkmen from Turkmenistan either.

Oghoul's only daughter is disabled and she doesn't even imagine the possibility for her to get married. Therefore, when discussing her children's marriage, she only spoke about the marriage of her boys.

> They must first find a job to support their families before they marry. Sometimes young people don't think about these things and as soon as they find their ideal wives they want to get married and ask the family's opinion. I am not against this, but only if they are economically independent. Today, a wedding costs a lot of money. The boy must have the necessary capital unless he has a rich father. The bride's dowry is determined by the example of other girls in her family, then gold jewelry is bought for the bride and there are also the expenses for the wedding party. The bride's parents provide the dower (jahiziyyeh) that is composed of all the furniture, for the house. The boy has to provide the housing.

The Turkmen wedding traditions resemble those of the Persians but are very different from Baluch traditions where the groom pays the bride's parents, the wedding party, the dower, and all other expenses.

Despite the diversity of traditions among various ethnicities, social and cultural changes have had important impact on demographic behavior of all Iranian women. As can be seen in our interviews and surveys, there is a sharp decrease in the number of children born to the younger generation compared to the generation of their parents, including in rural areas and among non-Persians, non-Shi'ites.

However, the country's demographic and social transformations are questioned by conservatives, led by the Leader Ali Khamenei, for whom women are primarily mothers and wives. Aiming to double the population, now at approximately 83 million, 75 percent of whom are urban dwellers and 49 percent under thirty years of age,[26] the Leader summoned Rohani's government in 2015 to put an end to family planning, which had been enforced since 1989. This order contravenes the very constitution of the Islamic Republic, which recognizes women as social, economic, and political actors beyond their maternal role. Rural women whose number of children was significantly higher than urban dwellers had adopted the family planning campaign motto "fewer children, better life." As mentioned earlier, the campaign and free distribution of contraceptive devices had greatly contributed to reduce population growth from 3.9 percent per year to 1.2 percent currently and the fertility rate from 7 to 1.6 children per woman. Following the Leader's order, the free distribution of contraceptives in urban clinics and rural dispensaries was banned in 2015, exposing poor women to the risk of unwanted pregnancies. Voluntary female and male sterilization is criminalized and doctors who perform it are subject to imprisonment. However, these injunctions have failed to gain the support of women as illustrated by the steady decline in the fertility rates. Between 2018 and 2019, for example, births diminished by 170,000. The Islamic Parliament's Research Center published a report entitled *The Promulgation of the Motion on Population and the Promotion of the Family in the Eleventh Parliament.* It stated that according to the data provided by the civil registry, there were 1,196,135 births in 2019, the lowest figure in the past decade. This figure shows a 12 percent decrease compared with 2018, and a 22 percent decrease compared with 2014.[27]

The number of early marriage, however, has increased by 10 percent as a result of increasing poverty and the Islamic regime encouraging early marriage through financial incentives. In 2021, the government decided to grant 100 million tomans to young married couples. It should be emphasized that according to the Statistical Center of Iran, in 2020–1, there were 31,379 girls aged ten to fourteen who married, a 10 percent increase compared to the previous year. Likewise, according to the Organization of Well-being (Behzisti), in 17 percent of all marriages in the country, brides were below the age of eighteen and 5 percent of women married were below fifteen.[28]

However, the strong trend in society among youth cannot be altered with these changes in population policy.

Permissive Upbringing

Mothers who are now more than ever in charge of their children's education have largely rejected authoritarian methods of education (high control, low support), opting for permissive upbringing, which consists of a low control and a high support toward children. It is through their intervention in their children's education, which is one of the rare spheres where women's contribution is recognized by the authorities and their own husbands that frustrated mothers do invest themselves entirely. As the following tables show, from amongst the mothers who declared having opted for their children's freedom with parental advice, the highest rate belongs to the Turkmen (46 percent) and the lowest to the Baluch (14 percent). The highest rate among those who have opted for discussion and persuasion method belongs to the Arabic speakers (71 percent) and the lowest rate to the Baluch speakers (50 percent).

Table 4.14 Rate of mothers fifteen years and older who have adopted discussion and persuasion method, by ethnic language (2002).

Local and ethnic language	Rate
Baluch	50
Arabic	71
Turkmen	50
Lori	60
Persian	64
Mazandarani	67
Azari	63
Kurdish	66
Gilaki	61
Average	63

Source: *Socio-economic Characteristics Survey of Iranian Households (2002)*, Statistical Center of Iran, National Center for Scientific Research (France), French Research Institute in Iran. Tehran, Statistical Center of Iran, 2003, P. 172.

Table 4.15 Rate of mothers fifteen years and older who have opted for their children's freedom with parental advice, by ethnic and local language (2002).

Local and ethnic language	Rate
Baluch	14
Arabic	18.5
Turkmen	46
Lori	24
Persian	30
Mazandarani	22
Azari	29
Kurdish	24
Gilaki	24
Average	27.5

Source: *Socio-economic Characteristics Survey of Iranian Households (2002)*, Statistical Center of Iran, National Center for Scientific Research (France), French Research Institute in Iran. Tehran, Statistical Center of Iran, 2003, P. 172.

Sadigheh who lives in a village in Sistan-Baluchistan said: "My daughters talk to me a lot. We have a good relationship." Kaniz said:

We try, as much as possible, to have a friendly relationship with the children but when I am exhausted or upset, I yell at them. And the cause is exclusively their homework, their studies. I tell them, study for yourself, to secure your future. To become somebody in this society. I tell them, look at us. We both have income but because we didn't study, we are poor. But I have friendly relationship with my children. They tell me everything, they tell me confidences. They tell me what happened at school, with their friends, on the way to school. They ask me for my opinion, for advice. To say that we have a friendly relationship. I tell them, my children this is the right way. I tell them to respect their teachers. We do everything we can for our children.

Contrary to many others, Dornâz and Zobeideh both punish their children. Dornâz's eldest son declared: "She hits us." To justify the corporal punishment Dornâz and Zobeideh argued: "Our children are not like yours, like the children of the other side [educated middle or upper class Tehranis). Our children are not polite. Did you see that? He entered the room and didn't even say hello to you. We don't have your patience. From morning to night, we spend our life cloistered with these children and lose our patience when they do not obey. We punish them and tell them why we do so."

Sadigheh spanks her son and says that her father used to punish them, but not her mother. Her father explained that her mother had no right. "Among the Sistanis, mothers are not allowed to punish their children. They report it to their husbands and the husband punishes." Sadigheh said she was more influenced by her father and was closer to her father. "When I had a problem, I used to tell my father. But my mother also advised us. For example, she would encourage us to study and tell us that if she is in a miserable situation it is because she is illiterate."

Marzieh thinks that "the education of children should be a joint affair of the spouses. In my family, my father used to help my mother. Even today, he never lets my mother do housework alone. I was influenced by this education and try, despite my low level of education, to advise my children. To tell them that they should not waste their time. That it is necessary to study."

Marzieh's husband is a teacher. She gets along well with her husband who seems to have a relatively liberal attitude. He helped her with childcare and put the house in his wife's name. This is quite rare in Iran and even less so in this province. "I owe a lot to my husband. Everything I have today is thanks to my husband." Both husband and wife make decisions together and have adopted the permissive type of upbringing with the children. No violence or corporal punishment. Just discussion and persuasion. Effat, her daughter, and Fatemeh, her friend, declared: "We have friendly relationships with our parents. We talk a lot. Parents don't force us to do things. They advise us. We make decisions after discussing them together."

Jahan from the village of Esboo Mahaleh in Golestan said she has always been kind to her children. "I have always talked with them. They have always respected me and they are all very obedient. I am very satisfied with them. We never punished them. We never had to punish them because they were all so good. My children are closer to me than to their father. If they want money, they tell me and I get them money from their father."

Bibi Latifeh declared never have inflicted corporal punishment on the children. "We ask them not to do any more mischief. We discuss with them." The eldest daughter intervenes: "Let's say it was verbal punishment!"

Oghoul from Gonbad Kavoos declared however, "When I was very upset, I would either give them corporal punishment (spankings) or I would argue with them. I would try to scare them. But most of the time I would talk to them and explain to them why they shouldn't do certain things."

Fatemeh from the village of Keykha in Sistan declared: "I never punish my children. I talk to them. I always explain to them what is in their best interest to do."

The type of education Hâjar and her husband give to their children is rather authoritarian. The husband is very strict with the children. Hâjar said:

> First we try to discuss with them in order to persuade them but if they continue to disobey, we punish them. We give them corporal punishment. They are beaten with sticks on their hands and feet. In the village, the children go out and do whatever they want. Mischief, dangerous games. We prefer our children to play at home. I don't allow them to go out. My husband is very nervous and punishes them but then he regrets it.

Maryam C from Esboo Mahaleh said: "As I am illiterate myself, I want my children to study. We do not differentiate between boys and girls. If later on the children wish to learn something else (foreign language, computer, etc.) we put our means at their disposal. It is good that they learn more subjects. My husband and I would like our children to get an education. I would rather spend on their education than on the house. We are workers and we are content with the means we have."

Her mother who attended the conversation proudly stated: "I worked hard on the land so that my children could get an education. Look at my daughter who has a high-school diploma, my other daughter who has a bachelor's degree, my boys too. Now I'm sick and can't do much."

Maryam C said they do not inflict corporal punishment on their children. They talk with the children. If they overdo it, she spanks them. "My parents never used corporal punishment on us either. If we didn't listen to our mother and when she was tired, she would give us a little spanking."

Her sister Zeynab stated: "Some parents are stupid and think they can educate their children by adopting a very severe type of education. Their children are afraid of them and there is no friendly relationship between these parents and their children. But corporal punishment never gives a good result. It gives the opposite result." During her studies, she went to her university in Gorgan every day and came back in the evening. From time to time, she stayed overnight in Gorgan at her sister's house. She helped her parents with the farming or did housework as she could. "This is the life of the village. The children participate in their parents' work and help with the housework. The farm work is mostly in the summer. So you can go to school and help your parents in the summer too."

As a well-educated woman, Zeynab clearly enjoyed a great deal of prestige and gave advice, especially regarding the education of children, to her sister and her family without interfering directly in her sister's life. For her, the best age for marriage is twenty-four to twenty-six for girls and twenty-four to thirty for boys. "Given the social, economic and cultural problems, the age of marriage has increased. To get married, one must have a certain financial level and the mental maturity to face the responsibilities." She believes that financial issues lead to social problems. "A young person who has a job and is able to support himself and his family will not seek illegal activities." On her celibacy she said:

In my family, nothing is imposed on us. We discuss things, they tell me what they think, but I make the final decision. I liked to study and want to continue studying. I wasn't thinking about marriage. I had suitors but I didn't like any of them. I didn't see any cultural characteristics in them that would interest me or lead to our understanding. The people of our village are open, especially now with the modern means of communication people have much more information and this leaves the way open for the education of women. Being close to the city is very important. In our village, many women have obtained their high school diploma.

Bibi Latifeh's husband thinks that children need to study. "We give them advice but they decide. For example, we advised our second daughter to choose natural science but she chose math." Bibi Latifeh explained: "We wrongly thought that there is no opportunity for girls in math." They both want the children to continue their studies but say you have to have the financial means. The husband declared: "I myself had been admitted to university but did not have the means or financial support and therefore could not continue my studies. I was married and had two children." Both parents say they do not differentiate between their daughters and sons. "If the girls are admitted to university in a different town, and if we can afford it financially, we will agree that they move to another city to study and stay in the student dorm."

Our survey illustrates the predominance of permissive upbringing and the rejection of laws by the majority of Iranian mothers. Of 7,640 mothers in our sample only 162, 2 percent declared using violence and physical punishment against their children; 385 or 5 percent declared themselves authoritarian, against 4,827 or 63 percent who said they had opted for discussion and persuasion; and 2,100 or 27.5 percent had opted for their children's freedom of decision-making along with parental advice. It is interesting to note that 2,998, or 39 percent, of the mothers in our survey were illiterate, but only 3 percent of them had physically punished their children. No mother with higher education declared inflicting violence and physical punishment.

A fewer number of children has liberated women from continuous childbearing and child rearing, allowing them to think and act for their own selves. The adoption by mothers of permissive upbringing seems to be a form of protest against the patriarchy. They react to the patriarchal system, values, and norms propagated by the Islamic regime, and reinforced by laws. It also illustrates the rejection by many Iranian parents of the civil code and the penal law based on Islamic laws that consider children as their parents', especially their father's, belongings. According to Article 1179 of the civil code, parents are entitled to punish their children physically. Likewise, according to Article 220 of the penal law, if a child is killed by his/her father or his/her paternal grandfather, the murderer will only pay the blood money to the heirs of the child, and might, upon court's decision, be imprisoned for a short period.[29] In recent years, several fathers assassinated their daughters whom they suspected of having "illicit" relationships. They are aware that the maximum sentence they risk is a three-year imprisonment. These cases are exceptions to the rule, in comparison to permissive upbringing which has become a dominant form of child education. The value of children and their well-being is at the center of the concerns of parents, who now mobilize their resources to respond to their children's needs and their often consumerist demands. It has also led to the establishment of a dialogue between parents and children, and the parents' respect for their children's opinion. Child centeredness and permissive upbringing lead children to enjoy an unprecedented individual freedom within their families. They gain autonomy (despite financial dependency of some) and construct an individualized identity. On the other hand, the economic crisis of recent decades and the failure of the Islamic regime to follow through on the revolution's promises, especially those of social justice and freedom, have led parents and grandparents (who belong to the generation of the revolution) to feel guilt toward the younger generation who are suffering from unemployment and cultural and political repression. Consequently, instead of generational conflicts between parents and children, we are faced with relationships based on respect and understanding between them.

The outcome is the rejection by the youths of obedience to authority and the emergence of a political and cultural counter-weight to authoritarian rule. This new reality has gained momentum in the public sphere where the concepts of tolerance, dialogue, and freedom have gained tremendous popularity, while authoritarianism and violence along with the institutions that generate them are rejected. The weakening of patriarchal power within family that represents an institutional domain contributes to the weakening of the Islamic state's institutions and grip of power and is likely to question gender inequality.

Opinion Poll

In addition to our quantitative and qualitative surveys, we also introduced an opinion poll for the first time in a major survey taken by the Statistical Center of Iran. The results show that profound changes have occurred in the lives of Iranian women, increasing their awareness and weakening perceptions concerning men's authority in the family institution and the patriarchal order founded on male domination.

Women's Access to Education

Although the official ideological discourse values women mainly as mothers and wives, until 1993 women's access to several university majors such as management, some branches of medicine, engineering, and law was prohibited, young women's quest for education continued and they increasingly enrolled in universities. The number of public universities has increased to over ninety in 2019, and the number of students in institutions of higher education increased from 175,000 in 1976 (30 percent of whom were women) to 4 million in 2016 (nearly 60 percent of whom were women). The semi-public, semi-private Azâd University (established in 1970 under the Shah) and less competitive than public universities has opened branches throughout the country. In spite of high registration fees at Azad University that represent a significant investment for some families, it had 1.7 million students in 2020.[30] The active presence of young women in education made possible, thanks to the expansion of schooling in urban and rural areas, led the older generation, overwhelmingly illiterate, to tremendously valorize women's education. As could be seen in the qualitative survey, many poor and illiterate respondents attributed their inferior status in their families and society to a lack of educational credentials, which they believed also prevented them from becoming autonomous from their fathers or husbands. They, therefore, advocated their daughters' education as a crucial means to their empowerment. As Table 4.16 shows, 86.5 percent of our respondents believed that men and women should have equal access to education. The rate is 81 percent for illiterate women, 92 percent for literate women, and 98 percent for highly educated women.

Contrary to the educated urban middle-class women who overwhelmingly choose their husbands either at university, at work, or through friends,[31] many women in our survey, including some younger ones, had no other choice but to marry the man their parents (especially fathers) had chosen for them. Some had been promised after their birth to their cousins, others were given to men with better financial and social conditions. Some others were given to the first suitor because parents were so poor; they couldn't provide for the basic needs of their daughters. Therefore, women's marriage had been either forced or arranged.

Table 4.16 Opinion of ever-married women fifteen years and older on the equality of rights concerning equal access to education, by ethnic and local language (2002).

Local and ethnic language	Rate (%)
Baluchi	60
Arabic	77
Turkmen	96
Lori	81
Persian	90
Mazandarani	87
Azari	89.5
Kurdish	92
Gilaki	88
Average	86.5

Source: *Socio-economic Characteristics Survey of Iranian Households (2002)*, Statistical Center of Iran, National Center for Scientific Research (France), French Research Institute in Iran. Tehran, Statistical Center of Iran, 2003, P. 160.

Table 4.17 Opinion of ever-married women fifteen years and older on the equality of rights between men and women concerning free choice, by local and ethnic language (2002).

Local and ethnic language	Rate (%)
Baluchi	53
Arabic	88
Turkmen	100
Lori	85
Persian	95
Mazandarani	97
Azari	83
Kurdish	95
Gilaki	94
Average	90

Source: *Socio-economic Characteristics Survey of Iranian Households (2002)*, Statistical Center of Iran, National Center for Scientific Research (France), French Research Institute in Iran. Tehran, Statistical Center of Iran, 2003, P. 160.

They rarely chose their husbands out of free choice. However, as can be seen, 90 percent of women were for free choice. The rate is 94 percent for literate women (99 percent for women with a high school diploma or with university education) and 84 percent for illiterate women. The rate is 100 percent for Turkmen and 53 percent for Baluch women. This shows that women are overwhelmingly distancing themselves from family, tribal, ethnic, or religious traditions, if not in reality at least in their minds and desires. At the same time as this desire to choose one's partner freely is established, these young women reconduct the injunctions made to women to preserve and ensure their virtue within a gendered social order. This is done through the construction of a virtuous femininity. This highlights the complexity of the subordination/resistance relationship, and the capacity for action of subjects in terms of their ability to introduce changes in social reality.

Housework and Childcare: Women's Exclusive Responsibility?

Women also question the gender division of labor within the family. Only 30.5 percent of women thought that housework is women's exclusive responsibility. The rate was 19 percent for literate mothers and 42 percent for illiterate ones. Among women with higher education, only 5 percent believed the housework to be women's responsibility.

The distinction between public and private that obscures the exploitative and dependent relationship of women to men has been challenged as a political distinction (thus implying the power of men over women). As the now abundant literature defining unpaid work as the material basis for patriarchal exploitation has shown, the domestic and family sphere is not reduced to "outside work"; it is the framework of production, of invisible, unpaid, unrecognized but real work.

Concerning childcare, only 15 percent of women in our survey believed it is a woman's exclusive responsibility. The rate was 9 percent for literate women and 5 percent for highly educated women.

Fatemeh and Effat are young Persians in Zâhedân. They agree that women have the same potential as men in education and work, and think that husbands and wives should help each other with housework and childcare.

Maryam D in Zâhedân said that regarding decisions about the children and the house, she makes them after having informed her husband: "My husband is too old. When he comes home, he doesn't want to discuss the children's problems or things like that. I inform him, but I make the decisions about the children."

Bibi Latifeh, a Turkmen in Gonbad Kavoos, said: "I make decisions about the house myself, but since I don't have the financial means, I ask my husband for the relevant expenses. For the education of the children, we make decisions together. For all decisions, we make them together."

Table 4.18 Rate of ever-married women fifteen years and older who think that housework is women's exclusive responsibility, by ethnic language (2002).

Local and ethnic language	Rate (%)
Baluchi	63
Arabic	51
Turkmen	23
Lori	45
Persian	20
Mazandarani	29
Azari	27
Kurdish	34
Gilaki	29
Average	30.5

Source: *Socio-economic Characteristics Survey of Iranian Households (2002)*, Statistical Center of Iran, National Center for Scientific Research (France), French Research Institute in Iran. Tehran, Statistical Center of Iran, 2003, P. 168.

Table 4.19 Rate of ever-married women fifteen years and older who think that childcare is women's exclusive responsibility by local and ethnic language (2002)

Local and ethnic language	Rate (%)
Baluchi	48
Arabic	35
Turkmen	04
Lori	39
Persian	01
Mazandarani	09
Azari	16
Kurdish	18
Gilaki	12
Average	15

Source: *Socio-economic Characteristics Survey of Iranian Households (2002)*, Statistical Center of Iran, National Center for Scientific Research (France), French Research Institute in Iran. Tehran, Statistical Center of Iran, 2003, P. 168.

Hâjar in Esboo Mahaleh declared: "When I'm very busy or have to go out shopping, I leave the children at home and my husband looks after them. But I do the cooking and everything else. My husband works a lot and is tired. When he comes home, he eats and then he rests."

Maryam C said she made decisions together with her husband. "We consult each other, we discuss. For the purchase of the land and the construction of our house, about the upringing of the children. My husband sells products but brings the money home and gives it to me. Then we spend it together. But I do the housework, cooking, childcare, everything. My husband does not help me at all."

In both rural and urban areas, and among middle-class and lower-class women, the bulk of housework and childcare is carried out by women, including working women. In school books, motherhood and domestic work are interpreted as the main function of the woman, while the man is presented as a social being who even spends his free time outside the home. As mentioned earlier, the Islamic laws and policies play a crucial role in enforcing the gender division of labor, women's dependency on men and public gender regime. Faced with an all-out ideological, political, and market impediments toward women's employment in formal sector of the state-run economy, many have no other choice but to work for the informal sector with no social protection.

Gender and Work, Gender and Politics

Gender and Work

In addition to the family as an institutional domain in Iran's Islamic gender regime, political and economic domains participate in maintaining the neo/patriarchal domination and social gender relations. Iran's rentier economy limits female economic participation. To this is added the ongoing attempts of the government and religious authorities to further impose gender segregation and limit women's access to the job market. This policy is likely to increase women's financial dependency on men and the state financial aid (both private and public neo/patriarchy), depriving them of autonomization. My observations and interviews with working women show the impact of women's revenue-earning activities and women's money on their self-esteem and the decision-making authority they gain within their family and society.

> A number of conditions must be met to establish gender economic equality. The first is women's freedom, the second is the relation between family and employment, the third is the criticism of male domination through the reversal of the burden of proof [...] Thinking about the relationship between family and the city is a fundamental condition for the production of economic and professional equality. It must be thought of in a political analogy. It is also one of the conditions for economic equality.[1]

The articulations between gender, work, and politics can only be analyzed by addressing issues such as the relationship between family and work, family socialization, the level of education and training, economic modes of production, the relationship to technology and tools, and the role of the state and other institutional actors.

Women, especially those belonging to the lower and middle classes, increasingly aspire to join the work force and matrimonial and family relations undergo change as and when women have access to a better education, economic independence, and social participation. It is noteworthy to mention that for the first time in Iran's history, the number of highly educated women is higher than that of men: 41.3 percent of all women six years and over had at least a high school diploma against 40.6 percent for men.[2] Likewise, the number of female students is higher than that of males in all university majors with the exception of technical and engineering sciences.

In our survey, 77 percent of women are for men and women's equal access to work. The rate is 71 percent for illiterate women, 81 percent for literate women, and 88 percent for highly educated women.

According to the results of my surveys, women's paid activity is a crucial means to modifying the power relations between women and men both within the family and in society although it does not lead to gender equality.

In addition to the limits set on their freedom by their own religious or tribal traditions, Baluch women in Baluchistan also feel they are discriminated against by the state, laws, and local authorities. Several educated unemployed women in Zâhedân and Iranshahr mentioned job discrimination against Baluch women in favor of Persians.

The work has been recomposed and redefined by its two dimensions: one professional, the other domestic. In Iran, as elsewhere, employers use the qualities acquired by women in the domestic sphere without being aware of it, as such skills are considered to be innate and not acquired. The technical and social division of labor is thus juxtaposed with the gender division of labor. The latter is characterized by the prioritized assignment of men to the productive sphere and women to the reproductive sphere, as well as the simultaneous capture by men

Table 5.1 B.A. Students at higher education institutes by field of study and gender, 1398–99/2020–21.

Field of study	Total both genders	Male	Female
	3,182,989	1,638,746	1,544,243
Medicine	243,008	98,148	144,860
Humanities	1,573,122	718,037	855,085
Basis Sciences	206,339	64,812	141,527
Technical and Engineering	810,720	613,969	196,751
Agriculture and Veterinary	117,883	55,698	62,185
Arts	231,917	88,082	143,835

Source: Iran Statistical Year Book 1398, P. 681.

Table 5.2 Opinion of ever-married women fifteen years and older on women's equal access to work, by local and ethnic language (2002).

Local and ethnic language	Rate (%)
Baluchi	48
Arabic	53
Turkmen	73
Lori	74
Persian	80
Mazandarani	66
Azari	78
Kurdish	86
Gilaki	90
Average	77

Source: *Socio-economic Characteristics Survey of Iranian Households (2002)*, Statistical Center of Iran, National Center for Scientific Research (France), French Research Institute in Iran. Tehran, Statistical Center of Iran, 2003, P. 160.

of functions with high social added value. However, the domestic and family sphere should not be reduced to the existing structures outside environments of work. It is the framework of a production, of an invisible, unpaid, unrecognized, but very real work.

Following Danièle Kergoat, I argue that the gender division of labor is a power-based relationship to the detriment of women:

> Gender division of labor, which is a form of social division of labor, assigns men to the sphere of production and women to the sphere of reproduction. Gender division of labor has two organizing principles: separation (between men's work and women's Work); and hierarchy (a man's work is more valuable than a woman's). These principles are applied through legitimizing the essentialist ideology. As a result, men obtain valued social functions in political, religious, military or economic realms.[3]

This is the reason why the distinction between public and private, which conceals the relationship of exploitation and dependence of women on men, has been challenged as a political distinction (implying the power of men over women).

"Men use their wealth to endow women" [Qur'an, Surah IV al-Nisa, Women, verse 34]. This authority in the family institution guarantees the man a privileged economic and social status that is enshrined in the traditions and laws of Iran, where women are far from enjoying full citizenship. Indeed, the Iranian civil code which legally determines the relationship between men and women grants excessive privileges to men (Article 1106) on the ground, emphasizing that economic function is a main attribute men carry. In return, the law recognizes him as head of the family and obliges his wife to obey him (tamkin, Article 1105 of the civil code). The financial dependence of women on men is so central to the Iranian legal system that it is one of the few cases in which a woman can file for a divorce, if the husband refuses to pay his wife's alimony (nafaqeh) and the household expenses. Another example is the inheritance law, according to which men inherit twice as much as women. Muslim theorists and religious authorities alike justify this inequality by arguing that women are supported financially by their male relatives, fathers, or husbands and that their financial needs are less than those of men who are responsible for providing for their family and their wives.[4] The dominant culture and employers adhere to this view and therefore prefer to hire men.

In other words, men's authority over women in both the public and the private spheres is recognized and sanctioned by law because men are perceived as having an economic function. For this very reason, if women succeed in assuming economic functions outside the family institution, the Islamic laws on the subject would also be questioned. Many Iranian religious authorities now acknowledge women's economic activity outside the household but continue to consider housework and childcare as women's main responsibility. The Islamic Republic's Supreme Leader, Ayatollah Ali Khamenei, declared: "Islam authorizes women to work outside the household. Their work might even be necessary but it should not interfere with their main responsibility that is childrearing, childbearing and housework. No country can do without women's work force but this should not contradict women's moral and human values. It should not weaken women, nor compel them to bend or to stoop low."[5]

However, in order for a woman to work, she needs her husband's authorization if he pays her alimony. Moreover, only the financial and economic dimension of women's activity is recognized to the detriment of its social dimension. This is clearly stated by a traditionalist:

> Islam prefers that women take care of housework … But if the husband's earnings are not enough to meet his family's needs then his wife is authorized to work in order to complete her husband's earnings provided that her work corresponds to her condition as a woman and that she preserves her chastity. If the costs of marital life prevent a young man from getting married, then woman's work outside the family becomes even compulsory in order to enhance marriage which is the tradition of our Prophet.[6]

The traditionalist's resistance to the financial independence of women can be explained by the fact that the status of women depends on the control they can exercise over their property and their workforce.[7]

Sadigheh, a Persian from the village of Keykha, said: "I have an income and I decide how to spend it. I spend it on the house, on the children. I decide myself what to buy."

On the impact of women's financial independence, Soraya, a young, Baluch-educated woman, thinks that it alone cannot empower women. It can prevent small-scale tensions between the spouses but cannot change the husband's behavior unless the woman is highly educated. At least as educated as her husband. "If a woman is empowered, her husband will respect her."

Some Baluch working women agreed with Mrs. Peymani, who said: "I have never had the feeling of being financially independent. I have never been to a bank myself to withdraw money. My husband signs for me and withdraws my salary from the bank. I wish my daughters would gain their autonomy from their husbands."

Likewise, on the question of working women's financial independence, Ashraf, a Baluch school principal in Iranshahr, said:

> Many women do have revenue earning activities but are not financially independent. Most of my Baluch colleagues for example are forced to hand their check books to their husbands. If they refuse, they will be beaten. This is also the case of my eight aunts who all work but do not have access to their own money. These men want to dominate their wives. One of my colleagues told me that she has never been to a bank or has never spent her salary herself. Another one told me she didn't even know how to cash a check in a bank. Here, most men are unemployed and some are drug addict. Women provide for the needs of their family. Some work outside as employees, others work at home and sell their products.

It is therefore of crucial importance that working women pocket the money.

Women's access to decision-making positions helps to strengthen the social position of women from the educated and active middle and upper classes, but social inequalities between women and men will not disappear by women adapting to the "male" model of work, which presupposes the existence of a free worker, owner of his own workforce that he would sell freely. As Carole Pateman argued, in the contractualist societies, the contract is indissociably sexual and social.[8]

In Iran, 40 percent of women working in the formal sector of the economy are highly educated but they rarely find themselves in decision-making positions. Women hold more positions in the education (40 percent) and health (12.5 percent) due to the policy of gender segregation imposed in these sectors. To fill this gap and given the outcry from women's rights activists over the absence of women ministers in Hassan Rohani's second government (presented to the Islamic Parliament in August 2017), the High Council of Administration declared its intention to allocate 30 percent of decision-making positions in the administration to women by the end of the Sixth Development Plan (2017–22). Rohani also pretended to encourage young people's access to decision-making positions by prohibiting the appointment of people over fifty-five years of age or with more than twenty-five years of seniority. These measures, however, have not been enforced.

As Carole Pateman argued, the definition of free and equal individuals presupposes their belonging to the public sphere and thus founds the exclusion of women from the social contract.[9] In other words, civil liberty depends on patriarchal law. The contracting individuals are therefore not neutral but gendered. The patriarchy is not the relic of an ancient world, for it is constitutive of the "social contract," of liberal modernity. This model also defines the differentiated access to social rights and to the effective exercise of citizenship. It condemns a large majority of women to choose between dependence on men, which Sylvia Walby calls "private patriarchy," and the dependence on the state, which she calls "public patriarchy."[10] According to Walby, citizenship involves the transfer of the patriarchal model from the private to the public sphere.

Wage-based labor is thus a financial alternative to women's traditional dependence in the private sphere. It is a crucial component of the transformation of gender relations, even if it does not succeed in protecting women from poverty. The state has contributed for several years to the change in women's domestic roles through the professionalization of a number of tasks that were previously assigned to the private sphere, such as teaching, childcare, and health care. However, it is still necessary that women be able to move from private to public patriarchy, and therefore have their husband's authorization to work outside the home.

Among the women surveyed in both urban and rural areas, whether educated or illiterate or with low literacy levels, those who had a paid activity in the formal or informal sector and pocketed their earnings themselves, all valued their work despite the sometimes very difficult working conditions. It is important to note that both domestic and international official statistics, including those of the World Bank, do not take into account women's employment in the informal sector and only provide figures for the formal sector. This is mostly regulated by the state, it being the largest employer of educated women in rentier economies like Iran. Indeed, according to the Statistical Center of Iran, 58 percent of the work force in 2020 was active in the informal sector of the economy. Of the total of 23,263,047 active people aged fifteen and over, 13,495,676 were employed in the informal sector. The percentage was 66.5 for Sistan-Baluchistan and 61.6 for Golestan provinces. They constitute of an army of cheap and available labor, and are devoid of social security, retirement, and every social protection. The share of women in the informal economy is higher than that of men. According to the Statistical Center of Iran, 63 percent of active women work in the informal sector.[11] Many work in garment industry, while others are a part of the service sector, especially in sale and care activities. Moreover, millions of women work for family businesses in both urban and rural areas with no pay. Of the 6 million people working in the latter sector (dairy products, agricultural products, carpet weaving, etc.), over 90 percent are women. Those who work but are not salaried or do not earn revenues do not consider themselves as workers but only as housewives. Because they do not pocket the money, they do not qualify themselves legitimate to take part in decision making within the family. The power relations are therefore to their detriment. For this very reason, it is important to raise not only the issue of women's work but also women's money. Many working women emphasized that paid work which provided them with financial autonomy, also gave them authority within the family, allowing them to participate in household decision making. This paid work was also valued as a way to break out of isolation, establish social relationships, and socialize outside the family.[12]

The analysis of family dynamics and women's daily lives has proven to be an excellent way to capture the profound changes experienced by ordinary Iranians, and the relationship between society and the state.

Since 1979, public policy has reinforced gender relations through family and employment policies. Women's employment outside the home has been discouraged unless it is essential to the survival of her family. The home is considered the best place for women.

During both terms of the populist President Mahmood Ahmadinejad's (2005–13) presidency, women's rights and economic activity outside the home had been under concerted and constant attack. Women who wanted or needed to work were pressured not to seek employment outside the home, but to work at home as hairdressers, tailors, cooks, designers, carpet weavers, etc.

By transforming their homes into workplaces, they were thus forced to combine domestic and professional tasks. The only exceptions were sectors such as primary and secondary education or certain branches of medicine (such as gynecology) where, due to gender segregation, women are supposed to exclusively serve the female population. Measures have also been taken to limit the access of women with high levels of education to positions of responsibility.

These measures reflect the government's attempts to create a solution for male unemployment, especially among young men aged fifteen to twenty-nine, whose (official) unemployment rate of 21.4 percent was twice as high as that of working men. The government also attempted to find a solution to the crisis of traditional masculinity aggravated by the high unemployment rates of young men. Masculinity refers to men's sense of identity and their individual and collective rights within material relationships that are grounded in family/domestic relationships. Traditional masculinities are constructed as bread winners, also assuming control over income and resources as well as over women. The identity of men as providers has legitimized women's exclusion from work outside the home.

However, the situation was much worse for young women aged fifteen to twenty-nine, whose unemployment rate was at 42 percent. In 2016 the official unemployment rate for men over ten years old was 10.5 percent compared to 21 percent for women.[13]

Despite multiple declarations of intent in favor of gender equality, the government of Hassan Rohani did not take any measures to facilitate women's economic activity or guarantee their rights within the family and society. In rentier economies like Iran, macroeconomic structures further compound the weight of social and political conservatism to block women's access to the formal economy. While the country has millions of highly educated women, only 17 percent of Iranian women over the age of fifteen work in the formal sector of the economy.

Working-class women work almost as much as men if not more; they are not confined to their homes; they are valued and respected by the community as both workers and mothers; and they have some economic independence. However, their activity is devalued by the Islamists because they do not correspond to the ideal of Islamic femininity based on the model of the wealthy classes for whom women's work is a choice and not an economic necessity.

Indeed, women's economic independence is likely to lead to an intellectual autonomy that would compete with and threaten men's authority within the family and the "social order." However, all these measures aimed at constraining women come up against economic realities, massive urbanization, and the dysfunction of social institutions due to the progressive withdrawal of the state from the social field and an ever-increasing poverty.

In the middle and working classes, women are thus forced to contribute to the household income, even if they continue to be considered by law financially dependent on their husbands.

The term "working poor" seemed paradoxical at the time, because poverty was associated with inactivity and unemployment.[14] Many young people, including graduates and from urban areas, are driven by economic necessity, to work in the informal sector of the economy, without a professional future or social rights. In Iran, as in elsewhere, there is a dualization of female employment with, on the one hand, high intellectual professions and, on the other hand, the precariousness and poverty of a growing number of working women. This includes ethnic women. We witness the appearance of a category of women affected by the generalization of part-time work, informal and precarious jobs, very poorly paid and not socially recognized, and unpaid work in the family business. As Sylvia Walby notes, "Women who are no longer limited to domesticity have the whole of society to roam and be exploited."[15] Indeed, the unequal social order persists and is reproduced through the gendered roles and symbolisms of social and economic life.

Positive attitudes about the authority and respect women can obtain from income-earning work was not limited to low-income women in large metropolitan areas but also was found among women in rural areas. For example, Jahân, a fifty-year-old housewife in Esboo Mahaleh near Gorgan, declared: "I agree with women's work outside the home. They must work in order to be financially independent. A woman who works is the honor of her husband."

Sadigheh, a Shi'ite from Zâhedân, declared:

> I would have liked to work but my husband is against it. He doesn't allow me to. He thinks that workplaces are not healthy for women. At first I wanted to work in the Pâsdârân. But my husband was against it. Back then the wives of the Pâsdârân were recruited without exams, but my husband did not agree. He told me that he saw vice with his own eyes ... After our son was born, he told me that if I work outside, our son will be deprived of motherly love. When my son grows older, I will ask my husband again, but I think he will be against it because he thinks the society is corrupt. It is true that we do not need my salary to live. But I like to work. To be a seamstress or a teacher. Last year I asked my husband to work with him, to be his secretary. He didn't accept. I get bored of staying at home. I am in favor of women's employment, their education and their political activities. They can represent women and their demands better than men.

Kaniz, who overvalued education, shared the same aspirations: "Girls can study better than boys. Women are much more capable than men in all activities. Women must work to be financially independent from their husbands. To build their lives, both must work." Kaniz works in the cafeteria of the local university and is very proud to be the breadwinner for her family, and to be in a position of authority. She said:

> My husband has a small retirement pension and is ill. It is thanks to my salary that we all can survive. I want my daughters to continue their studies and find a job before getting married. A woman should not rely financially on her husband. If I didn't work, we wouldn't be able to live. Then, after our death, the children will have our pensions and can continue their studies. You can't expect anything from illiterate people.

Sadigheh from the village of Keykha, and wife of a school principal, made no difference between men and women.

> Some women have the ability to be in important positions. Many women have the ability that men have. For example, I am a housewife, but I am the one who does the paperwork for my husband. I go everywhere, even to the security service bureau (harasat). In the administrations, everyone thinks that I am the school principal. But men, especially in villages and small towns, do not encourage women's activities … I know a little bit about women's rights, but the young people who are more educated know better than we do and can therefore defend their rights better.

Marziyeh, a Shi'ite housewife in Zâhedân, declared:

> Women can have the same abilities as men as long as they are educated. They do much more than men in the home. They also educate their children. It's like having two jobs. Society owes much more to women (than to men). I want my daughters to continue their studies and get highly educated. I think they also should find a job before getting married, because after marriage they won't have this opportunity. If I were educated like my husband, I could have found a job with higher income than what I earn now. Because I don't have any educational credentials, I had not many options and became a shopkeeper. My small shop is next to our house and I earn some money working some hours a day in the shop. I sell clothes and beauty supplies. I do everything myself. My husband does not interfere with my activity. I prepare the list of things I need to buy, then I go to the bazaar to purchase them and bring the goods to the shop. I spend the income I gain for the needs of my children, especially their education.

Bibi Latifeh, a Turkmen from Gonbad, said: "I agree with women's work outside the home. It is good to be financially independent and then to be present in the society. Being a teacher is very good."

However, her husband expressed a different opinion:

> I am not against women working outside the home, but I think that being a housewife also means that she has a job. From experience, I think it is better

for women to take care of the home. In our family, there are couples who both work outside the home and they have problems except when they have a mother or someone else in the home who does the housework. Then there will also be problems in the education and control of the children.

Hâjar, who lives in the village of Esboo Mahaleh, said:

I agree that women should study and find a good job. Besides, girls have better grades than boys at school. I think that a housewife also works and should have rights. But it seems to me that men have much more rights. It is true that men work more to earn the familiy's living, but women should also have rights. Some well-educated women are even capable of political activity. I don't see any problem.

Jahân's husband said: "Here women work in agriculture as much as men, maybe even more. For rice, women sow. But for cotton, all the steps are done by women. The men sell and collect the money. But we spend it on the house. The men work 365 days for the women, so the women must also work for whom"?

Jahan replied: "For the men!" Her husband said: "We have to work together to provide for our needs."

Maryam, thirty-seven, another resident of Esboo Mahaleh, a mother-of-three worked with her husband in cultivating tomatoes and cotton on land that they rent. "My husband sells the products, but he brings the money home and gives it to me."

According to our sample and observations, young and single Turkmen women shared that they were not allowed by their parents to work outside the home. If their parents possess agricultural land, they usually work on the land. They also learn handicrafts. But, once they are married, they can work outside of the home if their husband agrees. Young couples usually make decisions together, contrary to the older generation among whom the decision-making authority is exclusively held by the husband.

Oghoul's husband, a Turkmen from Gonbad, has a small business. She is a tailor and makes traditional Turkmen clothes at home. Like my other interviewees, she is proud to earn her own income and cherishes her financial independence, which allows her to make some minor decisions: "For example, if we are invited to a wedding, I can purchase the gift I want to give myself, with no need to ask my husband's money, opinion or permission. My husband tells me that I'm free to spend the money I earn from my work." However, she states that important decisions, including the purchase of their house, continue to be taken by her husband.

The social and cultural impact of women's income-earning activities still is limited, at best, to their own families and social environment. Moreover, the approval they receive has not had much of an effect on their responsibilities for domestic work and the education of children. Both of which remain almost exclusively women's domain. Many working women disapprove of this unequal division of labor at home, but for the sake of their children prefer to avoid tensions with their husbands and take on the housework. Laws, dominant ideology, and discourse along with social customs play a crucial role in maintaining the gender division of labor in the domestic and family sphere—essentially, maintaining unequal social relations between men and women.

Housework that is undertaken almost exclusively by women reinforces the practice of private patriarchy, keeping women in the private sphere, and contributes to the creation of professional inequalities for working women. Gender inequality also is reproduced in the job market through job discrimination and gender segregation who are perceived as mothers and wives throughout their professional lives. These intertwined processes thus help shape women's life experiences and maintain gendered social relations both at home and in society.

Djamileh, a forty-four-year-old Baluch mother of three daughters, works as a maternity ward nurse in Iranshahr. She was married at the age of twenty-four while she continued her studies with her husband's consent who then worked in a pharmacy. "He is a relative of my brother in law and is from a different tribe. My father was a school teacher and was polygamous. But he cherished education and encouraged us to study and to work. We are nine sisters from three different wives and we all work." Djamileh wants her daughters to pursue higher education and become autonomous. Like all other working women, Djamileh spends her salary for her family's expenditures. She says that in Baluchistan many men are unemployed and it is women who provide for their family's needs. Yet these unemployed men refuse to do the housework which is also working a woman's responsibility.

According to Madjid Malekshahi, genreal director of social protections of the Imam Relief Committee, 1,283,477 women heads of households and 2,352,842 households were under their protection in 2021. He added that 643,000 women heads of households are over sixty; 37,000 are between forty and sixty, 174,000 between thirty and forty; 79,000 between twenty and thirty; and 16,000 between fifteen and twenty. As many as 70,000 of these households live in urban areas, 58,000 in rural areas, and 3,000 are tribal.[16]

Masoumeh Ebtekar, who was President Rohani's vice-president in women's and family affairs, declared in April 2021 there were 4,500,000 women heads of households, 20 percent of whom were devoid of health insurance. She also estimated that almost 40 percent of poverty-stricken women heads of households do not benefit from insurance or any social protection.[17] Between 2011 and 2019 the number of women heads of households has increased by 27 percent, and the population in Sistan-Baluchistan have been marginalized due to the authorities' mismanagement and political and security reasons.[18]

However, gender-based social relations that are founded on a gendered division of labor can be changed through women's access to education, knowledge, technology, and related jobs.[19] Professional activities undertaken by women are likely to challenge men's authority both within the family institution and in the society. It undoubtedly will introduce a change in matrimonial harmony founded on the domination of men promoted by law. However, in the Iranian job market, the social and economic gap between college-educated active women with prestigious and well-paid jobs and less-educated women with part-time jobs in the formal or informal sectors of the economy is increasing. This adds to the heterogeneity of women and reinforces hierarchical power relations among them, which, in turn, hinders the alliance of various classes of women.

Nonetheless, in both urban and rural areas, women with a revenue-earning activity in the formal or informal sectors of the economy cherish their work. Their paid activity is a crucial means of changing the power relations both within the family and in society even though it does not lead to gender equality. It also contributes to the increase in women's awareness and interest in politics.

Despite the country's overall modernization, and women's achievements in Sunnite and/or non-Persian majority areas, regional disparities are paramount both in terms of uneven structural developments and the perception of women that are closely related to their real-life experiences. Many Baluch said they are discriminated against in matters of religion, medical care, housing, or job opportunities. Local authorities and the current government have no policy to stop ethnic segregation of the Baluch and the Turkmen. Saeid, a Sunni student from Zâhedân, declared:

> The future of my people is difficult to envisage. We are not really actors in our future, we are mainly thinking of providing for our basic needs, such as housing and food. The restrictions in terms of employment are a difficult obstacle to accept. Baluchistan is changing. But for the Baluch to really change, they would have to have other hopes than working as a trader in a bazaar. It's hard to be ambitious when you know that we'll always be left out of positions of responsibility … [20]

Although modernization processes have not led to social, economic, or cultural uniformity, they however have led to the reformulation of local/ethnic identities. Baluch and Turkmen have increasingly been influenced by the dominant cultural model presented on television or Persians they encounter every day. However, they also attempt to preserve their own identity, and especially emphasize their religious and linguistic difference.

At the same time, the integrative dimension of social change has renewed hierarchical relations and relations of domination. As a result, many Persian, Baluch, and Turkmen women, especially less-educated women, still yield to patriarchal traditions but do not consent. On the other hand, many women exert micropower within their families and environments in subtle ways. The way each woman performs should be explored in a more nuanced way through micro-sociological lenses. Another important impact of social transformation is that ethnic identities are overwhelmingly fragmented and mobilizations are increasingly located at identity-based intersections of gender, ethnicity, class, and religion.

Gender and Politics

Despite women's low political representation in national political institutions due to corporatism in polity, the involvement of educated women in politics is now widely accepted. "Ordinary" urban and rural women from all ethnicities and religions participate more in local politics because the stakes are relevant to their daily life and preoccupations. Although some Turkmen and Baluch women still understand politics as an essentially male-oriented activity, the representation of Baluch women in city and village councils has increased sharply recently. Nonetheless, their political participation is structured by the inequalities they face as women and ethnic minorities. In general, voting patterns are largely shaped by ethnic/religious affiliations.

Although women's partaking in politics, especially as voters, saw a sharp growth in the 1997, 2001, 2013 Presidential elections, 1999 local, and 2000 and 2016 legislative elections, the representation of women in national political institutions remains slim (thirteen women MPs in the reformist majority sixth Parliament elected in 2000 and seventeen in the tenth elected in 2016) and is overwhelmingly limited to the kin of the power elite. During the 2016 legislative elections, women's rights activists, both secular and religious, launched a campaign called "To End the Male-dominated Parliament." Thanks to the mobilization of women voters, eighteen women candidates, mostly from civil society, were elected, the majority of them in provincial cities. Shockingly, one elected candidate from Isfahan was disqualified because she had shaken hands with a man. The challenge has been to work to change discriminatory laws affecting women: The Constitutional Law, the Civil Code, which institutionalizes inequality in the domestic sphere and places women under the guardianship of men; the Penal Code, according to which the value of a woman's life is half that of a man's; the Inheritance Law, which grants women half the share of men; and discrimination in hiring. Moreover, although women massively voted for reformist candidates hoping that they would implement change in their legal status and condition, women's issues have been largely absent from debates between reformers and conservatives. Despite fundamental differences in their views, a consensus exists among them to perpetuate male domination and patriarchal system. According to some reformers the question of women and their legal and citizenship rights is not intertwined with the building of democracy, and therefore does not constitute an urgent issue![21] Likewise, the law continues to consider women as minors and places them for life under the guardianship of their fathers or husbands. Although the thirteen female members of the sixth parliament were gender conscious and quite active in proposing motions to ameliorate women's status (modification of the civil code, facilitating women's access to divorce, sending female students abroad, increasing the minimum age of marriage for girls from nine to eighteen, or adhering to the CEDAW), only a few legal changes have been implemented. The Guardian Council disapproved these laws arguing that they were incompatible with Islam. Finally, the minimum age of marriage and the age of penal responsibility for girls were increased to thirteen. President Khatami excluded government intervention to promote women's status arguing that the development of the civil society inevitably would contribute to satisfying women's demands and would provide women with the means to transform their demands into laws.[22] Despite the crucial role played by women in his election and re-election in 2001, Khatami conceded to conservative pressures by refusing to nominate women as ministers in his cabinet.

The persistence of gender inequality during his presidency and the sixth parliament largely disillusioned women activists who had strongly supported him and the reformers. Faced with severe criticisms by these women parliamentarians, President Khatami contented himself by saying that he was sorry. Women being disillusioned by the reformers further radicalized women activists who withdrew temporarily from the political sphere, as illustrated in their lack of mobilization in the 2004 legislative elections. These women exclusively relied on their own selves to promote women's status and the equality of rights.

The policies of the Islamic state had remained ambiguous with regard to women. The roots of this doctrinal ambiguity can be found in the very foundations of the Islamic regime which claimed to be both republican and Islamic. Its republican component praised gender equality, while its Islamic component advocated gender inequality. The failure of President Rohani like Khatami to implement change demobilized women voters. The electoral component of the regime blew up when the Leader nominated Ibrahim Raissi as the next president prior to the 2021 elections. The Islamic Republic has thus given way to the Islamic regime.

The thrusting aside of women from national politics has led many ordinary women to mistrust politics and to prefer social activities. Nonetheless, the growing plight of women toward gender equality or against gender discriminations has also led women to discover politics as a powerful agent toward implementing change in their status. As a result, in some parts of the country where women are either more politicized or more educated, women's involvement in politics and in decision-making government positions is now accepted. As Table 5.3 shows, 53 percent of women in our survey agreed with equal access for women and men to political activities. The highest rates belonged to Kurdish-speaking women (with 62.5 percent) and Persian-speaking women (with 59 percent) and the lowest rate belonged to Baluchi- and Turkmen-speaking women (23 percent). While the traditional behavior of Baluchi women with regards to politics follows their general views on other issues, Turkmen women's understanding of politics as an essentially male-oriented activity is contradictory to their more egalitarian views, as illustrated in other tables. Concerning the opinion of women on the equal access of men and women in decision-making government positions, the average rate is 52 percent, with the highest rate belonging to Kurdish-speaking women (64 percent) and the lowest belonging to Baluchi speakers (23 percent).

Kaniz, an illiterate Shi'ite woman in Zâhedân, declared: "Women, if they want to, are capable in political activities but on condition that they are educated. Highly educated women can do anything they want."

Marziyeh, a Shi'ite from Zahadan, said: "I will vote for a woman candidate in elections if she is good. Women have more potential than men." But her daughter Fatemeh thinks that men are better suited to occupy the positions of president or leader as they are more used to be active in the society, she says. Effat, her friend, thinks that there is no difference between men and women.

Djamileh, a Baluch nurse in Iranshar, stated: "When my sister Esmat registered her candidacy in Bampur for local and municipal elections, people were gossiping, but my father encouraged her to run for the elections. And she was elected. The first challenge for women candidates is to convince their families that they are as capable as male candidates."

Table 5.3 Opinion of ever-married women fifteen years and older on women's equal access to political activity, by local and ethnic language (2002).

Local and ethnic language	Rate (%)
Baluchi	23
Arabic	28
Turkmen	23
Lori	45
Persian	59
Mazandarani	41
Azari	51
Kurdish	62.5
Gilaki	54
Average	53

Source: *Socio-economic Characteristics Survey of Iranian Households (2002),* Statistical Center of Iran, National Center for Scientific Research (France), French Research Institute in Iran. Tehran, Statistical Center of Iran, 2003, P. 161.

Saideh, a Baluch social assistant, said bitterly: "I was a candidate in the first local and municipal elections in 1999 in the village where my family is from. Many men had sworn to divorce their wives (zan talâq) if I were elected. They did everything to prevent my election."

Likewise, Zeynab, an educated woman from Esboo Mahalah, argued:

The number of women in decision-making positions is very low. They don't let women hold important positions. In our country, traditions and traditional thinking and culture are still important, especially in villages or remote places. Women are limited in their action. They don't have much freedom and can't do all the jobs. For example, they are told that they are sentimental and therefore cannot be judges. In the speeches of the intellectuals, they ask for freedom of choice for women but in practice they do not have this choice. It takes time to change this mentality that women are not capable of having certain responsibilities. Even though we see that women are stronger in management and leadership than men. So why can't they lead the country?

As Table 5.4 shows, 69 percent of women in our survey were in favor of equality in decision-making positions at the local level. In terms of the spoken local language the lowest rate belonged to Baluchi women (33 percent) and the highest rate belonged to Kurdish women (77 percent) followed by Persians (73.5 percent).

Table 5.4 Opinion of ever-married women fifteen years and older on women's equal access to decision-making posts at local level, by local and ethnic language (2002).

Local and ethnic language	Rate (%)
Baluchi	33
Arabic	59
Turkmen	64
Lori	59
Persian	73.5
Mazandarani	57
Azari	71
Kurdish	77
Gilaki	69
Average	69

Source: *Socio-economic Characteristics Survey of Iranian Households (2002)*, Statistical Center of Iran, National Center for Scientific Research (France), French Research Institute in Iran. Tehran, Statistical Center of Iran, 2003, P. 161.

Table 5.5 Opinion of ever-married women fifteen years and older on women's equal access to decision-making posts at national level, by local and ethnic language (2002).

Local and ethnic language	Rate (%)
Baluchi	23
Arabic	25
Turkmen	21
Lori	47
Persian	54
Mazandarani	38
Azari	54
Kurdish	64
Gilaki	58
Average	52

Source: *Socio-economic Characteristics Survey of Iranian Households (2002)*, Statistical Center of Iran, National Center for Scientific Research (France), French Research Institute in Iran. Tehran, Statistical Center of Iran, 2003, P. 161.

My interviewees suggest that women's involvement in politics should start at the local level where elections are less politicized and women can better identify with the stakes that are more related to the everyday life of the population at hand. Indeed, women approving of women partaking in local politics is related to their daily life experiences where women usually play a more important role in managing the household, children's education, and are therefore more familiar with daily problems and needs of the population.

The first local-municipal elections in Iran were held in 1999 under President Khatami. According to Article 100 of the Constitution, social, economic, cultural, health, education, well-being, etc., programs should be applied with the cooperation of the local population, and the management of the affairs of each village, town, region, province is supervised by the councils. The aim was to elect 120,000 representatives in 37,000 villages and 721 towns. As many as 7,276 women (or 2.2 percent of the total 333,000 candidates) presented their candidacy, 11 percent of whom or 1,176 were elected: 6.4 percent or 300 in urban areas and 18.7 percent or 876 in rural areas. Tehran had the most important number of candidates (540 or 18 percent of women candidates) and Qom had the lowest (0.6 percent). Women obtained the highest number of votes in twenty towns. In Tehran, municipal council they won three seats out of fifteen. In Shiraz, one woman won the second highest number of votes. In Bahar in Hamadan province and in Urmiyeh three women won the highest number of votes. In Saveh, women won four of the seven seats, and in Kerman two seats out of four. In Guilan province, out of thirty-seven women candidates twenty-five were elected (68 percent). In twenty-eight chieftowns (at the time Iran had twenty-eight provinces, their number is now thirty-one), fifty-two candidates were elected and fifteen among them arrived in first or second position. These results show that not only do women electors trust women candidates, so do male electors, especially the more educated and active ones.

Women's candidacy and their success in rural areas illustrate the extent of the overall change in post-revolutionary Iran. Zinat Daryayi, then in her early thirties, was among the village Sunnite women who challenged traditional perception that sees political involvement and decision-making authority as an exclusive right of men. She won the highest number of votes in her village Salakh in Qeshm island, Hormozgan province, South of Iran, one of the most traditional and less-developed parts of the country. As an auxiliary nurse Zinat had been struggling for years to improve health and educational conditions in her village and had also in vain advocated the construction of a girl's high school in her village. "Each time I advocated the construction of a high-school, local authorities told me that the issue was irrelevant to my work and responsibilities." The 1999 local elections offered the much awaited opportunity to Zinat. "I had been an auxiliary nurse for 13 years. People knew me and trusted me. Many women participated in the elections to vote for me."

However, patriarchal resistance against women gaining positions of power is still very high: "Usually the person who obtains the highest number of votes becomes president of the local council. But other representatives were still not ready to accept a woman as the president of the council. Under their pressure I accepted to step down on the condition that my husband, who had been supportive of me, my opinions and activities for many years and who had won the third number of votes in the village, become president of the local council." Following her election, the first project Zinat successfully undertook was to construct a girl's high school in Salakh, allowing village girls to continue their studies.

Likewise, in 1999 local elections, Baluch were overwhelmingly elected to these councils and obtained the majority. In Sistan Baluchistan province, out of 8,006 elected representatives, almost 80 percent of all councils were won by Baluch, both men and women. In Zâhedân, Khâsh, Sarâvân, Nikshar, Châhbahâr, and Sarbâz, the rate of Baluch representatives was between 98 percent and 100 percent. A Baluch member of Zâhedân city council declared: "Following the election of President Khatami the Baluch complained about the discriminations against the Baluch. When Khatami travelled to Zâhedân and held meetings with local administrators, he realized that out of 50 only 5 were Baluch! When administrators are nominated, Baluch are either absent or rarely represented. However, when they come to office through elections, they constitute the overwhelming majority."[23] It is noteworthy to mention that reformist political parties become active only during the national elections. The Mosharekat Party (The Participation Front Party of Islamic Iran), then led by Mohammad Reza Khatami, President Khatami's brother, opened branches in Iranshahr and Khâsh. Some of our interviewees declared that tribalism is still very strong in Baluchistan and complained about lack of meritocracy. The educated youth who belong to small tribes have only a scarce chance to get elected to local councils. They thus oppose tribal structures and found civil society organizations to conduct social and cultural activities. A civil society activist in Khâsh declared: "We support meritocracy and struggle against tribalism and even Molavis (Sunnite clergy) who want to decide for us."[24] Our survey showed that a growing number of Baluch urban families debated amongst themselves and voted for their candidates without listening to the chieftains. Education, urbanization, social activities, and access to urban jobs and men's migration to other parts of the country for better job opportunities all participate in the weakening of tribalism.

Despite an average 20 percent drop in the rate of voters' participation in the 2003 municipal and local elections (49.96 percent), compared to the 1999 elections (64.42 percent), women's representation saw an 80 percent increase, mainly in villages and small towns. Likewise, in 2006 municipal elections, forty-six women, most of whom were highly educated and active, were elected in small, medium, and large towns. From among thirty chief towns, women obtained either the first or second number of votes: in Shiraz, Zanjan, Ardebil, Hamedan, Arak, Urmiyeh, and Qazvin women obtained the highest number of votes. In Ahwaz, Bandar Abbas, Sanandaj, Khorram Abad, Rostam Abad, and Qom, they obtained the second highest number of votes. In these elections, women obtained 43 seats from a total of 269 seats in municipal councils of chief towns (or 16 percent). In Qazvin and Hamedan, four women were elected to the municipal council; in Tehran, Arak, Urmiyeh, and Zanjan, the number of women elected was three.

Maryam from Esboo Mahaleh declared: "We participate in the elections. We decide together who to vote for. We discuss with my parents, in-laws, etc. and we all vote for the same candidate."

Zeynab declared:

I don't make a difference between male and female candidates. Here we did not have a female candidate. The women elected to the Sixth parliament have certainly done some things, on the cultural and sports level. But the changes were not up to the expectations of the population, neither in domestic nor in foreign policy. It must be said that the MPs' hands are tied. Certain thoughts prevail that prevent things from happening. But I still vote in elections. I want to participate in the fate of my country and want to be involved in the decisions. I want to know what is going on. What will be our future?

Fatemeh, from the village of Keykha in Sistan, agreed with the involvement of educated active women in political activities.

Fatemeh M, from Zahadân, said she voted for women and thinks that women have the same potential as men in political activities.

Roqiyyeh, from the village of Keykha, her husband, and their children participate in elections and said they are willing to vote for a woman candidate if she is good. "Sometimes we all vote the same way, sometimes not." Roqiyyeh agreed that women should have access to decision-making positions and said they have the potential.

Shahnâz, a Baluch in Zâhedân, declared: "Today, women are showing their capacity in all aspects. I think they can participate in all activities, including politics. But for that, they need to be educated." However, her son added: "Yes, but the Baluch will not let their women participate in political activities. As for the women, they can't say anything because according to the traditions it is the man who says the first and the last word." Shanâz emphasized: "We have always participated in voting. We decide together who to vote for. If there is a woman candidate, we will see if she is good and vote for her."

The ethnic/religious criteria are decisive for the vote. The Sistanis (Persians) vote for the Sistani candidates and the Baluch for the Baluch candidates. Shahnâz's son said: "We vote for the Baluch candidates so that they improve the living conditions in this province. But nothing is done." He also expressed how young voters have been misled and deceived by the reformists: "I started voting as soon as I reached the voting age. I participated in all elections and voted for Khatami. But next time I am not sure if I will go to vote."

Bibi Latifeh, a Turkmen of Gonbad Kavoos, did not agree with the political activity of women without knowing why. "I don't agree but I haven't really thought about this issue."

Her husband was against. "A woman should take care of her own life and think about the welfare of her children and her husband. Those who want to be in politics should not be married or have children."

I asked what if she has the means to take care of her children or have someone to take care of the housework? Bibi Latifeh answered: "In that case, if she has the means and her husband agrees, why not." But her husband still disagreed: "It is very difficult to be politically active. A man can take it but a woman cannot."

In Gonbad Kavoos, our Turkmen interviewees said they all participated in the voting. Even those who could not travel voted with the mobile offices. But the voting remains very community based. Turkmen all voted for Turkmen.

Jahan too said they participated in all elections. However, the voting behavior of Persians seemed different. Contrary to many Baluch and Turkmen who said they discussed amongst one another and voted as a singular group for their fellow co-religionist. Persians do not proceed the same way. The vote is more individual. As Jahan and her husband mentioned:

> We vote for the one who works well and is honest whether the person is a man or a woman. We agree on the political activity of women. There is no difference between men and women. We do not agree as a family to vote for a specific candidate. It is up to each one to decide. We don't argue but we are in a village and the environment is small. People say that this candidate is better than the others. But we never impose on each other one candidate over the others.

It is noteworthy to mention that the number of women elected to village and city councils increased from 783 in 1999 to 1,491 in 2006 and to 6,092 in 2013, the same year Rohani won the presidential elections.

For Kheyr Bibi from Zâhedân, the candidacy of a woman (Shi'ite) is not a problem for them, but Baluch women are not allowed to run. "If a Baluch woman runs for election, she will be disowned by her family. But I think that a woman should also have rights. She has the right to live, to choose." Zobeideh, her neighbor, was not against women's political activity but, like Kheyr Bibi, said that it was impossible for Baluch women to run.

Both women were wrong in their judgments and tended to generalize the norms of their own environment to all Baluch women because in several Baluch towns and villages such as Iranshahr, Zâhedân, Khâsh, and Bampur, several women had already been elected to city and village councils. Their number increased to 200 in 2013 and three Baluch women were appointed as city governors under the first Rohani government. Nonetheless, the political participation of Baluch women is structured by the inequalities they face as women, and as ethnic/religious minorities. Moreover, most of the elected Baluch women, especially in urban areas, were the educated middle class; they were supported by their families and their election was accepted because their profiles corresponded with the ideal model of women.

In 2017, during the fifth local council elections, the number of Baluch women elected to city and village councils increased sharply to 415. For example, in the fourteen villages of Khâsh,[25] two out of every three council members were women. "In Afzalâbâd, a village in Khâsh district, all 10 candidates on the council ballot were women."[26] However, some Persian journalists, both male and female, who covered the results of these elections, refused to believe in the capabilities of Baluch women. They refused to conceptualize the power of ordinary Baluch women and to confer on them the status of social and political agency. Their ethnocentric attitudes denied Baluch women their own realities, their own experiences in the construction of gender, ethnicity, religion, and the right to determine the meanings and goals of their own lives. They even fueled rumors inferring the lack of qualified male candidates as a result of high rates of drug addiction and imprisonment among men in the province, to be the reason of Baluch women's electoral success. The highly educated Persian women whose dominant discourse has been to save subaltern women could not accept the agency of the barely educated rural Baluch women and their rise to local power. The rumors were so widespread that even some foreign observers mentioned them in their articles.[27]

Despite the attempts to downplay the importance of Baluch women's ratings in the elections, their success was more likely the result of their own efforts and those by the Baluch civil society composed mainly of the youth fostering a greater political representation of women. Some of the Baluch women like Maryam Ahmadzehi, mayor of Afzalabad village, became role models for Baluch women. Here is what some of the villagers said of her efforts to better their life: "The day Ahmadzehi became Mayor, the village was in ruins, but things have changed a lot since then" (a local school headmaster). Another villager said: "Roads have been paved, new parks have been created and the village has been connected to the electricity grid." One of the candidates for the Afzalabad village council argued: "Her efforts motivated all of us to study and work."[28]

In his interview with the reformist newspaper *Sharq*, published on September 7, 2021, Molavi Abdolhamid declared: "In Zahedan, We have a city council of eleven members three of whom are women. One is a university professor, one is a cultural activist and one is a former Mayor. We asked Mr. Rohani [the former President] to nominate at least a woman and a Sunnite in his cabinet but he refused. I proposed the same idea to Mr. Raissi [the current President]."

However, the significant performance of women in elections in Sistan-Baluchistan and some other cities and villages in local 2017 elections did not shake the dominance of men. It failed to pave the way for more gender conscious women to win parliamentary seats and key positions in the government.

The neo/patriarchal political system and its logic of domination through nepotism and co-optation were further reinforced after the "presidential elections" of June 18, 2021. It took place amidst all-out political, economic, and social crises, and saw the lowest participation rate in the political life of the Islamic regime. In the face of a political system that has substituted the appointment to the election, the abstention of the majority of voters (52 percent according to official statistics) reflected a strong political act that intended to delegitimize the Islamic regime. In addition to the abstention, there were 3.7 million invalid ballots (second after Raissi votes). The architecture of the presidential elections was designed to elect Ibrahim Raissi, head of the judiciary, appointed by the Leader and supported by a large coalition of ultraconservatives and part of the Revolutionary Guards (Pâsdârâns), several of whom were candidates but withdrew to support him. The factional and plebiscitary character of the political system or its "republican" component is thus replaced by an Islamic regime. Under Ibrahim Raissi's presidency, the ultraconservatives further restrict individual and collective freedoms and continue to impose conservative and religious values through repressive measure. The political and religious power has been talibanized. In order to maintain the social order and assure its hegemony, the state pursues a repressive policy against active social groups. It continues to apply a social policy aimed at the voluntary servitude of individuals who benefit from state aid, and at the same time, it denies the population political citizenship, locking them out of the decision-making processes. But, as the record of the past four decades has shown, society will continue to gain ground through its resilience and will attempt through its actions to influence the structures and the system.

While I proof read my book, the Islamic regime is being challenged by the overwhelming majority of the population as evidenced by street protests, strikes in universities and schools, businesses, factories and the oil and petrochemical industries, despite the fierce repression of opponents, including children. For the first time in Iran's history, women from various social groups, ethnicities and religions, are at the forefront of the protests. The discrepancies between the demands of a modern society and an ideological power with archaic institutions and laws that reinforce social inequalities and has led the country into a deep and all-encompassing economic, political, social, cultural and environmental crisis explain the rejection of the Islamic regime. A country marked by a long history and an ethnic, religious, linguistic, gender and class diversity that Iranians in struggle are trying to save from destruction and death. Hence the slogan Woman, Life, Freedom.

Conclusion

This work has highlighted the experiences of non-Persian Sunnite women and other subaltern women, especially in Sistan-Baluchistan and Golestan provinces, who have largely been excluded from what is considered knowledge of women in Iran. It also attempted to examine the articulations between four distinct but associated processes in the making of unequal social relations in contemporary Iran, namely gender, ethnicity, class, and religion. Women who are supposed to reproduce the existing boundaries of groups are at the heart of the processes of national and ethnic/religious re-construction. My research rejected a distinction between micro- and macro-levels of analysis and combined quantitative and qualitative methods that aided in the ability to grasp the articulations between social determinants and women's individual subjectivities.

This work is critical of nationalist/Islamist discourses and policies that, throughout the twentieth and the twenty-first centuries, have tended to marginalize entire segments of the population for their ethnic, religious, or gender belongings. Since the advent of the modern nation-state under Reza Shah in the 1920s, the Persian language has appeared as the most permanent foundation of nationalism and its drive to uniformity. Westernized nationalism inspired by European Orientalism intended to erase ethnic identities in favor of Persianity. Persian language and a pre-Islamic past made Iranian nationalism an attractive ideology, later endorsed by the Pahlavi dynasty. In 1971, the organization of Persepolis ceremonies for the 2,500th anniversary of the Iranian monarchy, and the change in Calendar accordingly marked Iran's separation from the Islamic world. Orientalism and nationalist ideology also made use of male-dominant discourse and attempted to stabilize the hierarchical social order and the so-called "natural" stability of gender categories.

Under the Pahlavis, religion was not a decisive factor in determining social hierarchy. However, official aspirations to uniformity invited all members of ethnic groups to conform their way of life to a new model defined in a Persianized and pro-Western manner. Each nonconforming element was regarded as a sign of backwardness and a possible threat to the modern nation and territorial integrity. Homogenizing identity tended to erase linguistic, ethnic, cultural differences and replace them with a uniform language, culture, literature, art, and ethnicity. Western-oriented nationalism under the Pahlavis served to enforce the power of Persian men over women, and ethnic and religious minorities. Four layers of significance were assigned to women in nation-building projects: their capacity to give birth, their assigned role as primary caregivers to children; their representation as the symbols of the nation; and finally their bodies as metonyms for the homeland.

The model of an ideal woman was that of a Persian, urban-middle-class, modern, unveiled, educated but modest woman: a good mother and wife. The goal was to create national identities by bringing together membership of the political nation-state and identification with the national/Persian-centered culture. This type of nation-state building aimed at cultural and linguistic uniformity of a multi-ethnic Iran, which was supposed to promote allegiance to the Pahlavi regime. Regional, tribal, and ethnic uprisings and movements were crushed under both Reza Shah in the 1920s and 1930s and Mohammad Reza Shah in the 1940s.

Under the Islamic regime, Islamist/nationalism has intended to crush non-Shi'ite religious identities. In recent decade, the expansion of education has led to the hegemony of the Persian language. However, aspirations of religious/ethnic minorities to be included in the national political community have been shattered due to the all-out discrimination mainly based on religion that has impeded the completion of the nation-state building project.

The Shi'ite dimension of Iranian identity was emphasized to the detriment of other dimensions, and other religious groups, especially the Sunnites but also non-Muslims and Bahais. The political system is founded on Shi'ism as the political ideology of the state apparatus, and the implemented state policies consolidated social hierarchy founded on religious and gendered social relations. Cultural/religious difference between some ethnic-religious minorities and Persian-Shi'ites is often used to mark an essentialized hierarchy or what can be called *cultural racialization*. The expansion of education (in Persian) throughout Iran has contributed to the hegemony of the Persian language. Therefore, ethnicization or cultural racialization is based on religious difference rather than linguistic one. If the religious frame of reference can lead to racialized assignment and ethnicization, it sometimes activates forms of ordinary mobilization of resistance or individual and collective resilience. Moreover, the hegemony of Persian language has not led to the erasure of non/Persian languages. Recurrent demands for these languages to be taught at schools and universities, especially in non-Persian majority provinces, have been renewed.

Under the Islamic regime, nationalism and Shi'ism have steadily strengthened and reinforced the masculinity of the men of the Shi'ite nation and its corollary, Shi'ite femininity—a femininity in which the main components are vulnerability, sacrifice, and purity. The model of an ideal woman is that of an urban-middle-class, Shi'ite, veiled, educated but modest woman: a good mother and wife. In both monarchical and Islamist models, women belonging to religious and ethnic minorities, especially Sunnites, are excluded from the state-initiated construction of modern women.

However, Iran as a modern nation-state is existing in the condition of cultural hybridity. Contrary to the essentialist approach to ethnicity according to which ethnic groups are natural and unchanging, ethnic relations are above all social relations. Economic and political inequalities produce ethnicity, ethnic groups, and ethnic claims. However, ethnicity might also be the necessary place or space from which marginalized people speak. Ethnicity thus becomes a resource in the hands of actors who appropriate it and mobilize a category built from the outside. On the other hand, the economic, cultural, and political stranglehold of Shi'ites/Persians over Sunnites propels some of the latter to show their "Persian/Shi'ite credentials" by distinguishing themselves from other Sunnites.

In this study I examined various dimensions of the question of ethnic boundaries:

- Geographical boundaries that both separate and divide ethnic groups (Baluch in Iran, Pakistan, Afghanistan; Turkmen in Iran and Turkmenistan, etc.). They rarely marry their ethnic counterparts who live beyond national geographical boundaries.
- Boundaries between ethnic/religious minority groups and the majority groups whose members qualify themselves as "non-ethnic." Persians/Shi'ites differentiate themselves from other ethnic/religious groups, feel superior to others, claim to represent the universal, and require that their dominant norms be respected. This process of othering is supported by both central and local authorities who are Persian/Shi'ites.
- Boundaries founded on social hierarchies that are paramount amongst the same ethnic groups, based on rural-urban-tribal, social class, educational level, wealth, etc., divides.
- Boundaries between ethnic groups themselves (for example, Baluch and Turkmen in Golestan province). According to our observations, although Turkmen are Sunnite, they feel superior to the Baluch and tend to side with the Persian majority who are also Shi'ite and control resource distribution.

Contrary to ethnic/religious minorities, Persian/Shi'ites do not perceive themselves as belonging to an ethnicity. As our research illustrates, they instead identify with the dominant groups even though they are critical of their social and economic conditions. Therefore, social class is overshadowed by religious and ethnic affiliations. The same can more or less be argued for religious/ethnic minorities who, faced with discrimination and marginalization imposed by the majority, tend to side with other members of their community regardless of class interests. Ethnic minorities are denied legitimate access to the state's resources and cannot achieve their expectations. If ethnicity traditionally appears as the result of an identity assignment, which aims to differentiate "us" (Persan/Shi'ites) and "the others" (ethnic and religious minorities) who are supposed to be the only bearers of ethnic identity and attribute, it becomes a resource in the hands of actors who appropriate it and mobilize a category built from the outside.

As shown through interviews, the propensity of these "ordinary" individuals to essentialize religious differences between Shi'ites and Sunnites as a natural entity is also shared by individuals belonging to religious minorities. Therefore, under the current circumstances, religious boundaries between Shi'ites and Sunnites are more preponderant than class or ethnicity. The ethnicization of Sunnite religion in everyday life is paramount and the local and central authorities contribute tremendously to enforce religious divisions in order to divide the have nots and to rule. This process of othering reinforces the ethnicized social order that is already set in place. This ethnicized hierarchy, however, is not hermetically sealed, as there is considerable differentiation and fluidity within it. Moreover, like other power relations it can be changed. In fact, this model of power is increasingly challenged by aspirations for full citizenship rights of both marginalized men and women brought about by social, economic, and cultural change.

The book also qualifies the Islamic regime a gender regime defined as a series of gendered and interconnected relations and institutions that together constitute a system.[1] I argued that the Islamic gender regime operates across four institutional domains: family, polity, economy, and civil society. As interviews and discussions show, in spite of public policies that aim to reinforce gender power relations, the weakening of patriarchal order within the families, women's partaking in social and economic activities, and local politics tend to weaken the grasp of the public gender regime and the gender social order. In recent years, minority women's access to education and professional activities and local political representation have led some Sunnite religious authorities (molavis) to endorse women's active role in society.

As a specialist of Turkey stated, "A search for a path to go beyond identity politics, without totally condemning them, should not be based upon the idea of rejecting identities as political subjects. Instead, there is a need to articulate a theory of power which allows us to develop counter-political strategies based on intersubjective, intersectional analysis [...]."[2] Intersectionality is meaningful in better identifying the various interactions of ethnicity, class, religion, and gender in the context of discrimination. While I believe that intersectionality is likely to theorize social inequalities, I opt for the relative autonomy of systems of social inequalities. According to the results of my fieldwork, social inequalities (of gender, class, religion, ethnicity) do not have the same trajectories of change even though they feed and influence each other. For example, social class is not necessarily intertwined with religion. Some Shi'ites in my survey lived in the same neighborhoods and shared more or less the same social conditions of poverty as the Baluch. However, they belonged to the dominant religion and the national majority, thus identifying with the privileged in comparison to the Baluch. In contrast, the educated middle-class Baluch women were culturally closer to their Persian counterparts than to Baluch lower-class women or conservative women belonging to the chieftain families. Here, the ethnic/religious component of identity construction is less influential than gender and social class along with educational credential components. Women's education leading to the rise of the ethnic educated professional middle classes is a quite new phenomenon and has not followed the same trajectory as ethnicity. Likewise, Baluch and Turkmen are discriminated against due to their Sunnite religion rather than to their ethnicity. In Golestân province, for example, villages such as Safiâbâd were constructed by the Housing Foundation (Bonyâd-i Maskan) to relocate Azaris from Khorasan and Sabzevâr who are not Persian but are Shi'ites, while the same authorities usually refuse to construct modern villages for Baluch or Turkmen. In a Shi'ite majority society, Sunnism has become a crucial marker of identity, especially since the advent of the Islamic regime which, in fact, has made Shi'ism, not Islam, the official religion of the country. Religion has therefore become a grid for reading the uneven social relations that tend to justify domination. Intersectionality is not a demand for identity, not a theory initiating a process of discovering a complex world. Intersectionality can and should have the capacity to theorize social inequalities in a way to make the social change easier.[3]

Shi'ite-centric prejudice has also led to the tightening of control wherein ethnic and religious minorities exert on their women as symbolic agents of group identity, biological and cultural reproducers of ethnic community, in charge of transmission of ancestral values to their children, symbols of ethnic unity and its own essence. Concomitantly, social transformations of the past several decades have pushed children and the youth at the center of their families. They are now much more educated than before, speak Persian fluently, and cherished and valued by their families.

It is through the process of primary socialization which operates in families from early age that ethnicity is inscribed in individuals. The family is also a place where gender identity is formed. Individual subjectivity, gender, religious, ethnic, or class, is inseparable from the experience that produces it. In some cases, the parents transformed the religion, both Shi'ite and Sunnite, into a natural and hereditary attribute.

However, the family institution is a site of power, and by analyzing family dynamics and women's everyday life, we can better understand the politics of ordinary Iranians and the relationship between state and society. The underlying assumption is that the private and public spheres are not separable worlds, but rather they are interconnected and are elements of the same socio-economic system.

The religious and political elite attempted to Islamize the family through the Islamic laws in order to make this institution a place of rapprochement between society and the Islamic state. These laws tend to regulate and naturalize the social relations of gender, maintaining the binarity oppositions. In addition to laws, they attempted to enforce the patriarchal family by means of a public policy which encourages marriage, especially among young people, in addition to a recent return to pro-birth policy that was enforced during the first decade of the Islamic regime. The womb has become "the predominant biopolitical space"[4] for the Islamic state to practice sovereignty. These policies, however, have failed, thanks to the better education of women, postponing the age of the first marriage, economic crisis, youth unemployment, the high costs of living and housing, and the modernization of women's social, cultural, and demographic behaviors.

The number of poor has increased steadily. Yet poverty affects women more than men, particularly the women heads of households. Wage labor is a financial alternative to women's traditional dependence in the private sphere. It is a crucial component of the transformation of gender relations, even if it does not succeed in protecting women from poverty. Among the women surveyed in urban and rural areas, whether educated or illiterate or with low literacy levels, those who had a paid activity in the formal or informal sectors all valued their work despite the sometimes very difficult working conditions.

Micropolitical practices made possible by the access of ethnic, rural, and lower-class women to education and professionalization played a crucial role in the intellectual empowerment of ethnic activists. The thrusting aside of women from national politics has led many ordinary women to mistrust politics and to prefer social activities or local politics. The ethnic/religious affiliations are decisive criteria for voting. The significant performance of women in Sistan-Baluchistan and other cities and villages in the 2017 local elections shows that their fellow voters trust women. Nevertheless, their victory did not shake the dominance of men, nor did it pave the way for more gender conscious women to win parliamentary seats and key positions in the government.

Within a global gender regime, and specific social, religious, and cultural context, ethnic/minority women deploy specific strategies of subtle resistance, of appropriation to try to alleviate the inequalities relative to the gendered social order. In a silent, dispersed, and diffused manner, Baluch, Turkmen, and subaltern Persian women develop other ways to cope with or challenge the patriarchal order. As Saba Mahmood argued: "Effecting change in the world does not necessarily mean challenging power or undoing norms. It is entirely possible to articulate change by putting existing norms into action."[5] Many minority women have a good understanding of gender, class, ethnic/religious discriminations, but because of the everyday constrictions placed on their lives, they cannot risk struggling against them all. If clan solidarities favoring endogamous marriages persist, a key reason would be that as the groom is a relative, the risk of mal treatment, conjugal violence, etc., toward a woman might be less than with non-relatives.

These ordinary women, however, are undoubtedly in the process of becoming agents of social change. The most crucial change is their better education, and their access to the institutes of higher education, their professionalization, and their new perceptions. These almost ordinary citizens, who, in their daily lives, practice creative strategies against inequalities, think and act in relation to their immediate environments. The consequences of their thinking and actions may, however, be national because they aim to compete with both the homogenizing Western-centric and Islamist-centric perspectives. If given the chance, they have the potential to produce a non-hegemonic universality in national bodies and politics.

These women, whose process of subjectivation interacts with unequal social relations, mobilize the interactional networks of relationships as well as the cultural resources of both Persian/Shi'ite and Baluch, Turkmen/Sunnite environments for strategic purposes. Many now refuse any assigned identities which give them a choice between the absolute Other or the domesticated Other, and they can claim their inclusion in the local, national, and global sphere of politics. The subtle struggle of these "ordinary" women has not been recognized and taken seriously, mainly because strategies they deploy and their repertoire of action are very different from the ones mobilized by women's rights activists in large towns, especially Tehran.

In Iran as elsewhere in the Middle East and beyond, women's rights movements have been overwhelmingly limited to urban upper and educated middle class often Persian women. However, this domination has been challenged by the emerging social activists in Sunnite regions, many of whom have had access to higher education and have become professionals, entrepreneurs, teachers, or medical doctors. Some have been elected to local councils, and some even became mayors. These women have become role models for other minority women. The number of activists from subaltern ethnic social groups, who have had access to Persian-dominated women's rights associations, remains very low, and minority, marginalized voices and discourses are still largely concealed in feminist activities in both Iran and within the diaspora. Mainstream Feminist social activities have added issues relevant to subaltern women as variables to analyze without re-conceptualizing the knowledge systems based on urban Persian/Shiite middle-class experiences. This token inclusion means that women's rights activists and specialists have not yet learnt to unlearn. Following Teresa de Lauretis it can be argued: "feminist theory begins when the feminist critique of ideologies becomes conscious of itself and turns to question its own body of writing and critical interpretations, its basic assumptions and terms, and the practices which they enable and from which they emerge."[6]

It is necessary to grasp the meaning, subjectivities, agency, and practices deployed by women belonging to ethnic and religious minorities as well as other subaltern groups. In their daily lives, they attempt to implement subtle change within their own families and social environment while avoiding conflict with their husbands, fathers, etc., who also suffer from all-out class, ethnicity, religious, discrimination. These women refuse to abandon their affiliations and social identifications to enter the public sphere dominated by Persian/Shi'ite's, with an Islamist political elite that have made the Sunnites a problem.

Despite class, religion, ethnicity, sexuality, or rural-urban divide, many women share experiences and question the gender inequalities in both the family and society. They are likely to build a collective body of wisdom but they should first share their experiences. To do so, women, both activists and ordinary women from different religious and ethnic belongings, need to engage in a substantial critical approach to Islamist/Shi'ite ideology of the state and to the rise of the new nationalism among its opponents.

It is therefore urgent to acknowledge the diversity and plurality of experiences of oppression and injustice and to include multiple and discordant voices, in the historical and cultural dialogue, in order to achieve a non-hegemonic definition of Iranian national identity. The claims of minority groups are relevant to inequalities in the distribution of economic, political, and cultural power, and represent real social issues. Ethnic identity should not be securitized for, as this research clearly shows, it is not incompatible with national belonging. The Islamic state policies have tended to securitize and marginalize ethnic/religious minorities and exclude them from the national identity which the state defines exclusively as Shi'ite. The Iranian national identity is composed of a multiplicity of belongings: genders, religions, ethnicities, social classes. Likewise, the orientalist discourse on national identity that is overwhelmingly present in the new nationalist discourse needs to be scrutinized and criticized.

Finally, and as Kimberlé Crenshaw argued, we need to change the way we look at the discrimination that structures policy. Placing the marginalized at the center is the most effective way to resist efforts that divide or fragment experiences and overlook potential collective action.[7]

Notes

Introduction

1   Azadeh Kian, *Les femmes iraniennes entre islam, Etat et famille*, Paris, Maisonneuve & Laros, 2002.

2   Azadeh Kian and Bernard Hourcade, "Nommer les banlieues de Téhéran," in H. Rivière d'Arc (ed.), *Nommer les nouveaux territoires urbains*, Paris, Editions de la Maison des Sciences de l'Homme, 2001, PP. 189–210.

3   In Iran, all Persians are Shi'ite but all Shi'ites are not Persian. For example, Azeris, the second largest ethnicity, after Persians are also Shi'ite.

4   Azadeh Kian, "Social and Cultural Change and the Women's Rights Movement in Iran," in A. Sreberny and M. Torfeh (eds.), *Cultural Revolution in Iran: Contemporary Popular Culture in the Islamic Republic*, London & New York, I.B.Tauris, 2013, PP. 43–57.

5   As Elisabeth Cunin has pointed out in her study of migration: Elisabeth Cunin, "La globalisation de l'ethnicité?," *Autrepart*, No. 38, 2006, PP. 3–13. See Kian & Hourcade, " Nommer les banlieues de Téhéran." Ibid.

6   Kian & Hourcade. Ibid.

7   See, for example, Farideh Koohi-Kamali, *The Political Development of the Kurds in Iran: Pastoral Nationalism*, New York, Palgrave Macmillan, 2003; Shahrzad Mojab (ed.), *Women of a Non-State Nation: The Kurds*, Costa Mesa, Mazda Publishers, 2001; Abbas Vali, *The Forgotten Years of Kurdish Nationalism in Iran*, London, Palgrave Macmillan, 2019.

8   Sahar Shakiba, Omid Ghaderzadeh, and Valentine Moghadam, "Women in Iranian Kurdistan: Patriarchy and the Quest for Empowerment," *Gender and Society*, Vol. 35, No. 4, 2021, PP. 616–42.

9   Shakiba, Ghaderzadeh, Moghadam. Ibid. P. 636.

10   Fatemeh Karimi's, *Genre et militantisme au Kurdisatn d'Iran. Les femmes kurdes de Komala 1979–1991*, Paris, L'Harmattan, 2022, P. 84.

11   Temporary marriage is specific to the twelver Shi'ism. It can be concluded between a single woman and a man who can be married. The duration of the marriage and the financial compensation for the temporary wife are determined by the partners. The aim of temporary marriage is not child bearing but if children are born into this type of marriage, the genitor should recognize them, give them his name and children can inherit from their father. No divorce is possible in temporary marriage.

12 Some results of the quantitative survey are published in Azadeh Kian, "From Motherhood to Equal Rights Advocates: The Weakening of Patriarchal Order," in *Iranian Studies*, Vol. 38, No. 1, March 2005, PP. 45–66. Reprinted in Homa Katouzian and Hossein Shahidi (eds.), *Iran in the 21th Century*, London, Routledge, 2008.

13 Iran Statiscal Yearbook, 1397/2018, P. 155. https://www.amar.org.ir/Portals/1/yearbook/1397/03.pdf.

14 Michel Foucault. *Le Pouvoir psychiatrique, Cours au Collège de France, année 1973–1974*, Paris, Éditions Gallimard/ Seuil. 2003. Michel Foucault, *Sécurité, territoire, population, Cours au Collège de France, année 1977–1978*, Paris, Éditions Gallimard/Seuil, 2004.

15 Armelle Testenoire, "Genre, stratification et mobilité sociale au sein des classes populaires," *Lien social et Politique*, No. 74, 2015, PP. 19–36.

16 Olivier Schwartz, "Peut-on parler des classes populaires?" *La vie des idées*. http://www.laviedesidees.fr/IMG/pdf/20110913_schwartz.pdf.2011: 23. The term continuum does not simply express a diversification of living conditions, but also the existence of an internal hierarchy between different strata perceived as such by those concerned. Yasmine Siblot, Marie Cartier, Isabelle Coutant (dirs.), *Sociologie des classes populaires contemporaines*. Paris, Armand Colin, 2015.

17 Judith Butler, "Performative Agency," *Journal of Cultural Economy*, Vol. 3, No. 2, 2010, PP. 147–61, DOI: 10.1080/17530350.2010.494117 & Judith Butler, *Gender Trouble. Feminism and the Subversion of Identity*, London & New York, Routledge, 1999 (re-edition).

18 Michel Foucault, "The Subject and Power," in H. Dreyfus and P. Rabinow (eds.), *Beyond Structuralism and Hermaneutics*, Chicago, University of Chicago Press, 1983, PP. 208–26.

19 Saba Mahmood, *Politics of Piety. The Islamic Revival and the Feminist Subject*, Princeton & Oxford, Princeton University Press, 2005.

20 Mahmood. Ibid. P. 18.

21 Azadeh Kian, "Gender, Ethnicity and Identity in Iran: Surrender without Consent. Baluchi Women in Changing Contexts," in Leif Stenberg and Eric Hooglund (eds.), *Navigating Contemporary Iran. Challenging Economic, Political and Social Perceptions*, London & New York, Routledge, 2012, PP. 117–38.

22 Nicole-Claude Mathieu, *L'anatomie politique, Catégorisations et idéologies du sexe*, Paris, Côtés-femmes, 1991.

23 Patricia Hill Collins, *On Intellectual Activism*, Philadelphia, Temple University Press, 2013, P. 16.

24 Norbert Elias, "Problems of Involvement and Detachment," *British Journal of Sociology*, Vol. 7, No. 3, 1956, PP. 226–52.

25 Norbert Elias, *The Civilizing Process*, Vol. 1: *The History of Manners*, Oxford, Basil Blackwell, 1978, P. 153.

26 Catharine Mackinnon, *Toward a Feminist Theory of the State*, Londres, Harvard University Press, 1989, P. 16.

27 Sandra Harding, "The Instability of the Analytical Categories of Feminist Theory," *Signs*, Vol. 11, No. 4, Summer 1986, PP. 645–64.

28 Danièle Kergoat, "La division sexuelle du travail et les rapports sociaux de sexe," in Hirata et al. (eds.), *Dictionnaire critique du féminisme*, Paris, PUF, 2000, PP. 66–71.

29 Teresa de Lauretis, *Théorie queer et culture populaire. De Foucault à Cronenberg*, trans. M. H. Bourcier, Paris, La Dispute, 2007, PP. 55–6 (my translation).

30 Ahmad Ashraf, "Theocracy and Charisma: New Men of Power in Iran," *International Journal of Politics, Culture and Society*, Vol. 4, NO. 1, 1990, PP. 113–52.

31 Stuart Hall, "The question of cultural identity," in S. Hall, D. Held, and T. McGrew (dirs.), *Modernity and Its Futures*, Cambridge, Polity Press in Association with the Open University, 1992, PP. 273–325.

32 Roland Pfefferkorn, "Rapports de racisation, de classe, de sexe." ... *Migrations Société*, 133, 2011, PP. 193–208. https://doi.org/10.3917/migra.133.0193.

33 Sylvia Walby, *Globalization and Inequalities: Complexity and Contested Modernities*, London, Sage, 2009, P. 301.

34 Sylvia Walby, "Varieties of Gender Regimes," *Social Politics*, Vol. 27, No. 3, 2020, P. 427.

35 Valentine Moghadam, "Theorization of Varieties of Gender Regimes and Feminist Movements," *Social Politics*, Vol. 27, No. 3, 2020, P. 479.

36 Valentine Moghadam, *Modernizing Women: Gender and Social Change in the Middle East*, Boulder, CO, Lynne Rienner Publishers, 1993, P. 111.

37 *The Combahee River Collective Statement*. https://www.blackpast.org/african-american-history/combahee-river-collective-statement-1977/.

38 bell Hooks, *Talking Back: Thinking Feminist, Thinking Black*, Boston, South End Press, 1989; Patricia Hill Collins, *Black Feminist Thought*, second edition, London & New York, Routledge, 2009.

39 Patricia Hill Collins, *Black Feminist Thought*, New York and London, Routledge, 2000, P. 28.

40 Collins. Ibid. P. 320.

41 Patricia Hill Collins & Sirma Bilge, *Intersectionality*, second edition, UK, Polity Press, Cambridge, 2016, 2020, P. 20.

42 Patricia Hill Collins, *Intersectionality as Critical Social Theory*, Durham & London, Duke University Press, 2019, P. 21.

43 Collins. Ibid. P. 22.

44 Gloria T. Hull, Patricia Bell Scott, and Barbara Smith, *All Women Are White, All the Blacks Are Men, But Some of Us Are Brave*, New York, Feminist Press, 1982.

45 Kimberlé Crenshaw, "Demarginalizing the Intersection of Race and Sex, a Black Feminist Critique of Antidiscrimination Doctrine, Feminist Theory and Antiracist Politics," *University of Chicago Legal Forum*, Vol. 1989, No. 1, Article 8, P. 27. http://chicagounbound.uchicago.edu/uclf/vol1989/iss1/8.

46 Crenshaw. Ibid. P. 31.

47 Crenshaw. Ibid. P. 33.

48 Candace West, "Goffman in Feminist Perspective," *Sociological Perspectives*, Vol. 39, No. 3, 1996, PP. 353–69.

49 Hae Yeon Choo and Myra Marx Ferree, "Practicing Intersectionality in Sociological Research: A Critical Analysis of Inclusions, Interactions, and Institutions in the Study of Inequalities," *Sociological Theory*, Vol. 28, No. 2, June 2010, PP. 129–49. https://doi.org/10.1111/j.1467-9558.2010.01370.x.

50 Walby, *Globalization and Inequalities*. Ibid.

51 Avtar Brah, *Diaspora, Border, and Transnational Identities, in Feminist Postcolonial Theory*, London: Routledge, 2003, P. 633.

52 Nancy Fraser, "Rethinking Recognition," *New Left Review*, Vol. 3, 2000, PP. 107–20. Here P. 109.

53 Fraser. Ibid. P. 119.

54 Nira Yuval Davis, "Beyond the Recognition and Redistribution Dichotomy: Intersectionality and Stratification," in H. Lutz, M. T. H. Vivar, and L. Supik (dirs.), *Framing Intersectionality. Debates on a Multi-Faceted Concept in Gender Studies*, Berlington, Ashgate, 2011, PP. 155–69.

55 Nira Yuval Davis, *The Situated Politics of Belonging*, London, Sage, 2006, P. 198.

56 Davis. Ibid. P. 166.

57 Stuart Hall, *Nouvelles ethnicités*, Paris, Amsterdam, 2007.

58 Kathy Davis, "Intersectionality as Buzzword. A Sociology of Science Perspective on What Makes a Feminist Theory Successful," *Feminist Theory*, Vol. 9, No. 1, PP. 67–85.

59 Davis. Ibid.

60 Sylvia Walby, "Globalization and Multiple Inequalities," in Esther Ngan-Ling Chow, Marcia Texler Segal, and Lin Tan (eds.), *Analyzing Gender, Intersectionality, and Multiple Inequalities: Global, Transnational and Local Contexts (Advances in Gender Research, Volume 15)*, Bingley, Emerald Group Publishing Limited, 2011, PP. 17–33.

61 Leslie McCall, "The Complexity of Intersectionality," *Signs*, Vol. 30, No. 3, 2005, PP. 1771–800.

62 Patricia Hill Collins, "Still Brave? Black Feminism and a Sovial Justice Project," in Patricia Hill Collins (ed.), *On Intellectual Activism*, Philadelphia, Temple University Press, 2013, PP. 49–62. Here P. 61.

63 Collins, *Intersectionality as Critical Social Theory*. Ibid. 2019.

64 Judith Butler, *Gender Trouble*, New York & London, Routledge, 1990, P. 143.

Chapter 1

1 Danielle Juteau, *L'ethnicité et ses frontières*, Montreal, Les presses de l'université de Montréal, 1999, P. 175.

2 Juteau. Ibid. PP. 11, 14–15, 26.

3 Milton J. Esman, *An Introduction to Ethnic Conflict*, Cambridge, Polity, 2004, PP. 30–40.

4 Stuart Hall, "The Local and the Global: Globalization of Ethnicity," in Anthony D. King, (ed.), *Culture, Globalization and the World-System: Contemporary Conditions for the Representation of Identity*, Minneapolis, University of Minnesota Press, 1997, P. 39.

5 Elisabeth Cunin, "La globalisation de l'ethnicité ?" *Autrepart*, No. 38, 2006, PP. 3–13, 4–5.

6 Hamid Ahmadi, *Ethnicity* and Ethnicism in Iran. From to Fiction to Reality (in Persian), Tehran, Ney, 1378/2000, PP. 51–2.

7 Aimé Césaire, *Discours sur le colonialisme, suivi de discours sur la Négritude*, Présence Africaine, 2000.

8 Shahrzad Mojab, "The Solitude of the Stateless: Kurdish Women at the Margins of Feminist Knowledge," in Shahrzad Mojab (ed.), *Women of a Non-state Nation: The Kurds*, Costa Mesa, Mazda Publishers, 2001, PP. 1–20. Here PP. 1 and 12.

9 Alam Saleh, *Ethnic Identity and the State in Iran*, New York, Palgrave Macmillan, 2013, P. 111.

10 Saleh. Ibid. P. 21.

11 Juteau, *L'ethnicité et ses frontières*. Ibid. PP. 20–2.

12 Nina Eliasoph, "Making a Fragile Public: A Talk Centered Study of Citizenship and Power," *Sociological Theory*, Vol. 14, No. 3, 1996, PP. 262–89.

13 Fiona Wilson and Bodil Folke Frederiksen (eds.), *Ethnicity, Gender and the Subversion of Nationalism*, London, Frank Cass, 1996, P. 12.

14 Richard Tapper, "Ethnicity, Order and Meaning in the Anthropology of Iran and Afganisatan," in Jean-Pierre Digard (ed.), *Le fait ethnique en Iran et en Afghanistan*, Paris, CNRS éditions, 1988, PP. 21–34. Here P. 31.

15 Fiona Wilson, "Race and Gender in Postcolonial Peru," in Fiona Wilson and Bodil Folke Frederiksen (ed.), *Ethnicity, Gender and the Subversion of Nationalism*. Ibid. P. 32.

16 Eric Hobsbawm, *Nations and Nationalism Since 1780: Programme, Myth, Reality*, Cambridge, Cambridge University Press, 1992, P. 8.

17 Mohamad Tavakoli-Targhi, "From Patriotism to Matriotism: A Topological Study of Iranian Nationalism, 1870–1909," *International Journal of Middle East Studies*, Vol. 34, No. 2, May 2002, PP. 217–38. Here P. 218.

18 Tavakoli-Targhi. Ibid. P. 220.

19 Nira Yuval-Davis, *Gender and Nation*, London, SAGE Publications, 1997.

20 Yuval-Davis, *Gender and Nation*, op.cit., P. 23. Lisa Bernstein, (M)Othering the
    nation. *Constructing and Resisting National Allegories through the Maternal Body*,
    Newcastel, Cambridge Scholars Publishing, 2008.

21 Ruth Miller, *The Limits of Bodily Integrity: Abortion, Adultery, and Rape Legislation
    in Comparative Perspective*, Aldershot, Ashgate, 2007, P. 149.

22 Paul Vieille and Morteza Kotobi, "Familles et unions de familles en Iran," *Cahiers
    internationaux de sociologie*, nouvelle série, No. 41, juillet-décembre 1966,
    PP. 93–104.

23 Paul Vieille, "Iranian Women in Family Alliance and Sexual Politics," in Lois Beck
    and Nikki Keddie (eds.), *Women in the Muslim World*, Cambridge, MA, Harvard
    University Press, 1978, PP. 451–72. Here P. 470.

24 Firoozeh Kashani-Sabet, *Conceiving Citizens. Women and the Politics of Motherhood
    in Iran*, New York, Oxford University Press, 2011, P. 190.

25 Nira Yuval-Davis et Floya Anthias, *Woman-Nation-State*, London, Macmillan,
    1989, PP. 1–15.

26 Afsaneh Najmabadi, *Women with Mustaches and Men without Beards. Gender
    and Sexual Anxieties of Iranian Modernity*, Berkeley et Los Angeles, University of
    California Press, 2005.

27 Mohamad Takavoli-Targhi, "From Patriotism to Matriotism." Ibid. P. 233.

28 Afsaneh Najmabadi, "The Erotic Vatan as Beloved and Mother." *Comparative
    Studies in Society and History*, Vol. 39, 1997, PP. 442–67. Here P. 450.

29 Najmabadi, *Women with Mustaches and Men without Beards*. Ibid.

30 Afsaneh Najmabadi, "Is Our Time Remembered"? *Iranian Studies*, Vol. 29, 1996,
    PP. 85–109.

31 Janet Afary, *The Iranian Constitutional Revolution, 1906–11. Grassroots Democracy,
    Social Democracy, and the Origins of Feminism*, New York, Columbia University
    Press, 1996.

32 Mostafa Vaziri. *Iran as Imagined Nation: The Construction of National Identity*, New
    York, Paragon House, 1993.

33 Reza Zia-Ebrahimi, "Self-Orientalization and Dislocation: The Uses and Abuses of
    the 'Aryan' Discourse in Iran," *Iranian Studies*, Vol. 44, No. 4, 2011, P. 448.

34 Zia-Ebrahimi. Ibid. P. 452.

35 Fernand Braudel. L'identité de la France, Paris, Flammarion, 1999.

36 Gayatri Chakravorty Spivak. *A Critique of Postcolonial Reason. Toward a History
    of the Vanishing Present*, Cambridge, MA, Harvard University Press, 1999. Partha
    Chatterjee, *The Nation and Its Fragments: Colonial and Post-colonial Histories*,
    Princeton, Princeton University Press, 1993.

37 Mirza Aqa Khan Kermani, *Seh Maktub* [Three Letters], Bahram Chubin (ed.),
    Frankfurt, 2005, PP. 180–1, 139. In Zia-Ebrahimi,"Self-Orientalization and
    Dislocation." Ibid. PP. 454 and 466.

38 Yusuf Ashtiani, *Tarbiyat-i nisvan* (Women's *Education*), Tabriz, 1900, in Afsaneh Najmabadi, "Crafting an Educated Housewife," in Lila Abu-Lughod, *Remaking Women. Feminism and Modernity in the Middle East*, New Jersey, Princeton University Press, 1998, PP. 102–3.

39 Ahmed Bey, "La femme persane," *La nouvelle revue*, No. 69, 1891, P. 378. http://gallica.bnf.fr/ark:/12148/bpt6k35977v/f387.image.r=.

40 Kashani-Sabet, *Conceiving Citizens*. Ibid. P. 57.

41 Najmabadi, *Women with Mustaches and Men without Beards*. Ibid. PP. 194–5.

42 Kashani-Sabet, *Conceiving Citizens*. Ibid. Janet Afary, *Sexual Politics in Modern Iran*. Cambridge, Cambridge University Press. 2009.

43 Azadeh Kian, "Modernité, genre et religion en Iran," in Florence Rocheford (ed.), *Le pouvoir du genre. Laïcités et religions 1905–2005*, Toulouse, Presses universitaires de Toulouse, 2007.

44 Kumari Jayawardena, *Feminism and Nationalism in the Third World*, London, Zed Books, 1986.

45 Parvin Paidar, *Women and the Political Process in Twentieth-century Iran*, Cambridge, Cambridge University Press, 1997.

46 Azadeh Kian and Lucia Direnberger (eds.), *Etat-nation et fabrique du genre, des corps et des sexualités*. Iran, Turquie, Afghanistan, Presses universitaires de Provence, collection penser le genre, 2019.

47 *Memories of Colonel Kossakovsky*, translated into Persian by Abbasgholi Jali, Tehran, Simorgh, 1977, P. 32.

48 Afary, *The Iranian Constitutional Revolution, 1906–1911*. Ibid.

49 Pavlovitch, *Enghelab-e mashroutiyyat-e iran va risheh ha-ye ejtemai va eghtesadi ye an*, op. cit., PP. 51–2.

50 Mangol Bayat-Philipp, "Women and Revolution in Iran 1905–1911," in Nikki Keddie and Lois Beck (eds.), *Women in the Muslim World*, Cambridge, Harvard University Press, 1978, PP. 295–308. And Afary. *The Iranian Constitutional Revolution, 1906–1911*. Ibid.

51 Afary. Ibid. and Paidar, *Women and the Political Process in Twentieth-century Iran*. Ibid. 1997.

52 Reza Arasteh, "The Struggle for Equality in Iran," *Middle East Journal*, Vol. 18, NO. 2, 1964, PP. 192, 195.

53 Zohreh T. Sullivan, "Eluding the Feminist, Overthrowing the Modern? Transformations in Twentieth Century Iran," in Lila Abu-Lughod (ed.), *Remaking Women. Feminism and Modernity in the Middle East*, New Jersey, Princeton University Press, 1998, P. 230.

54 Norbert Elias, *The Civilizing Process*, vol. 1: *The History of Manners*, Oxford, Basil Blackwell, 1978, P. 81.

55 Pascale Molinier, *L'énigme de la femme active. Égoïsme, sexe et compassion*. Paris, Payot, 2003, P. 48.

56 Raewyn Connell, "Masculinities and Globalization," *Men and Masculinities*, No. 1, 1998, PP. 3–23.

57 Zillah Eisenstein, *Against Empire. Feminisms, Racism, and the West*, New York/ London, Zed Books, 2004, P. 191.

58 Mansoureh Ettehadieh, "The Origins and Development of Women's Movement in Iran: 1906–41," in Lois Beck and Guity Neshat (dirs.), *Women in Iran. From 1800 to the Islamic Republic*, Chicago, University of Illinois, 2004.

59 Ernest Renan, *Qu'est-ce qu'une nation ? Conférence faite en Sorbonne le 11 mars 1882*, Paris, Calman Lévy, 1882, PP. 7–11. https://www.ens.psl.eu/sites/default/files/ Sujet%20oral%20SIL2018-4.pdf.

60 This statement is from the second-year primary school textbook in 1940. Mohamad Ali Akbari, *Tabar shenasi hoviyyat jadid irani* (The Genealogy of New Iranian Identity), Tehran, Entesharat elmi va Farhangi, 2005. P. 262.

61 Intellectuals such as Ahmad Kasravi (assassinated in 1945 by the Fadaiyan Islam, a fundamentalist group), Hassan Taqizadeh, Mohamad-Ali Jamalzadeh. See Paidar, *Women and the Political Process in Twentieth-Century Iran*. Ibid. PP. 114–15.

62 Manuel Castels, *Le pouvoir de l'identité*. French Translation, Paris, Fayard, 1999, P. 45.

63 Kosaku Yoshino, *Cultural Nationalism in Contemporary Japan: A Sociological Enquiry*, London, Routledge, 1992, P. 1. In Castels, *Le pouvoir de l'identité*. Ibid. P. 45.

64 Stuart Hall, *Representation: Cultural Representations and Signifying Practices*. London, Sage in association with the Open University, 1997.

65 Touraj Atabaki, and Erik J. Zürcher (eds.) *Men of Order: Authoritarian Modernization under Atatürk and Reza Shah*, London, I.B. Tauris, 2004, P. 8.

66 John Brouilly, *Nationalism and the State*, Chicago, Chicago University Press, 1993.

67 Ernest Gellner, *Nations and Nationalism*, Oxford, Basil Blackwell, 1983, P. 43.

68 Stuart Hall, "The Question of Cultural Identity," in Stuart Hall, David Held, Don Hubert, and Kenneth Thompson (eds.), *Modernity. An Introduction to Modern Societies*, Oxford, Blackwell Publishers, 1996.

69 Peter G. Lewis, "The Politics of Iranian Place-Names," *Geographical Review*, Vol. 72, No. 1, 1982, PP. 99–102. Here P. 101.

70 Firoozeh Kashani-Sabet, *Frontier Fictions. Shaping the Iranian Nation 1804–1946*. Princeton, Princeton University Press. 2000, P. 218.

71 Firoozeh Kashani-Sabet, "Color Blind or Blinded by Color? Race, Ethnicity and Identity in Iran," in Firat Oruc (ed.), *Sites of Pluralism. Community Politics in the Middle East*, London, Hurst & Company, 2019, PP. 153–80.

72 Paul Gilroy, "Wearing Your Art on Your Sleeve: Towards a Diaspora Theory of Black Ephemera," in D. A. Bailey and S. Hall (eds.), *The Critical Decade: Black British Photography of the 1980s, Ten 8,* Vol. 2, No. 3, P. 87. In Hall, *Modernity and Its Futures*. Ibid. P. 618.

73 Didier Fassin and Éric Fassin (eds.), *De la question sociale à la question raciale? Représenter la société française*, Paris, La Découverte, 2006, P. 40.

74 Étienne Balibar, "Y a-t-il un 'néo-racisme'?" in Étienne Balibar and Immanuel Wallerstein, *Race, nation, classe, Les identités ambiguës*, Paris, La Découverte, coll. "Poche," 1997, P. 28.

75 Balibar. Ibid. PP. 33, 34–9.

76 Gilles Riaux, "The Formative Years of Azerbaijani Nationalism in Post Revolutionary Iran," *Central Asian Survey*, Vol. 27, No. 1, 2008, PP. 45–8.

77 Mohamad Ali Akbari, *Tabar shenasi hoviyyat jadid irani* (The Genealogy of New Iranian Identity), Tehran, Entesharat elmi va Farhangi, 2005, P. 250.

78 Ernest Renan, *Qu'est-ce qu'une nation*, Paris, Bordas, 1992.

79 Pierre Nora, "Le nationalisme nous a caché la nation" (Nationalism has hidden the nation from us), *Le monde*, March 17, 2007.

80 Firat Oruc (ed.), *Sites of Pluralism. Community Politics in the Middle East*, London, Hurst & Company, 2019, P. 3.

81 Oruc. Ibid. P. 2.

82 James C. Scott, *Domination and the Arts of Resistance: Hidden Transcripts*, New Haven, Yale University Press, 1990.

83 Oruc, *Sites of Pluralism*. Ibid. P. 3.

84 Cosroe Chaqeri, *The Soviet Socialist Republic of Iran 1920–21: Birth of the Trauma*, Pittsburgh and London, University of Pittsburgh Press, 1995.

85 Yann Richard, "La fondation de l'armée nationale en Iran," in Y. Richard (ed.), *Entre l'Iran et l'Occident. Adaptation et assimilation des idées et techniques occidentales en Iran*, Paris, Maison des Sciences de l'Homme, 1989, P. 44.

86 Nikki Keddie, "Iranian Revolution in Comparative Perspectives," *American Historical Review*, Vol. 88, June 1983, PP. 579–98. Here P. 594.

87 Asghar Fathi, "Kasravi's Views on Writers and Journalists: A Study in Sociology of Modernization," *Iranian Studies*, Vol. 19, Spring 1986, PP. 167–77.

88 David Menashri, *Education and the Making of Modern Iran*, Ithaca and London, Cornell University Press, 1992, PP. 87–93, 110.

89 Menashri. Ibid. P. 110.

90 Azadeh Kian, *Secularization of Iran, a Doomed Failure? The New Middle Class and the Making of Modern Iran*, Louvain and Paris, Peeters and Institut d'Études Iraniennes, 1998.

91 Gellner, *Nations and Nationalism*. Ibid.

92 Stuart Hall, "New Ethnicities," in David Morley and Kuan-Hsing Chen (eds.), *Critical Dialogues in Cultural Studies*, London and New York, Routledge, 1996, PP. 442–51.

93 Homi Bhabha, "The Other Question. The Stereotype and Colonial Discourse," in K. M. Newton (ed.), *Twentieth-century Literary Theory*, London, Palgrave Macmillan, 1997, second edition, PP. 293–311. Here P. 293.

94 Fratz Fanon, *Racism and Culture, Toward the African Revolution*, London, Pelican, 1970, P. 44. In Bhabha, "The Other Question." Ibid. P. 305.

95 Edward Said, *Orientalism*, London, Routledge, 1978, P. 72.

96 Shahrough Akhavi, *Religion and Politics in Contemporary Iran*, Albany, State University of New York Press, 1980, P. 187. And Menashri, *Education and the Making of Modern Iran*. Ibid. P. 102.

97 Afary, The Iranian Constitutional Revolution. Ibid.

98 Ghassem Salami and Afsaneh Najmabadi (eds.), *Nehzat-e nesvan-e charq (The Eastern Women's Movement)*, Tehran, Shirazeh, 2005, P. 111.

99 Interview pour le magazine *Alam-e Zanan* publié en 1943, in Kashani-Sabet, *Conceiving Citizens*. Ibid. P. 145.

100 Mehrzad Boroujerdi, "Gharbzadegi. The Dominant Intellectual Discourse of Pre- and Post-Revolutionary Iran," in S. K. Farsoun and M. Mashayekhi (eds.), *Iran: Political Culture in the Islamic Republic*, London, New York, Routledge, 1992.

101 Azadeh Kian, *Secularization of Iran, a Doomed Failure? The New Middle Class and the Making of Modern Iran*, Louvain & Paris, Peeters & Institut d'Études Iraniennes, 1998.

102 Kian. Ibid. and Azadeh Kian, "Gendering Khomeini," in A. A. Moghadam (dir.), *A Critical Introduction to Khomeini*, Cambridge, Cambridge University Press, 2014, PP. 170–92.

103 Eric Hobsbawn, *Nations and Nationalism since 1780: Programme, Myth, Reality*, Cambridge, Cambridge University Press, 1991, P. 10.

104 Ahmad Kasravi, *Azari ya zaban-i bâstân-i Azarbaijan*, Bethesda, Iranbooks, 1993.

105 Taqi Arani, "Azarbaidjan ya yek mas'aleh-yi hayati va mamati-yi Iran," *Farhangestan*, Vol. 1, No. 5, 1924, P. 24.

106 *Constitution de la République islamique d'Iran 1979–1989*, translated into French by Michel Potoki, Paris, l'Harmattan, 2004, PP. 49, 51.

107 Seyed Mohammad Hachemi, *Human Rights and Fundamental Liberties* (in Persian), Tehran, Mizan, 2005, P. 588.

108 Laurent Perpigna Iban, "L'horizon bouché des sunnites du Baloutchistan iranien. Au cœur d'une région déstabilisée", *OrientXXI*, 8 juin 2016.

109 Eugene D. Genovese, *Roll Jordan Roll, The World the Slaves Made*, New York, Vintage Books, 1976, P. 7.

110 Iban. "L'horizon bouché des sunnites du Baloutchistan iranien. Au cœur d'une région déstabilisée". Ibid.

111 Nouchine Yavari-d'Hellencourt, "Ethnies et ethnicité dans les manuels scolaires iraniens," in Jean-Pierre Digard (ed.), *Le faits ethniques en Iran et en Afghanistan*, Paris, Editions du CNRS, 1988, PP. 247–65; here P. 251.

112 Yavari-d'Hellencourt. Ibid. PP. 252, 256, 261, 263.

113 Bernard Hourcade, "Ethnie, nation et citadinité en Iran," in Jean Pierre Digard (ed.), *Le fait ethnique en Iran et en Afghanistan*, PP. 161–74. Here P. 172.

114 David Menashri, *Post-revolutionary Politics in Iran, Religion, Society, and Power*, London, Franck Cass, 2001, P. 81.

115 Gilles Riaux, "La radicalisation des nationalistes azéris en Iran," *CEMOTI*, Vol. 37, 2004, PP. 15–42.

116 Azadeh Kian, *La Republique islamique d'Iran. De la maison du Guide à la raison d'Etat*. Paris, Michalon, 2005.

117 Shahram Rafizadeh, "Protest against the State's interference in Sunnite Schools," in *Rooz*, 2008.05.06. http:www.roozonline.com/archives/2008/05/post_7257.php. Rooz was a Persian and English news website first published on the web on May 10, 2005. It stopped publication in 2015.

118 Interview of Reyhaneh Tabatabayi with Molavi Abdolhamid, in Daily *Bahar*, Téhéran, June 25, 2013.

119 Interview of Reyhaneh Tabatabayi with Molavi Abdolhamid. Ibid.

120 http://fr.euronews.com/2016/02/24/iran-tous-les-hommes-d-un-village-executes-pour-trafic-de-drogue/.

121 Sadigheh Sheikhzadeh, *Bar rasi-yi chalesh-i jame'i-yi ahl-i sonnat-i baluch ba nizam-i siyasi-yi jomjoori-yi islami-ye iran*, *(A Study of the Challenges of the Baluch Sunnite Community with the Political System of the Islamic Regime of Iran)*, Dissertation, Tehran, Department of Law and Political Science, University of Tehran, 2006, P. 607.

122 Alam Saleh, *Ethnic Identity and the State in Iran*, New York, Palgrave Macmillan, 2013, P. 21.

123 Ahmadi, *Ethnicity and Ethnicism* in Iran. Ibid. P. 377.

124 Ali al-Taie, *Bohran-i hoviyyat-i qomi dar iran*, *(Ethnic Identity Crisis in Iran)*, Tehran, Shadegan Publications, second edition, 1382/2003, PP. 200–1.

125 Mateo Mohammad Farzaneh's, *Iranian Women & Gender in the Iran-Iraq War*, Syracuse, Syracuse University Press, 2021 is a welcome attempt but its scope is limited to women warriors or women who participated in war efforts.

Chapter 2

1   Hassan Afrakhteh, "The Problems of Regional Development and Border Cities: A Case Study of Zahedan, Iran," *The International Journal of Urban Policy and Planning*, Special Issue. Urbanization and the Iranian Revolution, Vol. 23, No. 6, December 2006, PP. 423–32. Here pages 423–4.

2   Afrakhteh. Ibid. P. 429.

3   Fredy Bémont, Les villes de l'Iran? Volume II, Paris 1973, PP. 254–5.

4   Fredy Bémont's interview in 1972 with a group of exiles. Ibid. P. 255.

5   Iran Statistical Yearbook, 1398/2020, P. 23.

6 Sima Soltani, "Zâhedân" Budget and Planning Organization of Sistan and Baluchistan, 1999, PP. 43–51, cited in Afrakhteh, "The Problems of Regional Development and Border Cities", The International Journal of Urban Policy and Planning, Special Issue. Urbanization and the Iranian Revolution. Vol. 23, No. 6, December 2006, PP. 423–32.

7 Brian Spooner, "Who Are the Baluch ? A Preliminary Investigation into the Dynamics of an Ethnic Identity from Qajar Iran," in Edmund Bosworth and Carole Hillenbrand (eds.), *Qajar Iran. Political, Social and Cultural Change 1800–1925*, Edinburgh, Edinburgh University Press, 1983, PP. 93–110. Here PP. 107–8.

8 Spooner. Ibid. PP. 93, 95.

9 Spooner. Ibid. PP. 96–7.

10 Philip Carl Salzman, *Black Tents of Baluchistan*, Washington & London, Smithsonian Institution Press, 2000, P. 358.

11 William Irons, "Why Are the Yomuts Not More Stratified?" in C. Chang and H. Koster (eds.), *Pastoralists at the Periphery: Herders in a Capitalist World*, Tucson, University of Arizona Press, 1994.

12 Spooner, "Who Are the Baluch?" Ibid. PP. 100–1.

13 Fredrik Barth, "Ethnic Processes on the Pathan-Baluch Boundary," in G. Redard (ed.), *Indo-Iranica: mélanges présentés à Georg Morgenstierne*, Wiesbaden, O. Harrassowitz, 1964, PP. 13–20. In Spooner, "Who Are the Baluch?" Ibid. P. 101.

14 Spooner. Ibid. P. 102.

15 *Seday i Ghalam*, First Year, No. 4, December 2002, PP. 8–10. The journal and the NGO have both disappeared.

16 Philip Carl Salzman, *Black Tents of Baluchistan*, Washington & London, Smithsonian Institution Press, 2000, PP. 36–7.

17 Salzman. Ibid. P. 39.

18 Salzman. Ibid. P. 41.

19 Hamid Ahmadi, *Qomiyyat va qom garayi dar iran*, (*Ethnicity and Ethnicism in Iran*). Ibid. PP. 106, 139.

20 Hamid Ahmadi's Interview with Mahmood Zand-Moghadam, "Baluchistan-i iran. Hoviyyat, târikh va taghyir" (Iranian Baluchistan: Identity, History and Change), in Hamid Ahmadi (ed.), *Iran. Hoviyyat, meliyyat, qomiyyat (Iran. Identity, Nationality, Ethnicity)*, Tehran, Center for Research and Development of Human Sciences, 2005, PP. 306–42.

21 Zand-Moghadam. Ibid. PP. 313–14.

22 Zand-Moghadam. Ibid. P. 333.

23 Thierry A. Brun, C. Geissler, and C. F. Bel, "Le Balouchistan iranien. Un réservoir de travailleurs sous-alimentés pour les Emirats," *Tiers-Monde*, tome, Vol. 18, No. 69, 1977, Migrations et développement, P. 133.

24 Brun et al. Ibid. PP. 131–8. Here P. 131.

25 Brun et al. Ibid. PP. 136–7.

26 Ahmadi, *Qomiyyat va qom garayi dar iran*, (*Ethnicity and Ethnicism in Iran*). Ibid. Ahmadi. Ibid. PP. 258–62.

27 Ahmadi. Ibid. P. 278.

28 Zand-Moghadam, "Baluchistan-i iran. Hoviyyat, târikh va taghyir." Ibid. PP. 317–19.

29 Zand-Moghadam. Ibid. P. 319.

30 Spooner, "Who Are the Baluch ?" Ibid. P. 109.

31 Zand-Moghadam, "Baluchistan-i iran. Hoviyyat, târikh va taghyir." Ibid. P. 323.

32 Zand-Moghadam. Ibid. P. 264.

33 Zand-Moghadam. Ibid. PP. 338, 340.

34 Zand-Moghadam. Ibid. P. 318.

35 Organization of Management and Planning, Statistical Year book, 1382 & 1384, P. 501.

36 Interview with Djamshid Ordoni from Sistan and Baluchistan Health Center, in *Sharq*, August 25, 2004.

37 Selected findings of the 2016 National Population and Housing Census, table 34.

38 Accessed on April 17, 2020.

39 Sadigheh S's interview. Khâsh, 2008.

40 Afshin Shahi and Ehsan Abdoh-Tabrizi, "The Shi'te State and the Socioeconomic Challenges of the Sunni Communities in Iran. Historical and Contemporary perspectives," in Firat Oruc (ed.), *Sites of Pluralism. Community Politics in the Middle East*, London, Hurst & Company, 2019, PP. 87–113.

41 Ilna. September 13, 2014, in Shahi and Abdoh-Tabrizi. Ibid. P. 106.

42 Shahi and Abdoh-Tabrizi. Ibid. PP. 108–9.

43 Shahi and Abdoh-Tabrizi. Ibid. P. 109.

44 Djavad Salehi-Isfahani, "Poverty and Income Inequality in the Islamic Republic of Iran," *Revue internationale des études du développement*, Vol. 1, No. 229, 2017, PP. 113–36. Here P. 115.

45 Salehi-Isfahani. Ibid. P. 120.

46 Ali Ranjipour, "Poverty in Iran: an Introduction," *Iranwire*, March 2, 2020. https://iranwire.com/en/features/5829. Hossein Raghfar, "26 Million Iranians Suffer Absolute Poverty, Says Prominent Economist," *Radio Farda*, April 10, 2018. https://en.radiofarda.com/a/iran-million-suffer-from-poverty/29156808.html.

47 Parviz Fatah quoted in *Radio Farda*, December 15, 2019.

48 Hossein Raghfar, "26 Million Iranians Suffer Absolute Poverty, Says Prominent Economist." Ibid.

49 Ministry of Labor: "Thirty Six Million People Are Poor," Radio Zamaneh, August 21, 2021. https://www.radiozamaneh.com/682386.

50 IRNA, quoted by Radio Farda, September 14, 2015. www.radiofarda.com.

51 Davoud Shahpari Sani, Rasoul Sadeghi, Javad Hadadi, Razieh Khajenexad, Mohammadreza Hosseini, and Hossein Mahmoudian, "The Analysis of Demographic, Social and Economic Situation of Female-Headed Households

in Iran" (in Persian), *Zan va Jame'i* (Woman and Society), Vol. 12, No. 47, 2021, PP. 1–18. Here P. 11.

52 Ali Ranjipour, "Poverty in Iran: Sistan and Baluchistan". *Iranwire*, March 2, 2020, https://iranwire.com/en/features/5841.

53 "Re-opening of Schools: A Huge Wave of Drop Outs of Poor Pupils," *Radio Zamaneh*, September 8, 2021, https://www.radiozamaneh.com/684621.

54 Laurent Perpigna Iban, "L'horizon bouché des sunnites du Baloutchistan iranien. Au cœur d'une région déstabilisée," OrientXXI, June 8, 2016.

55 *Sharq*, September 7, 2021. https://news.gooya.com/2021/09/post-55714.php. According to Molavi Abdolhamid in Zahedan a Sunnite theology school for women has opened, called Hazrat Ayesheh with almost 1,000 theology students.

56 Maryam Dehkordi's interview with Ziba Azizi, *Iran Wire*, Monday, August 31, 2020. https://iranwire.com/fa/features/40773.

57 Maryam Dehkordi's interview with Ziba Azizi. Ibid.

58 Sadigheh Sheikhzadeh's interview. 2007.

Chapter 3

1 Selected findings of the 2016 National Population and Housing Census, https://www.amar.org.ir/english/Population-and-Housing-Censuses. Accessed on April 17, 2020.

2 Ali Ranjipour, "Poverty in Golestan," March 2020, Iranwire https://iranwire.com/en/features/5917.

3 Alain de Bures, *La horde enracinée. Turkmènes d'Iran*, Paris, L'Asiathèque, 1992, P. 475.

4 Louis Bazin, "Les turcophones d'Iran: aperçus ethnolinguistiques," in *Le fait ethnique*, PP. 43–54.

5 Mateo Mohammad Farzaneh, *Iranian Women & Gender in the Iran-Iraq War*, Syracuse, Syracuse University Press, 2021.

6 Farzaneh. Ibid. P. 5.

7 Farzaneh. Ibid. P. 142. See also P. 262.

8 Peyman Vahabzadeh, *A Guerrilla Odyssey: Modernization, Secularism, Democracy, and the Fadai Period of National Liberation in Iran. 1971–79*, Syracuse, Syracuse University Press. 2010, P. 68. Also see Ahmad Khajehnejad, Ghobar Sahra (Dust of the Desert), Gorgan, Surah Mehr, 2020.

9 Houchang Chehabi, Peyman Jafari, and Maral Jefroudi (eds.), *Iran in the Middle East: Transnational Encounters and Social History*, London & New York, I.B.Tauris, 2015, P. 189.

10 Chehabi, Jafari, Jefroudi. Ibid. P. 189.

11 Vahabzadeh, *A Guerrilla Odyssey*. Ibid. P. 68.

12 William Samii, "The Nation and Its Minorities: Ethnicity, Unity and State Policy in Iran," *Comparative Studies in South Asia, Africa and the Middle East*, Vol. XX, Nos. 1 & 2, 2000, PP. 128–42; here P. 139.

13 Oghuz, confederation of Turkic peoples whose homeland, until at least the eleventh century AD, was the steppes of Central Asia and Mongolia. The Seljuqs, who comprised one branch of the Oğuz, controlled an empire stretching from the Amu Darya to the Persian Gulf and from the Indus to the Mediterranean Sea by the end of the eleventh century. Speakers of the southwestern branch of the Turkic language subfamily are also sometimes referred to as Oğuz Turks. The Oghuz tribes had been the main source of the Ottoman Empire's economic and political power for many years. https://www.britannica.com/topic/Oguz.

14 Bazin, "Les turcophones d'Iran: aperçus ethnolinguistiques." Ibid. PP. 43–54. Here P. 46.

15 In 1260 the Mogol Empire split into four groups called khanates. These four khanates were the Yuan Dynasty based in China, the Golden Horde in Russia/Pontic Steppes, the Ilkhanate in Persia/Middle East, and the Changhatai in Central Asia. Charles Melville, "The Fall of Amir Chupan and the Decline of the Ilkhanate, 1327–37: A Decade of Discord in Mongol Iran." Papers on Inner Asia, No. 30. 90 PP. Bloomington, Indiana University, Research Institute for Inner Asian Studies, 1999.

16 Yves Porter, *Les iraniens. Histoire d'un peuple*, Paris, Arman Colin, 2006, PP. 186–718.

17 Porter. Ibid. PP. 188–9.

18 Sussan Babaie, Kathlyne Babayan, Ina Baghdiantz-mccabe, and Massumeh Farhad, *Slaves of the Shah. New Elites of Safavid Iran*, London & New York, I.B.Tauris, 2004, PP. 6–7.

19 Babaie, Babayan, Baghdiantz-mccabe, and Farhad. Ibid.

20 Michael Axeworthy, *The Sword of Persia. Nader Shah, From Tribal Warrior to Conquering Tyrant*, London and New York, I.B.Tauris, 2009, P. 25.

21 Axeworthy. Ibid. P. 21.

22 Axeworthy. Ibid. P. 18.

23 Axeworthy. Ibid. P. 19.

24 de Bures, *La horde enracinée*. Ibid. P. 474.

25 William Irons, *The Yomut Turkmen: A Study of Social Organization among a Central Asian Turkic Speaking Population*, Ann Arbor, Anthropological papers, The University of Michigan, 1975, P. 25.

26 Irons. Ibid. P. 29.

27 Today, the Astan-i Qods foundation that also supervises the shrine of Imam Reza (the 8th Shi'ite Imam and the only one to be buried in Iran) is the richest and the most powerful foundation in the country.

28 Afsaneh Najmabadi, *Hikâyat-i dokhtarân-i Ghoochân* (The Tale of Ghoochan Girls), Tehran, Roshangaran, 1995, PP. 20–1, 23.

29 Najmabadi. Ibid. PP. 11–12.

30 Najmabadi. Ibid. PP. 28–9.

31 Najmabadi. Ibid. PP. 49, 57.

32 Eric Hobsbawm and Terence Ranger (eds.), *The Invention of Tradition*, Cambridge, Cambridge University Press, 1983, PP. 1, 12.

33 Irons, *The Yomut Turkmen*. Ibid. P. 90.

34 Irons. Ibid. PP. 88–9.

35 Irons. Ibid. PP. 92–3.

36 Irons. Ibid. P. 104.

37 Irons. Ibid. P. 139.

38 Irons. Ibid. PP. 143, 104–5.

39 Organization of Civil Registration (Sazman Sabt Ahval). October 14, 2021. In "Child Marriage has increased by 10 percent in Iran," Radiozamaeh, https://www.radiozamaneh.com/682222.

40 Maryam Dehkordi, "Zoleikha Adeli, an Entrepreneur Who Introduces Turkmen rugs in the World." Influential Women of Iran. Iran Wire, August 25, 2020. https://iranwire.com/fa/features/40570.

41 From Maryam Dehkordi's interview with Zoleikha Adeli. Ibid.

42 Quoted in Thierry A. Brun, C. Geissler, and F. Bel, "Le Balouchistan iranien. Un réservoir de travailleurs sous-alimentés pour les Emirats," in *Tiers-Monde*, tome Vol. 18, No. 69, 1977. Migrations et développement. PP. 131–8 (here P. 132) doi: https://doi.org/10.3406/tiers.1977.2692, https://www.persee.fr/doc/tiers_0040-7356_1977_num_18_69_2692.

43 Max Weber, *Economie et société*, vol. II, Paris, Plon, 1995, P. 130.

44 Andrew P. Vayda, "Actions, Variations and Change: The Emerging Anti-essentialist View in Anthropology." in R. Borofsky (ed.), *Assessing Cultural Anthropology*, New York, McGraw-Hill, 1994, P. 321. In Salzman, *Black Tents of Baluchistan*. Ibid. P. 351.

45 Leïla Enayatzadeh, *Bâz tajarod-i zanân* (Women's Celibacy), Tehran, Djamei'a Shenasan, 2017, P. 151. In Fatemeh Karimi. *Genre et militantisme au Kurdistan d'Iran. Les femmes kurdes de Komala 1979–1991*. Paris, L'Harmattan, 2022, P. 53.

46 A. Qaemi, *Tashkil-e khanevadeh dar Eslam*, Tehran, Amiri, 1994, P. 70.

47 Paola Tabet, *La construction sociale de l'inégalité des sexes. Des outils et des corps.* Paris, L'Harmattan, 2000, PP. 21–3.

48 Sohrab Sardashti is a professional photographer. He was born in 1981 in Gorgan, Golestan province. His pictures were taken in the years 2010–11.

49 Gellner, *Nation and Nationalism*. Ibid.

50 Anthony D. Smith, *Nationalism and Modernism*, London & New York, Routledge, 1998.

51 Deniz Kandiyoti, "Bargaining with Patriarchy," *Gender and Society*, Vol. 2, No. 3, September 1988, PP. 274–90.

52 Homi Bhabha, *Les lieux de la culture. Une théorie postcoloniale*, French translation, Paris, Payot, 2007.

Chapter 4

1 The Maghreb countries, Moghadam argued, are characterized by strong feminist movements, the visibility of women in the professions (especially the judiciary), and reformed family law. Valentne Moghadam, "Gender Regimes in the Middle East and North Africa: The Power of Feminist Movements," *Social Politics*, Vol. 27, No. 3, 2020, P. 468.

2 Moghadam. Ibid. PP. 468–9.

3 According to 2006 National Census of the Population and Housing, from the then thirty Iranian provinces, only in five of them the majority of the population was still rural: Sistan-Baluchistan (50.40 percent), Golestan (51 percent), Kohguilouyeh va BoyerAhmad (52.3 percent), Hormozgan (53 percent), and Northern Khorasan (51.6 percent). The five most urbanized provinces are: Qom (93.91 percent), Tehran (91. 34 percent), Esfahan (83.32 percent), Yazd (79.71 percent), and Semnan (74.70 percent). The 2016 National Census of the Population and Housing shows that from among the thirty-one provinces, only in Sistan-Baluchistan the majority of the population was still rural. The population growth rate in rural areas of this province has increased by two points.

4 Statistical Center of Iran 1986, P. 3. In Rasmus Elling and Kevan Harris, "Difference in Difference: Language, Geography, and Ethno-racial Identity in Contemporary Iran," *Ethnic and Racial Studies*, Vol. 44, No. 12, 2021, PP. 2255–81. Here P. 2259.

5 Rasmus Elling and Kevan Harris, "Difference in Difference: Language, Geography, and Ethno-racial Identity in Contemporary Iran," *Ethnic and Racial Studies*, Vol. 44, No. 12, 2021, PP. 2267–8.

6 "A Huge Group of Pupils Have Been Prevented from Going to School," *Radio Zamaneh*, December 19, 2020, https://www.radiozamaneh.com/562102.

7 "Withdrawal of One Million Students from School According to the Ministry of Education, Five Million According to Unofficial Statistics," *Radio Farda*, November 9, 2021. https://www.radiofarda.com/a/iran-shadapp/31551409.html.

8 Lila Abu-Lughod, *Veiled Sentiments*, Berkeley and Los Angeles, University of California Press, 1986.

9 Claude Lévi-Strauss, *Les structures élémentaires de la parenté*, Paris, Mouton et Maison des sciences de l'homme, 1967 (first edition 1949), P. 135.

10 Rouhollah Khomeini, *Resaleh-yi Tawzih ol-Masail,* Tehran, Qadr-i Velayat, 1375/1996, second edition, Question number. 2459, P. 279.

11 Ali Qaemi. *Tashkil-i khanevadeh dar Islam* (The Formation of the Family in Islam), Tehran, Amiri, 1994, P. 16.

12 Qaemi. Ibid. P. 9.

13 Janet Afary and Jesilyn Faust (eds.), *Iranian Romance in the Digital Age: From Arranged Marriage to White Marriage,* London and New York, I.B. Tauris, 2021.

14 B. Spooner, "Who Are the Baluch? A Preliminary Investigation into the Dynamics of Ethnic Identity from Qajar Iran," in Edmund Bosworth and Carole Hillenbrand (eds.), *Qajar Iran, Political, Social and Cultural Change 1800–1925,* Edinburgh, Edinburgh University Press, 1983, PP. 93–110.

15 Elham Shirdel, Mohammadreza Hasani, and Fateme Hami Kargar, "Barsakht-i Ezdevaj-i Beyn-i mazhabi-yi Movafagh va Zamineh hay-i Sheklgiri-yi an: Motale'e-yi Keyfi-yi Beyn-i Zojeyn dar Ostan-i Sistan va Baluchistan" "Construction of a Successful Inter-religious Marriage and the Context of Its Formation: A Qualitative Study between Couples in Sistan and Baluchistan Province" (in Persian), *Sociology and Social Institutions*, Vol. 8, No. 18, Autumn-Winter 2021, PP. 373–97.

16 Shirdel, Hasani, and Kargar. Ibid. P. 386.

17 Shirdel, Hasani, and Kargar. Ibid. P. 394.

18 Shirdel, Hasani, and Kargar. Ibid. P. 388.

19 Shirdel, Hasani, and Kargar. Ibid. P. 386.

20 Shirdel, Hasani, and Kargar. Ibid. P. 387.

21 Shirdel, Hasani, and Kargar. Ibid. P. 390.

22 Nafaqeh includes housing, food, clothing, and furniture (article 1204 of the civil code). Article 1106 of the civil code states that in a permanent marriage, the husband must provide a nafaqeh to his wife. If he refuses to do so, his wife can file for a divorce.

23 According to ISNA, Iran's student news agency, October 9, 2017.

24 Qaemi. *Tashkil-i khanevadeh dar Islam* (Formation of the Family in Islam). Ibid. PP. 195–200.

25 Twelver shi'ism authorizes temporary marriage called sigheh or mut'eh. The length of temporary marriage varies from couple of minutes to ninety-nine years. Shi'ite men who marry temporarily can also have up to four wives. But a woman married temporarily cannot contract another marriage at the same time.

26 Statistical Center of Iran, *Selected Results of the 2016 National Population and Housing Census,* www.amar.org.ir. 2017.

27 Tehran, Office of Studies on Education and Culture, 2020. In "The Birth Rate Has Reached the Lowest in Ten Years," *radiozamaneh*, July 1, 2020, www.radiozamaneh.com/515610.

28 "Child Marriage Has Increased by Ten Percent in Iran," *Radio Zamaneh*, August 19, 2021, https://www.radiozamaneh.com/682222.

29 Shirin Ebadi, *Hoquq-i Kudak* (The Rights of the Child), Tehran, Rowshangaran, third edition, 1992, PP. 58–9, 190, 194–5.

30 http://educationiran.ir/en/Universities. And https://wenr.wes.org/2017/02/education-in-iran.

31 Azadeh Kian, *Les femmes iraniennes entre islam, Etat et famille*, Paris, Maisonneuve & Larose, 2002. And Janet Afary and Jesilyn Faust (eds.), *Iranian Romance in the Digital Age: From Arranged Marriage to White Marriage*, London and New York, I.B. Tauris, 2021.

Chapter 5

1 Geneviève Fraisse, "Des conditions de l'égalité économique," in *Travail et pauvreté: la part des femmes, Travail, genre et sociétés*, Vol. 1, No. 1999, PP. 149–55. here P. 153.

2 *A Selection of Labor Force Survey Results*, Tehran, Statistical Center of Iran, 2018, P. 23.

3 Danièle Kergoat, "Division sexuelle du travail et rapports sociaux de sexe" [Sexual division of labor and gender social relations], in H. Hirata (ed.), *Dictionnaire critique du fe´minisme* [Critical dictionary of feminism], second edition, Paris, PUF, 2004, PP. 35–44.

4 Morteza Mottahari. *Nezâm-e Hoquq-e Zan dar eslam* (Women's Rights in Islam), Téhéran, 1372/1993, seventeenth edition.

5 From Ayatollah Khamenei's sermon on December 16, 1992. In *Cheshmeh-ye Nour*, Tehran, 1995, P. 269.

6 Seyyed Javad Mostafavi, *Behesht-i Khanevadeh (The Family Paradise)*, Qom, Qods, tenth edition, Vol. I, 1995, P. 117.

7 For a discussion, see R. L. Blumberg, "A General Theory of Gender Stratification," *Sociological Theory*, 1984, PP. 23–101.

8 Carole Pateman. *Le contrat sexuel*, 1988, French translation, Paris, La Découverte, 2010.

9 Carole Pateman. Ibid.

10 Sylvia Walby, "La Citoyenneté est-elle sexuée?" in T. H. Ballmer-Cao et al. (eds.), *Genre et politique*, Paris, Gallimard, 2000, PP. 51–82.

11 Sa'id Saber, "The Big Share of the Black Economy in Exploitation" (in Parisan), Radio Zamaneh, November 2, 2021, https://www.radiozamaneh.com/691431.

12 Azadeh Kian *Les femmes iraniennes entre islam, État et famille*, Paris, Maisonneuve et Larose, 2002. Azadeh Kian, "Gender Social Relations and the Challenge of

Women's Employment," *Middle East Critique*, Vol. 23, No. 3, 2014, PP. 333–47, http://dx.doi.org/10.1080/19436149.2014.943594.

13 *A Selection of Labor Force Survey Results.* Tehran, Statistical Center of Iran, 2016, P. 5.

14 Tania Angeloff, "Des miettes d'emploi: temps partiel et pauvreté," in "Travail et pauvreté: la part des femmes," *Travail, genre et sociétés*, Vol. 1, No. 1, 1999, PP. 43–70.

15 Sylvia Walby, *Theorizing Patriarchy*, Oxford, Blackwell, 1997, P. 201.

16 "Sistan-Baluchistan, Khorasan and Hormozgan have the most numerous needy women," Ibid.

17 "Sistan-Baluchistan, Khorasan and Hormozgan have the most numerous needy women," *Radio Zamaneh*, August 12, 2021. https://www.radiozamaneh.com/680746.

18 "Sistan-Baluchistan, Khorasan and Hormozgan have the most numerous needy women." Ibid.

19 Paola Tabet, *La construction sociale de l'inégalité des sexes: Des outils et des corps* [Social construction of sexual inequality: The tools and bodies], Paris, L'Harmattan, 1998.

20 Laurent Perpigna Iban, "L'horizon bouché des sunnites du Baloutchistan iranien." Ibid.

21 See among others Abbas Abdi's interview "Religious Intellectualism and More Urgent Questions than the Women's Questions" (Rawshanfikri-yi dini va masa'il-i fawritar az masa'il-i zanan), *Zanan*, No. 58, 2000, P. 38.

22 Khatami's interview with *Zanan*, No. 34, April–May 1997, PP. 2–5.

23 Sadigheh Sheikhzadeh's interview. Zâdedân, December 4, 2008.

24 Sadigheh Sheikhzadeh's interview. Ibid.

25 The population of Khâsh is 173,000 and is located 185 km south of Zâhedân.

26 https://globalvoices.org/2017/07/27/what-do-election-results-signal-about-womens-political-participation-in-iran/.

27 https://financialtribune.com/articles/people/65161/increasing-number-of-iranian-women-in-local-governance.

28 "Tamami zanan-i yek roosta," (All the Women of a Village), *Tabnak*, 14 farvardin 1396/April 3, 2017. Tabnak.ir/fa/news/681321.

Conclusion

1 Sylvia Walby, *Globalization and Inequalities: Complexity and Contested Modernities*, London, Sage, 2009, P. 301.

2 Betül Yarar, "Reflecting on the Oppositional Discourses against the AKP's Neoliberalism and Searching for a New Vision for Feminist Counter Politics," in

Azadeh Kian and Buket Turkmen (eds.), *Transformations of the Gender Regime in Turkey, Les Cahiers du CEDREF*, No. 22, 2018, PP. 23–67, https://doi.org/10.4000/cedref.1101.

3 Collins, *Intersectionality as Critical Social Theory*. Ibid.

4 Ruth Miller, *The Limits of Bodily Integrity: Abortion, Adultery, and Rape Legislation in Comparative Perspective*, Aldershot, Ashgate, 2007, P. 149.

5 Jean-Michel Landry, "Repenser la norme, réinventer l'agencéité (Rethinking the Norm, Reinventing Agency), Interview with Saba Mahmood," translated into French by Fabienne Boursiquot, *Anthropologie et société*, Traverse, Vol. 34, No. 1, 2010, P. 223, https://doi.org/10.7202/044205ar.

6 Teresa de Lauretis, "Displacing Hegemonic Discourses: Reflections on Feminist Theory in the 1980s," *Inscriptions*, Vol. 3, No. 4, 1988, P. 138.

7 Kimberlé Crenshaw, "Demarginalizing the Intersection of Race and Sex, A Black Feminist Critique of Antidiscrimination Doctrine, Feminist Theory and Antiracist Politics," *University of Chicago Legal Forum*, Vol. 1989, No. 1, Article 8, P. 27, https://chicagounbound.uchicago.edu/uclf/vol1989/iss1/8.

Bibliography

Abu-Lughod, Lila. *Veiled Sentiments*, Berkeley and Los Angeles, University of California Press, 1986.

Afary, Janet. *The Iranian Constitutional Revolution, 1906–11. Grassroots Democracy, Social Democracy, and the Origins of Feminism*, New York, Columbia University Press, 1996.

Afary, Janet and Faust, Jesilyn (eds.) *Iranian Romance in the Digital Age: From Arranged Marriage to White Marriage*, London and New York, I.B. Tauris, Bloomsbury Publishing, 2021.

Afrakhteh, Hassan, "The Problems of Regional Development and Border Cities: A Case Study of Zâhedân, Iran," *The International Journal of Urban Policy and Planning*, Special Issue. Urbanization and the Iranian Revolution, Vol. 23, No. 6, December 2006, PP. 423–32.

Ahmadi, Hamid. *Qawmiyyat va Qawm garayi dar Iran. az afsaneh ta vagheiyyat* (*Ethnicity and Ethnic Tendencies in Iran*, From *Tale to Reality*), Tehran, Nashr Ney, 1378/1999.

Ahmadi, Hamid. *Ethnicity and Ethnicism in Iran. From to Fiction to Reality* (in Persian), Tehran, Ney, 1378/2000.

Ahmadi, Hamid, "Unity within Diversity: Foundations and Dynamics of National Identity in Iran," *Critique: Critical Middle East studies*, Vol. 14, No. 1, Spring 2005, PP. 127–47.

Akbari, Mohamad Ali. *Tabâr shenâsi hoviyyat jadid irani* (The Genealogy of New Iranian Identity), Tehran, Entesharat elmi va Farhangi, 2005.

Alkan, Hilal, "The Sexual Politics of War: Reading the Kurdish Conflict through Images of Women," in Azadeh Kian and Buket Turkman (eds.), *Transformations of the Gender Regime in Turkey*, Les Cahiers du CEDREF, Paris, 2018, PP. 68–92, https://doi.org/10.4000/cedref.1111.

Al-Taie, Ali. *Ethnic Identity Crisis in Iran* (in Persian), Tehran, Shadegan Publications, second edition, 1382/2003.

Angeloff, Tania, "Des miettes d'emploi: temps partiel et pauvreté," in "Travailet pauvreté: la part des femmes," *Travail, genre et sociétés*, Vol. 1, No. 1, 1999, PP. 43–70.

Arasteh, Reza, "The Struggle for Equality in Iran," *Middle East Journal*, Vol. 18, No. 2, 1964, PP. 189–205.

Ashraf, Ahmad, "Theocracy and Charisma: New Men of Power in Iran," *International Journal of Politics, Culture and Society*, Vol. 4, No. 1, 1990, PP. 113–52.

Atabaki, Touraj and Zürcher Erik, J. (eds.) *Men of Order: Authoritarian Modernization under Atatürk and Reza Shah*, London, I.B. Tauris, 2004.

Axeworthy, Michael. *The Sword of Persia. Nader Shah, From Tribal Warrior to Conquering Tyrant*, London and New York, I.B.Tauris, 2009.

Babaie, Sussan, Babayan, Kathlyne, Baghdiantz-mccabe, Ina and Farhad, Massumeh. *Slaves of the Shah. New Elites of Safavid Iran*, London and New York, I.B.Tauris, 2004.

Bahramitash, Roksana and Salehi Esfahani, Hadi (eds.) *Veiled Employment: Islamism and the Political Economy of Women's Employment in Iran*, Syracuse, Syracuse University Press, 2011.

Barth, Fredrik, "Ethnic Processes on the Pathan-Baluch Boundary," in G. Redard (ed.), *Indo-Iranica: Mélanges Présentés à Georg Morgenstierne*, Wiesbaden, O. Harrassowitz, 1964, PP. 13–20.

Bayat-Philipp, Mangol, "Women and Revolution in Iran 1905–1911," in Nikki Keddie and Lois Beck (dirs.), *Women in the Muslim World*, Cambridge, Harvard University Press, 1978, PP. 295–308.

Bazin, Louis, "Les turcophones d'Iran: aperçus ethnolinguistiques," in J. P. Digard (ed.), *Le fait ethnique en Iran et en Afghanistan*, Paris, Editions du CNRS, 1988, PP. 43–54.

Bémont, Fredy. *Les villes de l'Iran. Des cités d'autres fois à l'urbanisme contemporain*, Volume II, Paris, Author's print, 1973.

Bernstein, Lisa. *(M)Othering the nation. Constructing and Resisting National Allegories through the Maternal Body*, Newcastel, Cambridge Scholars Publishing, 2008.

Bey, Ahmed, "La femme persane," *La nouvelle revue*, No. 69, 1891, http://gallica.bnf.fr/ark:/12148/bpt6k35977v/f387.image.r=.

Bhabha, Homi. *The Location of Culture*, London and New York, Routledge, 1994.

Bhabha, Homi, "The Other Question. The Stereotype and Colonial Discourse," in K. M. Newton (ed.), *Twentieth-century Literary Theory*, New York, Palgrave Macmillan, 1997, second edition, PP. 293–311.

Bhabha, Homi. *Les lieux de la culture. Une théorie postcoloniale*, French translation, Paris, Payot, 2007.

Blumberg, R. L., "A General Theory of Gender Stratification," *Sociological Theory*, Wiley, 1984, PP. 23–101, https://www.jstor.org/stable/i211057.

Boroujerdi, Mehrzad, "Gharbzadegi. The Dominant Intellectual Discourse of Pre- and Post-revolutionary Iran," in S. K. Farsoun and M. Mashayekhi (eds.), *Iran: Political Culture in the Islamic Republic*, London, New York, Routledge, 1992.

Bose, Christine, "Intersectionality and Global Gender Inequality," *Gender & Society*, Vol. 26, No. 1, 2012, PP. 67–72.

Brah, Avtar. *Cartographies of Diaspora:Contesting Identities*, London, Routeledge, 1996.

Brah, Avtar and Phoenix, Ann, "Ain't I a Woman? Revisiting Intersectionality," *Journal of International Women's Studies*, Vol. 5, No. 3, 2004, PP. 75–86.

Braudel, Fernand. *L'identité de la France*, Paris, Flammarion, 1999.

Brouilly, John. *Nationalism and the State*, Chicago, Chicago University Press, 1993.

Brun, Thierry, Geissler, A. and Bel, F., "Le Balouchistan iranien. Un réservoir de travailleurs sous-alimentés pour les Emirats," *Tiers-Monde*, tome, Vol. 18, No. 69, 1977. Migrations et développement. PP. 131–8, DOI: https://doi.org/10.3406/tiers.1977.2692.

Bures, Alain de. *La horde enracinée. Turkmènes d'Iran*, Paris, L'Asiathèque, 1992.

Butler, Judith. *Gender Trouble. Feminism and the Subversion of Identity*, London and New York, Routledge, 1990/1999 (reedition).

Butler, Judith, "Performative Agency," *Journal of Cultural Economy*, Vol. 3, No. 2, 2010, PP. 147–61, DOI: 10.1080/17530350.2010.494117.

Castells, Manuel. *L'Ère de l'information, la société en réseau*, Paris, Fayard, 1998.

Castels, Manuel. *Le pouvoir de l'identité*, French Translation, Paris, Fayard, 1999.

Chaqeri, Cosroe. *The Soviet Socialist Republic of Iran 1920–21: Birth of the Trauma*, Pittsburgh and London, University of Pittsburgh Press, 1995.

Chatterjee, Partha. *The Nation and Its Fragments. Colonial and Postcolonial Histories*, Princeton, Princeton University Press, 1993.

Chehabi, Houchang, Jafari, Peyman and Jefroudi, Maral (eds.) *Iran in the Middle East: Transnational Encounters and Social History*, London and New York, I.B.Tauris, 2018.

Choo, Hae Yeon and Ferree, Myra Marx, "Practicing Intersectionality in Sociological Research: A Critical Analysis of Inclusions, Interactions, and Institutions in the Study of Inequalities," *Sociological Theory*, Vol. 28, No. 2, June 2010, PP. 129–49. https://doi.org/10.1111/j.1467-9558.2010.01370.x.

Crenshaw, Kimberlé, "Demarginalizing the intersection of race and sex, A Black Feminist Critique of Antidiscrimination Doctrine, Feminist Theory and Antiracist Politics," *University of Chicago Legal Forum*, No. 1, 1989, Article 8. http://chicagounbound.uchicago.edu/uclf/vol1989/iss1/8.

Cronin, Stéphanie. *The Army and the Creation of the Pahlavi State in Iran*, 1910–1926, London, I.B.Tauris, 1997.

Cronin, Stephanie. *Social Histories of Iran. Modernism and Marginality in the Middle East*, Cambridge, Cambridge University Press, 2021.

Cunin, Elisabeth, "La globalisation de l'ethnicité?" *Autrepart*, No. 38, 2006, PP. 3–13.

Davis, Kathy, "L'intersectionnalité, un mot à la mode. Ce qui fait le succès d'une théorie féministe" ("Intersectionality as Buzzword. A Sociology of Science Perspective on What Makes a Feminist Theory Successful," *Feminist Theory*, Vol. 9, No. 1, PP. 67–85.

Dehkordi, Maryam, "Zoleikha Adeli, an Entrepreneur Who Introduces Turkmen rugs in the World," *Influential Women of Iran. Iran Wire*, 25 August 2020. https://iranwire.com/fa/features/40570.

Dehkordi, Maryam, "Interview with Ziba Azizi," *Iran Wire*, Monday, August 31, 2020. https://iranwire.com/fa/features/40773.

Delphy, Christine. *Penser le genre*, Paris, Sylleps, 2001.

Digard, Jean-Pierre (ed.). *Le fait ethnique en Iran et en Afghanistan*, Paris, Editions du CNRS,1988.

Digard, Jean-Pierre, Hourcade, Bernard and Richard, Yann. *L'Iran au XXe siècle*, Paris, Fayard, 1996.

Direnberger, Lucia and Kian, Azadeh (eds.) *Etat-nation et fabrique du genre, des corps et des sexualités*, Iran, Turquie, Afghanistan, Presses universitaires de Provence, collection penser le genre, 2019.

Dudoignon, Stephane. *Voyage au pays des Baloutches*, Paris, Editions Cartouche, 2009.

Ebadi, Shirin. *Hoquq-i Kudak* (The Rights of the Child), Tehran, Rowshangaran, third edition, 1992.

Eisenstein, Zillah. *Against Empire. Feminisms, Racism, and the West*, New York and London, Zed Books, 2004.

Elias, Norbert, "Problems of Involvement and Detachment," *British Journal of Sociology*, Vol. 7, No. 3, 1956, PP. 226–52.

Elias, Norbert. *The Civilizing Process, vol. 1: The History of Manners*, Oxford, Basil Blackwell, 1978.

Eliasoph, Nina, "Making a Fragile Public: A Talk Centered Study of Citizenship and Power," *Sociological Theory*, Vol. 14, No. 3, 1996, PP. 262–89.

Elling, Rasmus Christian. *Minorities in Iran. Nationalism and Ethnicity after Khomeyni*, New York, Palgrave, Macmillan, 2013.

Elling, Rasmus and Harris, Kevan, "Difference in Difference: Language, Geography, and Ethno-racial Identity in Contemporary Iran," *Ethnic and Racial Studies*, Vol. 44, No. 12, 2021, PP. 2267–8.

Esman, Milton J. *An Introduction to Ethnic Conflict*, Cambridge, Polity, 2004, PP. 30–40.

Ettehadieh, Mansoureh, "The Origins and Development of Women's Movement in Iran: 1906–41," in Beck, Lois and Neshat, Guity (dirs.), *Women in Iran. From 1800 to the Islamic Republic*, Chicago, University of Illinois, 2004.

Fanon, Fratz. *Racism and Culture, toward the African Revolution*, London, Pelican, 1970.

Farzaneh, Mateo Mohammad. *Iranian Women & Gender in the Iran-Iraq War*, Syracuse, Syracuse University Press, 2021.

Fassin, Didier (ed.). *De la question sociale à la question raciale? Repré-senter la société française*, Paris, La Découverte, 2006.

Fathi, Asghar, "Kasravi's Views on Writers and Journalists: A Study in Sociology of Modernization," *Iranian Studies*, Vol. 19, Spring 1986, PP. 167–77.

Foucault, Michel. "The Subject and Power," in Michel Foucault, H. Dreyfus and P. Rabinow (eds.), *Beyond Structuralism and Hermaneutics*, Chicago, University of Chicago Press, 1983, PP. 208–26.

Foucault, Michel. *Le Pouvoir psychiatrique, Cours au Collège de France, année 1973–1974*, Paris, Éditions Gallimard/ Seuil, 2003.

Foucault, Michel. *Sécurité, territoire, population, Cours au Collège de France, année 1977–1978*, Paris, Éditions Gallimard/Seuil, 2004.

Fraisse, Geneviève, "Des conditions de l'égalité économique," in *Travail et pauvreté: la part des femmes, Travail, genre et sociétés*, 1/1999, PP. 149–55.

Fraser, Nancy, "Rethinking Recognition," *New Left Review*, 3, 2000, PP. 107–20.

Gellner, Ernest. *Nations and Nationalism*, Oxford, Basil Blackwell, 1983.

Gilroy, Paul, "Wearing Your Art on Your Sleeve: Towards a Diaspora Theory of Black Ephemera," in D. A. Bailey and S. Hall (eds.), *The Critical Decade: Black British*

Photography of the 1980s, Ten. 8 Ltd., Birmingham, Vol. 2, No. 3, 1992, P. 87. In
S.Hall, "The question of cultural identity," in S. Hall, D. Held et T. McGrew (eds.),
Modernity and its Futures, Cambridge, Polity Press in association with the Open
University, 1992, P. 618.

Goffman, Erving, "The Arrangement between the Sexes," *Theory and Society*. Vol. 4,
No. 3 (Autumn, 1977), PP. 301–331.

Goffman, Erving. *Stigma. Notes on the Management of Spoiled Identity*, New York,
London, Toronto, Simon & Schuster, 1963.

Hachemi, Seyed Mohammad. *Human Rights and Fundamental Liberties* (in Persian),
Tehran, Mizan, 2005.

Hajjat, Abdellali and Mohammed, Marwan. *Islamophobie. Comment les élites françaises
fabriquent le « problème musulman »*, Paris, La Découverte, 2013.

Hall, Stuart, "The Question of Cultural Identity," in S. Hall, D. Held and T. McGrew
(eds.), *Modernity and Its Futures*, Cambridge, Polity Press, in association with the
Open University, 1992, PP. 273–325.

Hall, Stuart, "The Local and the Global: Globalization and Ethnicity," in Anthony D. King
(eds.), *Culture, Globalization and the World-System: Contemporary Conditions for the
Representation of Identity*, Minneapolis, University of Minnesota Press, 1997.

Hall, Stuart. *Representation: Cultural Representations and Signifying Practices*, London,
Sage in association with the Open University, 1997.

Hall, Stuart. *Nouvelles ethnicités*, Paris, Amsterdam, 2007.

Harding, Sandra, "The Instability of the Analytical Categories of Feminist Theory,"
Signs, Vol. 11, No. 4; Summer 1986, PP. 645–64.

Hill Collins, Patricia. *Black Feminist Thought*, London and New York, Routledge, second
edition, 2009.

Hill Collins, Patricia. *On Intellectual Activism*, Philadelphia, Temple University, 2013.

Hill Collins, Patricia, "Still Brave? Black Feminism and a Social Justice Project," in
Patricia Hill Collins On Intellectual Activism, Philadelphia, Philadelphia, Temple
University Press, 2013, PP. 49–62.

Hill Collins, Patricia. *Intersectionality as Critical Social Theory*, Durham, North
Carolina, Duke University Press, 2019.

Hill Collins, Patricia and Bilge, Sirma. *Intersectionality*, UK, Polity Press Cambridge,
2016, second edition, 2020.

Hobsbawm, Eric. *Nations and Nationalism since 1780: Programme, Myth, Reality*,
Cambridge, Cambridge University Press, 1992.

Hobsbawm, Eric and Ranger, Terence (eds.) *The Invention of Tradition*, Cambridge,
Cambridge University Press, 1983.

Hooks, bell. *Talking Back: Thinking Feminist, Thinking Black*, Boston, South End Press,
1989.

Hourcade, Bernard, "Ethnie, nation et citadinité en Iran," in Jean Pierre Digard (ed.), *Le
fait ethnique en Iran et en Afghanistan*, Paris, Editions du CNRS,1988, PP. 161–74.

Hourcade, Bernard, Mazurek, Hubert, Taleqani, Mahmoud and Papoli-Yazdi, Mohammad-Hosseyn. *Atlas d'Iran*, Paris, La documentation française, 1998.

Hull, Gloria T., Bell Scott, Patricia and Smith, Barbara. *All Women Are White, All the Blacks Are Men, But Some of Us Are Brave*, New York, Feminist Press, 1982.

Irons, William. *The Yomut Turkmen: A Study of Social Organization among a Central Asian Turkic Speaking Population*, Ann Arbor, Anthropological papers, The University of Michigan, 1975.

Irons, William, "Why Are the Yomuts Not More Stratified?" in C. Chang and H. Koster (eds.), *Pastoralists at the Periphery: Herders in a Capitalist World*, Tucson, University of Arizona Press, 1994, PP. 175–196.

Jali, Abbasgholi. *Memories of colonel Kossakovsky*, translated into Persian, Tehran, Simorgh, 1977.

Jayawardena, Kumari. *Feminism and Nationalism in the Third World*, Avon Bath, Press, 1986.

Juteau, Danielle. *L'ethnicité et ses frontières*, Montreal, Les presses de l'université de Montréal, 1999.

Kandiyoti, Deniz, "Bargaining with Patriarchy," *Gender and Society*, Vol. 2, No. 3, September 1988, PP. 274–90.

Karimi, Fatemeh. *Genre et militantisme au Kurdistan d'Iran. Les femmes kurdes de Komala 1979–1991*, Paris, L'Harmattan, 2022.

Kashani-Sabet, Firoozeh. *Frontier Fictions. Shaping the Iranian Nation 1804–1946*, Princeton, Princeton University Press, 2000.

Kashani-Sabet, Firoozeh, "Patriotic Womanhood: The Culture of Feminism in Modern Iran, 1900–1941." *British Journal of Middle Eastern Studies*, Vol. 32, No. 1, May 2005, PP. 29–46.

Kashani-Sabet, Firoozeh. *Conceiving Citizens. Women and the Politics of Motherhood in Iran*, New York, Oxford University Press, 2011.

Kashani-Sabet, Firoozeh, "Color Blind or Blinded by Color? Race, Ethnicity and Identity in Iran," in Firat Oruc (ed.), *Sites of Pluralism. Community Politics in the Middle East*, London, Hurst & Company, 2019, PP. 153–80.

Keddie, Nikki, "Iranian Revolution in Comparative perspectives," *American Historical Review*, Vol. 88, No. 3, 1983, PP. 579–98.

Kergoat, Danièle, "La division sexuelle du travail et les rapports sociaux de sexe," in Hirata et al. (eds.), *Dictionnaire critique du féminisme*, Paris, PUF, 2000, PP. 66–71.

Khajehnejad, Ahmad. *Ghobar Sahra (Dust of the Desert)*, Gorgan, Surah Mehr, 2020.

Khamenehi, Seyed Ali. *Cheshmeh-yi Nur*, Tehran, Ghadr-e velayat, 1995.

Khosrokhavar, Farhad. *Anthropologie de la revolution iranienne. Le rêve impossible*, Paris, L'Harmattan, 1997.

Kian, Azadeh. *Secularization of Iran, a Doomed Failure? The New Middle Class and the Making of Modern Iran*, Louvain & Paris, Peeters & Institut d'Études Iraniennes, 1998.

Kian, Azadeh. *Les femmes iraniennes entre islam, Etat et famille*, Paris, Maisonneuve & Laros, 2002.

Kian, Azadeh. *La Republique islamique d'Iran. De la maison du Guide à la raison d'Etat*, Paris, Michalon, 2005.

Kian, Azadeh, "Modernité, genre et religion en Iran," in Florence Rocheford (ed.), *Le pouvoir du genre. Laïcités et religions 1905–2005*, Toulouse, Presses universitaires de Toulouse, 2007, PP. 201–215.

Kian, Azadeh, "From Motherhood to Equal Rights Advocates: The Weakening of Patriarchal Order," *Iranian Studies*, Vol. 38, No. 1, March 2005, PP. 45–66. Reprinted in Homa Katouzian and Hossein Shahidi (eds.), *Iran in the 21th Century*, London, Routledge, 2008, PP. 86–106.

Kian, Azadeh, "Gender, Ethnicity and Identity in Iran: Surrender without Consent. Baluchi Women in Changing Contexts," in Leif Stenberg and Eric Hooglund (eds.), *Navigating Contemporary Iran. Challenging Economic, Political and Social Perceptions*, London and New York, Routledge, 2012, PP. 117–38.

Kian, Azadeh, "Social and Cultural Change and the Women's Rights Movement in Iran," in A. Sreberny and M. Torfeh (eds.), *Cultural Revolution in Iran: Contemporary Popular Culture in the Islamic Republic,* London and New York, I.B.Tauris, 2013, PP. 43–57.

Kian, Azadeh "Gender Social Relations and the Challenge of Women's Employment," *Middle East Critique*, Vol. 23, No. 3, 2014, PP. 333–47, http://dx.doi.org/10.1080/194 36149.2014.943594.

Kian, Azadeh. *Femmes et pouvoir en islam*, Paris, Michalon, 2019.

Kian, Azadeh and Hourcade, Bernard, "Nommer les banlieues de Téhéran," in H. Rivière d'Arc (éds.), *Nommer les nouveaux territoires urbains*, Paris, Editions de la Maison des Sciences de l'Homme, 2001, PP. 189–210.

Kian, Azadeh and Riaux, Gilles, "Crafting Iranian Nationalism: Intersectionality of Aryanism, Westernism and Islamism," in Susana Carvalho and François Gemenne (eds.), *Nations and Their Histories*, London, Palgrave. Macmillan, 2009, PP. 189–203.

Labor Force Survey Summary findings, Summer 1392 (2013) (Tehran: Statistical Center of Iran) and available online at: http://amar.org.ir/Default.aspx?tabid¼1242&articleT ype¼ArticleView&articleId.

Laurent Perpigna, Iban, "L'horizon bouché des sunnites du Baloutchistan iranien. Au cœur d'une région déstabilisée," OrientXXI, June 8, 2016. https://orientxxi.info/magazine/l-horizon-bouche-des-sunnites-du-baloutchistan-iranien,1361.

Lauretis, Teresa de. *Théorie queer et culture populaire. De Foucault à Cronenberg*, translated from English by M. H. Bourcier, Paris, La Dispute, 2007. Original title: *Queer theory and popular culture. From Foucault to Cronenberg*.

Lévi-Strauss, Claude. *Les structures élémentaires de la parenté*, Paris, Mouton et Maison des sciences de l'homme, 1967 (first edition 1949).

Lewis, Peter G. "The Politics of Iranian Place-Names," *Geographical Review*, Vol. 72, No. 1, 1982, PP. 99–102.

Mackinnon, Catharine. *Toward a Feminist Theory of the State*, Londres, Harvard University Press, 1989.

Mahmood, Saba. *Politics of Piety. The Islamic Revival and the Feminist Subject*, Princeton and Oxford, Princeton University Press, 2005.

McCall, Leslie, "The Complexity of Intersectionality," *Signs*, Vol. 30, No. 3, 2005, PP. 1771–800.

Melville, Charles, "The Fall of Amir Chupan and the Decline of the Ilkhanate, 1327–37: A Decade of Discord in Mongol Iran," Papers on Inner Asia, No. 30. Bloomington, Indiana University, Research Institute for Inner Asian Studies, 1999.

Menashri, David. *Education and the Making of modern Iran*, Ithaca and London, Cornell University Press, 1992.

Menashri, David. *Post-revolutionary Politics in Iran, Religion, Society, and Power*, London, Franck Cass, 2001.

Moghadam, Valentine. *Modernizing Women: Gender and Social Change in the Middle East*, Boulder, CO, Lynne Rienner Publishers, 1993.

Moghadam, Valentine, "Gender Regimes in the Middle East and North Africa: The Power of Feminist Movements," *Social Politics,* Vol. 27, No. 3, 2020, PP. 467–85.

Mojab, Shahrzad (ed.). *Women of a Non-state Nation: The Kurds*, Costa Mesa, Mazda Publishers, 2001.

Mojab, Shahrzad and Hassanpour, Amir. *Women of Kurdistan: A Historical and Bibliographical Study*, London, Transnational Press, 2021.

Miller, Ruth. *The Limits of Bodily Integrity: Abortion, Adultery, and Rape Legislation in Comparative Perspective*, Aldershot, Ashgate, 2007.

Molinier, Pascal. *L'énigme de la femme active. Égoïsme, sexe et compassion*, Paris, Payot, 2003.

Mostafavi, Seyed Djavad. *Behesht-i khanevadeh [Family paradise]*, vol I, tenth edition. Qom, 1995.

Mottahari, Morteza. *Nezâm-e Hoquq-e Zan dar eslam* (Women's Rights in Islam), Téhéran, Sadra, 1372/1993, seventeenth edition.

Najmabadi, Afsaneh. *The Tale of Ghoochan Girls* (in Persian), Tehran, Roshangaran, 1995.

Najmabadi, Afsaneh, "Is Our Time Remembered?" *Iranian Studies*, 29, 1996, PP. 85–109.

Najmabadi, Afsaneh, "The Erotic Vatan as Beloved and Mother," *Comparative Studies in Society and History*, 39, 1997, PP. 442–67.

Najmabadi, Afsaneh, "Crafting an Educated Housewife," in Lila Abu-Lughod (ed.), *Remaking Women. Feminism and Modernity in the Middle East*, Princeton, NJ, Princeton University Press, 1998.

Najmabadi, Afsaneh. *Women with Mustaches and Men without Beards. Gender and Sexual Anxieties of Iranian Modernity*, Berkeley and Los Angeles, University of California Press, 2005.

Nora, Pierre, "Le nationalisme nous a caché la nation" (Nationalism Has Hidden the Nation from Us), *Le monde*, March 17, 2007.

Oruc, Firat (ed.). *Sites of Pluralism. Community Politics in the Middle East*, London, Hurst & Company, 2019.

Paidar, Parvin. *Women and the Political Process in Twentieth-century Iran*, Cambridge, Cambridge University Press, 1997.

Pateman, Carole. *Le contrat sexuel*, 1988, French translation, Paris, La Découverte, 2010.

Pfefferkorn, Roland, "Rapports de racisation, de classe, de sexe....," *Migrations Société*, 133, 2011, PP. 193–208. https://doi.org/10.3917/migra.133.0193.

Porter, Yves. *Les iraniens. Histoire d'un peuple*, Paris, Arman Colin, 2006.

Qaemi, Ali. *Tashkil-i khanevadeh dar Islam* (The Formation of the Family in Islam), Tehran, Amiri, 1994.

Rafizadeh, Shahram, "Protest against the State's Interference in Sunnite Schools," in *Rooz*, 2008.05.06. http:www.roozonline.com/archives/2008/05/post_7257.php.

Raghfar, Hossein, "26 Million Iranians Suffer Absolute Poverty, Says Prominent Economist," *Radio Farda*, April 10, 2018. https://en.radiofarda.com/a/iran-million-suffer-from-poverty/29156808.html.

Ranjipour, Ali, "Poverty in Iran: An Introduction," *Iranwire*, March 2, 2020. https://iranwire.com/en/features/5829.

Ranjipour, Ali, "Poverty in Iran: Sistan and Baluchistan," *Iranwire*, March 2, 2020 https://iranwire.com/en/features/5841.

Renan, Ernest. *Qu'est-ce qu'une nation*, Paris, Bordas, 1992.

Riaux, Gilles. "La radicalisation des nationalistes azéris en Iran," *CEMOTI*, 37, 2004, PP. 15–42.

Riaux, Gilles. "The Formative Years of Azerbaijani Nationalism in Post-revolutionary Iran," *Central Asian Survey*, Vol. 27, No. 1, 2008, PP. 45–8.

Riaux, Gilles. *Ethnicité et nationalisme en Iran. La cause azerbaïdjanaise*, Paris, Karthala, 2012.

Richard, Yann, "La fondation de l'armée nationale en Iran," in Y. Richard (ed.), *Entre l'Iran et l'Occident. Adaptation et assimilation des idées et techniques occidentales en Iran,* Paris, Maison des Sciences de l'Homme, 1989.

Richard, Yann. *L'Iran. Naissance d'une république islamique*, Paris, Editions La Martinières, 2006.

Saber, Sa'id, "The Big Share of the Black Economy in Exploitation" (in Parisan), *Radio Zamaneh*, November 2, 2021. https://www.radiozamaneh.com/691431.

Said, Edward. *Orientalism*, London, Routledge, 1978.

Saleh, Alam. *Ethnic Identity and the State in Iran*, New York, Palgrave Macmillan, 2013.

Salehi-Isfahani, Djavad, "Poverty and Income Inequality in the Islamic Republic of Iran," *Revue internationale des études du développement*, Vol. 1, No. 229, 2017, PP. 113–36.

Salzman, Philip Carl. *Black Tents of Baluchistan*, Washington and London, Smithsonian Institution Press, 2000.

Samii, William, "The Nation and Its Minorities: Ethnicity, Unity and State Policy in Iran," *Comparative Studies in South Asia, Africa and the Middle East*, Vol. XX. Nos. 1 &2, 2000, PP. 128–42.

Schwartz, Olivier, "Peut-on parler des classes populaires?" *La vie des idées*. http://www.laviedesidees.fr/IMG/pdf/20110913_schwartz.pdf.2011:23.

Scott, James C. *Domination and the Arts of Resistance: Hidden Transcripts*, New Haven, Yale University Press, 1990.

Selected findings of the 2016. "National Population and Housing Census," https://www.amar.org.ir/english/Population-and-Housing-Censuses. Accessed on April 17, 2020.

Shahi, Afshin and Abdoh-Tabrizi, Ehsan, "The Shi'te State and the Socioeconomic Challenges of the Sunni Communities in Iran. Historical and Contemporary Perspectives," in Firat Oruc (ed.), *Sites of Pluralism. Community Politics in the Middle East*, London, Hurst & Company, 2019, PP. 87–113.

Shakiba, Sahar, Ghaderzadeh, Omid and Moghadam, Valentine, "Women in Iranian Kurdistan: Patriarchy and the Quest for Empowerment," *Gender and Society*, Vol. 35, No. 4, 2021, PP. 616–42.

Shirdel, Elham, Hasani, Mohammadreza and Hami Kargar, Fateme, "Barsakht-i Ezdevaj-i Beyn-i mazhabi-yi Movafagh va Zamineh hay-i Sheklgiri-yi an: Motale'e-yi Keyfi-yi Beyn-i Zojeyn dar Ostan-i Sistan va Baluchistan" "Construction of a Successful Inter-religious Marriage and the Context of its Formation: A Qualitative Study between Couples in Sistan and Baluchistan Province" (in Persian), *Sociology and Social Institutions*, Vol. 8, No. 18, Autumn-Winter 2021, PP. 373–97.

Siblot, Yasmine, Cartier, Marie and Isabelle, Coutant (eds.) *Sociologie des classes populaires contemporaines*, Paris, Armand Colin, 2015.

Smith, Anthony D. *Nationalism and Modernism*, London and New York, Routledge, 1998.

Soltani, Sima, *Zâhedân*, Budget and Planning Organization of Sistan and Baluchistan, 1999, PP. 43–51.

Spivak, Gayatri Chakravorty, "Can the Subaltern Speak?" in Cary Nelson and Lawrence Grossberg (eds.), *Marxism and the Interpretation of Culture*, Basingstoke, Macmillan Education, 1988, PP. 271–313.

Spivak, Gayatri Chakravorty. *A Critique of Postcolonial Reason. Toward a History of the Vanishing Present*, Cambridge, MA, Harvard University Press, 1999.

Spooner, Brian, "Who Are the Baluch? A Preliminary Investigation into the Dynamics of an Ethnic Identity from Qajar Iran," in Edmund Bosworth and Carole Hillenbrand (eds.), *Qajar Iran, Political, Social and Cultural Change 1800–1925*, Edinburgh, Edinburgh University Press, 1983, PP. 93–110.

Statistical Center of Iran. *A Selection of Labor Force Survey Results*, Tehran, Statistical Center of Iran, 2016.

Statistical Year Book, Tehran, Organization of Management and Planning, 1382 & 1384 (2003 & 2004).

Sullivan, Zohreh T., "Eluding the Feminist, Overthrowing the Modern? Transformations in Twentieth Century Iran," in Lila Abu-Lughod (dir.), *Remaking Women. Feminism and Modernity in the Middle East*, Princeton University Press, 1998, PP. 215–242.

Tabet, Paola. *La construction sociale de l'inégalité des sexes. Des outils et des corps*, Paris, L'Harmattan, 2000.

Taheri, Ahmad Reza, "The Sociopolitical Culture of Iranian Baloch Elites," *Iranian Studies*, Vol. 46, No. 6, November 2013, PP. 973–94, http://dx.doi.org/10.1080/00210 862.2013.810079.

Tapper, Richard, "Ethnicity, Order and Meaning in the Anthropology of Iran and Afganisatan," in Jean-Pierre Digard (ed.), *Le fait ethnique en Iran et en Afghanistan*, Paris, Editions du CNRS, 1988, PP. 21–34.

Tavakoli-Targhi, Mohamad, "From Patriotism to Matriotism: A Tropological Study of Iranian Nationalism, 1870–1909," *International Journal of Middle East Studies*, Vol. 34, No. 2, May 2002, PP. 217–38.

Taylor, Charles, "The Politics of Recognition," in Amy Gutmann and Charles Taylor (eds.), *Multiculturalism: Examining the Politics of Recognition*, Princeton, NJ, Princeton University Press, 1994, PP. 25–73.

Testenoire, Armelle, "Genre, stratification et mobilité sociale au sein des classes populaires," *Lien social et Politiques*, No. 74, 2015, PP. 19–36.

Vahabzadeh, Peyman. *A Guerrilla Odyssey: Modernization, Secularism, Democracy, and the Fadai Period of National Libertaion in Iran. 1971–79*, Syracuse, Syracuse University Press, 2010.

Varikas, Eleni, "Universalisme et particularisme," *Dictionnaire critique du féminisme*, Elena Hirata et al. (dirs.), second edition, Paris, PUF, 2004, PP. 241–245.

Vayda, Andrew P., "Actions, Variations and Change: the Emerging Anti-essentialist View in Anthropology," in R. Borofsky (ed.), *Assessing Cultural Anthropology*, New York, McGraw-Hill, 1994, PP. 320–347.

Vaziri, Mostafa. *Iran as Imagined Nation: The Construction of National Identity*, New York, Paragon House, 1993.

Vieille, Paul, "Iranian Women in Family Alliance and Sexual Politics," in Lois Beck and Nikki Keddie (eds.), *Women in the Muslim World*, Cambridge, MA, Harvard University Press, 1978, PP. 451–72.

Vieille, Paul and Kotobi, Morteza, "Familles et unions de familles en Iran," *Cahiers internationaux de sociologie*, nouvelle série, No. 41, juillet-décembre 1966, PP. 93–104.

Walby, Sylvia. *Theorizing Patriarchy*, Oxford, Blackwell, 1997.

Walby, Sylvia, "La citoyenneté est-elle sexuée?" in Ballmer-Cao, T. H. Mottier and V. Sgier (eds.), *Genre et politique. Débats et perspectives*, Paris, Gallimard, 2000, PP. 51–87.

Walby, Sylvia. *Globalization and Inequalities: Complexity and Contested Modernities*, London, Sage, 2009.

Walby, Sylvia, "Globalization and Multiple Inequalities," in Esther Ngan-Ling Chow, Marcia Texler Segal and Lin Tan (eds.), *Analyzing Gender, Intersectionality, and Multiple Inequalities: Global, Transnational and Local Contexts (Advances in Gender Research, Volume 15)*, Bingley, Emerald Group Publishing Limited, 2011, PP. 17–33.

Walby, Sylvia, "Varieties of Gender Regimes," *Social Politics*, Vol. 27, No. 3, 2020, PP. 414–31.

Weber, Max. *Economie et société*, vol. II, Paris, Plon, 1995.

West, Candace, "Goffman in Feminist Perspective," in *Sociological Perspectives*, Vol. 39, No. 3, 1996, PP. 353–69.

Wilson, Fiona and Frederiksen, Bodil Folke (eds.) *Ethnicity, Gender and the Subversion of Nationalism*, London, Frank Cass, 1996.

Yavari-d'Hellencourt, Nouchine, "Ethnies et ethnicité dans les manuels scolaires iraniens," in Jean-Pierre Digard (ed.), *Le faits ethniques en Iran et en Afghanistan*, Paris, Editions du CNRS,1988, PP. 247–65.

Yoshino, Kosaku. *Cultural Nationalism in Contemporary Japan: A Sociological Enquiry*, London, Routledge, 1992.

Yuval Davis, Nira, "Beyond the Recognition and Redistribution Dichotomy: Intersectionality and stratification," in H. Lutz, M. T. H. Vivar and L. Supik (dirs.), *Framing Intersectionality. Debates on a Multi-faceted Concept in Gender Studies*, Berlington, Ashgate, 2011, PP. 155–69.

Yuval-Davis, Nira and Anthias, Floya. *Woman-Nation-State*, London, Macmillan, 1989.

Yuval-Davis, Nira. *Gender and Nation*, London, Sage Publications, 1997.

Yuval Davis, Nira. *The Situated Politics of Belonging*, London, Sage, 2006.

Zand-Moghadam, Mahmoud, "Iranian Baluchistan: Identity, History and Change" (in Persian), in Hamid Ahmadi (ed.), *Iran. Identity, nationality, Ethnicity* (in Persian), Tehran, Center for Research and Development of Human Sciences, 2005, PP. 306–42.

Zia-Ebrahimi, Reza, "Self-orientalization and Dislocation: The Uses and Abuses of the 'Aryan' Discourse in Iran," *Iranian Studies*, Vol. 44, No. 4, 2011, PP. 445–72.

Zia-Ebrahimi, Reza. *The Emergence of Iranian Nationalism: Race and the Politics of Dislocation*, New York, Columbia University Press, 2016.

Index